When Charles Edward Stuart launched the last, and perhaps most famous, of the Jacobite Risings in the late summer of 1745, the British Army found itself ill-placed to respond. Its most effective troops were on the continent; regular units at home were weak, inexperienced or both; the Militia system was moribund and politically suspect. When the opposing forces first met in the field, the result was ignominious rout and retreat. Nevertheless, eight months after the Rising began, the Jacobite cause went down in crushing defeat at Culloden.

This collection of essays examines in detail some of the units that marched and fought for George II during this tumultuous period. Consideration is given to regular regiments of foot and dragoons as well as to the additional units raised for the emergency. In the latter category, different chapters examine the 'noblemen's regiments' added to the regular line as a piece of political jobbery, the militias raised by clans loyal to the House of Hanover, and the blue-coated volunteer regiments fielded to resist the Jacobite invasion of England. Emphasising the fact that this was a civil war, two of the chapters specifically address units and men raised in Scotland to fight the Jacobites.

The experiences of the units in question varied greatly; some took part in the pivotal battles of Prestonpans, Falkirk, and Culloden whilst others never fired a shot in anger. Taken together, however, these studies provide a new and fascinating insight into the military response to the Jacobite '45.

Andrew Bamford obtained his PhD in military history from the University of Leeds and now edits the From Reason to Revolution series for Helion & Co. His main research interests are the British Army during the Napoleonic Wars, and the European campaigns of the 1740s and 1750s. As well as numerous Napoleonic titles, he is the author of *The Lilies and the Thistle: French Troops in the Jacobite '45*, also published by Helion.

Rebellious Scots to Crush

The Military Response to the Jacobite '45

Edited by Andrew Bamford

Helion & Company

Helion & Company Limited
Unit 8 Amherst Business Centre
Budbrooke Road
Warwick
CV34 5WE
England
Tel. 01926 499 619
Email: info@helion.co.uk
Website: www.helion.co.uk
Twitter: @helionbooks
blog.helion.co.uk

Published by Helion & Company 2020
Designed and typeset by Mach 3 Solutions Ltd (www.mach3solutions.co.uk)
Cover designed by Paul Hewitt, Battlefield Design (www.battlefield-design.co.uk)

Text © Individual contributors 2020
Cover: Grenadier of Pulteney's 13th Foot and volunteer of the Derbyshire Blues. Original artwork by
Christa Hook (www.christahook.co.uk) © Helion & Co. 2020

ISBN 978-1-912866-74-8

British Library Cataloguing-in-Publication Data.

A catalogue record for this book is available from the British Library.

For details of other military history titles published by Helion & Company Limited, contact the above
address, or visit our website: http://www.helion.co.uk

We always welcome receiving book proposals from prospective authors.

Dedicated to the memory
of
Colonel Hugh Geoffrey Robert Boscawen
Coldstream Guards
February 7th 1954–December 22nd 2018
Soldier and Historian

Contents

List of Plates

List of Contributors

Dr Andrew Bamford obtained his PhD in military history from the University of Leeds and now edits the From Reason to Revolution series for Helion & Co. His main research interests are the British Army during the Napoleonic Wars, and the European campaigns of the 1740s and 1750s. As well as numerous Napoleonic titles, he is the author of *The Lilies and the Thistle: French Troops in the Jacobite '45*, published by Helion in 2018.

Lucy Bamford studied at the Courtauld Institute of Art, where she obtained a BA Honours in the History of Art in 2007. The following year, she was recruited to the role of Keeper of Art at Derby Museums and now holds a senior curatorial post within that organisation. Lucy's research interests are primarily focused on the life and work of the eighteenth-century artist, Joseph Wright of Derby, about whom she has mounted numerous exhibitions and displays as well as contributing essays to external exhibition catalogues both at home at abroad. Most recently she was the co-author of *Joseph Wright of Derby: an Introduction to his Life and Work Through the Collection at Derby Museums* (2017).

Dr Andrew Cormack FSA, FRHistS worked in military museums throughout his career. His edition of *The Journal of Corporal William Todd, 1745-1762* was published by the Army Records Society in 2001. He has contributed many articles on eighteenth-century subjects to the *Journal of the Society for Army Historical Research* and became its editor in July 2008. His PhD (2017) was a study of the Out-pension of the Royal Hospital, Chelsea, which he published as *'These Meritorious Objects of the Royal Bounty'; The Chelsea Out-Pensioners in the Early Eighteenth Century* in the same year.

Dr Arran Johnston is a self-employed historian and heritage consultant with a particular interest in battlefields and Scottish history. He was born in Derbyshire, where his fascination with the Jacobites of 1745 first began; an interest which would soon lead him to Scotland. Arran graduated from the University of Edinburgh with an MA(hons) in Ancient History and Latin, and then completed his doctoral research at the University of the West of Scotland, focussing on the Scottish diaspora. For more than ten years Arran has been heavily involved with the Battle of Prestonpans (1745) Heritage Trust and in 2015 he founded the Scottish Battlefields Trust to promote battlefield heritage across Scotland and to campaign for the protection of historic battlefield landscapes. Arran is the author of several books, including *On Gladsmuir Shall the Battle Be!: The Battle of Prestonpans 1745* (2017) and *Essential Agony: The Battle of Dunbar 1650* (2019), both published by Helion.

Dr Jonathan Oates has been interested in the Jacobite campaigns since he was 11 years old, especially its military aspects. In this he was encouraged by his late father; watching the few relevant films, reading the popular books, visiting the battlefields in Scotland and later record offices together. In 1990 his undergraduate dissertation at Reading University considered responses in Newcastle upon Tyne to the Jacobite insurrection of 1715. Eleven years later there was a doctoral thesis at the same institution concerning the responses in the north-eastern counties of England to the 1715 and 1745 Jacobite rebellions. His recent Jacobite titles from Helion include *The Crucible of the Fifteen: Sheriffmuir* (2017), *Killiecrankie and the Jacobite Campaign of 1689-1691* (2018), and *King George's Hangman: Henry Hawley and the Battle of Falkirk 1746* (2019). He recently completed a study of siege warfare during the '45, and is now researching the 1715 Battle of Preston.

Mark Price graduated from the University of Sheffield and has since followed a career in civil engineering in the public and private sector. He has maintained a lifelong interest in military history in general but more specifically the wars and armies of the 18th century. He has also appeared briefly, and sometimes forgettably, in the occasional historical television drama or documentary and is a sedentary member of the Society for Army Historical Research.

Jenn Scott studied politics at the University of Edinburgh and subsequently obtained an MA in Heritage from the University of Surrey. She is a Trustee of the of the Scottish Battlefield Trust. Her most recent publication is *I am Minded to Rise: The Clothing, Weapons and Accoutrements of the Jacobites in Scotland 1689-1719*, published by Helion in 2020.

Editor's Preface

Lord, grant that Marshal Wade
May by thy mighty aid
Victory bring
May he sedition hush
and like a torrent rush
Rebellious Scots to crush
God save the King

The title of this book is, of course, taken from the loyalist verse sung to the tune of God Save the King during the Jacobite Rising of 1745. I would suggest to readers, however, that the key word to note here is 'Rebellious' rather than 'Scots'. Sadly, the suppression of the last Jacobite Rising has all-too-often been painted as a conflict between England and Scotland, and, although serious historiography has now moved on from such a skewed interpretation of events and recognised the events of 1745-1746 as a civil war over dynastic succession, the popular perception has not necessarily caught up. In reality, of course, a great many Scots fought for King George rather than for King James, and two of the chapters in this work deal specifically with Scots units raised, from the Lowlands and Highlands respectively, for the Government cause. It is perhaps more useful, however, to consider these events not from a national perspective – be that nation be England, Scotland, or Great Britain – but from a local one. The '45 was an event shaped by circumstances that stretching beyond the British Isles, but, as we shall see throughout this book, the factors that shaped the response to it were often influenced far more by local and regional concerns than by national or international politics.

Perception is one problem affecting the study of the men who served the cause of George II and his Government. A further problem is, however, a lack of detail in many cases. Whether through bias of sympathies, or simply because they are too easily perceived as a homogenous red-coated entity rather than the romantic variety of their opposition, the experiences of the men who marched and fought under Cope, Wade, Hawley, and Cumberland have been somewhat neglected in comparison with those of their adversaries. Indeed, with respect to those units raised specifically to put down the Rising, our knowledge of their organisation, activities, and even their uniforms, has been left incomplete or confused by previous studies – albeit to some extent because the sources simply do not exist to enable definitive answers to be offered.

The purpose of this work is to outline the nature of the military response to the 1745 Rising – from the initial disjointed reactions, to the eventual victory at Culloden and the subsequent pacification of the Highlands – by means of case studies of some of the units involved. It is not intended to be a military history of the Rising, nor can the case studies – although they have been chosen so as to present the broadest possible cross-section – represent every unit or formation that took part. However, the Introduction serves to review the response in more general terms and thus provide the case studies with a greater degree of context, while Appendix I summarises what is known about the organisation and order of battle of the Government forces during the course of the Rising.

The backbone of the military response to the '45 was the regular British Army, both those units that were in the British Isles when the Rising began, and those veterans brought back from Flanders. However, although the first two chapters study units that fall into these categories, the regulars are not the primary focus of the book. There are works aplenty that discuss the British Army of the second quarter of the eighteenth century in far more detail than it would be possible to do here, and so these first two chapters should be understood as case-studies representative of a far greater body of troops. What has received less consideration – much less, in many cases – is the mobilisation of new forces after the Rising broke out. Therefore, although these forces were numerically and operationally far less significant, they nevertheless qualify for a more detailed treatment here because much of the information presented has not been made easily accessible elsewhere. Some of these new formations were added to the list of regular marching regiments, as detailed in Chapter 3; others were raised by local associations; whilst, as Chapter 5 points out, the Highlanders who were mobilised to fight for George II were brought out by their chiefs in a manner not dissimilar to that by which Jacobite clans came out for Prince Charles.

This title has been some years in the development, so that its eventual publication in the 275th anniversary year of the '45 Rising is by happy accident rather than design. Part of the reason for the delay was the sad passing of Hugh Boscawen, who was a major collaborator in developing the project. Having initially volunteered to write a chapter on the regiment raised by his ancestor and namesake, Hugh Boscawen, 2nd Viscount Falmouth, he soon became more heavily involved and was to have co-authored the Introduction with me. Sadly, his worsening illness prevented him making the contribution that he had wished to offer and his untimely death has deprived us of the work of a fine scholar of the period whose work and presence will be sorely missed. This book is, therefore, dedicated to his memory.

Without Hugh's privileged access to the Boscawen family papers, it sadly proved impossible to include a chapter on Viscount Falmouth's Regiment, but our mutual friend Andrew Cormack very generously stepped in at short notice to provide a survey chapter discussing all 13 of the so-called Noblemen's Regiments. To Andrew for stepping in, and to all the chapter contributors, I must express my gratitude for their patience in sticking with and supporting this project. Each contributor has, I know, incurred their own debts and has acknowledged them in their various chapters – and it is pleasing to note how many of those debts of gratitude are to fellow-members of the writing team – but there are also a number of individuals who have assisted with this project more widely and who I take the opportunity to thank here: Mr Allan Carswell, Dr J.A. Houlding, and Professor Keith McLay. Christa Hook produced two excellent figure plates to accompany the title, and was a pleasure to work with; thanks are also due to the members of the Pulteney's

13th Foot re-enactment group for helping to ensure that the details for the figure representing a grenadier of that regiment are as they should be. Lastly, my own contribution of a chapter to the main body of the book was a joint effort with my wife, Lucy – the first time that we have worked together in this way, and hopefully not the last – but she has assisted me in countless other ways in bringing this title together and I must thank her for support throughout the whole project.

Andrew Bamford
June 2020

Introduction

In order to place the following case-studies into their wider context, this Introduction attempts to provide a brief outline of Britain's land forces upon the outbreak of the '45 Rising, and of those raised in response to it. Details of the organisation and order-of-battle of those units directly concerned with the active campaigning can be found in Appendix I. Regiments were generally known and referred to by the names of their colonels, but a numbering system – with separate sequences for horse, foot, and dragoons – did exist and has been employed throughout this work for ease of cross-referencing. This will be found to be of particular benefit for those cases where there were multiple colonels with the same surname, the few unusual occasions where the same man held multiple colonelcies at the same time, and where colonelcies changed hands during the course of events. The last option could occur either due to the death of the colonel, or through his transfer to a more prestigious colonelcy: several regiments of foot changed colonel during the course of the Rising, whilst the 13th Dragoons lived up to its unlucky number and lost two colonels in succession, so that the regiment was known by three different names across the nine months under consideration. For the benefit of readers who may be more familiar with the regimental numbering of a later date, it should be remembered that the numbers above 41 for the foot, and all numbers for the horse, do not correspond to the regiments associated with them in the 1750s and afterwards, for reasons which will be explained.

The Regular Army[1]

Beginning with the mounted troops, the senior element was the Household Cavalry composed of four troops of Horse Guards and two of Horse Grenadier Guards. The Royal Horse Guards (Blues) did not at this date have Household status, but ranked as the senior of the eight regiments of horse; the other seven were those regiments which would later be

---

1   The survey that follows is primarily a summary of C.T. Atkinson, 'Jenkins' Ear, The Austrian Succession War and the 'Forty-Five: Gleanings from the Sources in the Public Record Office', *Journal of the Society for Army Historical Research*, Vol.XXII No 91 (Autumn 1944), pp.280-298, with additional material from Christopher Duffy, *Fight for a Throne: The Jacobite '45 Reconsidered* (Solihull: Helion, 2015); N.B. Leslie, *The Succession of Colonels of the British Army From 1660 to the Present Day* (London and Aldershot: Gale and Polden Ltd. for the Society of Army Historical Research, 1974); Stuart Reid, *Cumberland's Culloden Army 1745-46* (Oxford: Osprey, 2012). I am also obliged to Dr Andrew Cormack for sharing his insights based on study of the Establishments contained in the WO24 series in The National Archives.

re-designated as dragoon guards. After the horse came the dragoons, of which there were a total of 14 regiments. The bulk of the mounted regiments were organised on an establishment of six troops, although the 5th Dragoons and the two senior regiments of horse had nine. Two or three troops typically formed a squadron as a tactical unit, but there was no formal squadron organisation as such.

Standing outside of the numbered line of marching regiments of foot as the senior infantry element were the three regiments of Foot Guards. The 1st Foot Guards having 28 companies and the other two regiments 18 apiece, each of these regiments was able to field multiple battalions – three for the 1st Foot Guards and two for each of the others. However, the internal organisation of these battalions was rather more flexible than was the case with the marching regiments of foot.

If the organisations outlined above are simple enough, things begin to grow more complicated when we come to the regiments of foot. When Prince Charles landed in Scotland in July 1745 the numerical list extended to 63 regiments, with three more in the process of being raised. The first 40 regiments were old-established; the bulk of them represented the survivors of the great reduction of the Army at the close of the War of the Spanish Succession, and even the most junior of them had been in existence since 1717. Next, ranking as 41st, came the Royal Invalids, formed in 1719: there were also a number of independent companies of Invalids. Together with the units enumerated above, this represented the British Army as it stood prior to the outbreak of war with Spain in 1739; higher-numbered regiments represented the wartime expansion.

As befits a conflict that began as a colonial war, the bulk of the initial wartime increment was in the form of troops intended for operations overseas: a regiment of foot (Oglethorpe's 42nd) to garrison the colony of Georgia, 10 regiments of Marines, and a four-battalion American Regiment (disbanded after the Cartagena expedition). The Marines, intended for amphibious operations rather than service with the fleet, had their own numbering from 1st to 10th but also ranked as the 44th through 53rd Foot: six of them were authorised in December 1739, and four more in January 1741. Major General James Oglethorpe, who was Governor of Georgia as well as colonel of its garrison regiment, also raised a corps of Georgia Rangers for service there; as matters fell out, Oglethorpe himself was about to return from England to the Americas with two newly-raised mounted troops for this unit when the '45 Rising broke out, and he and his men were temporarily retained for service in the British Isles.

Filling the gap between Oglethorpe's and the Marines in the numerical listing was the British Army's first Highland regiment, formed by bringing together existing independent companies. Better known as the Black Watch, they were Murray's 43rd at the time of the Rising. After the formation of this unit in 1739, no more regiments were raised for European service until 1741 when a further seven regiments of foot were authorised; these ranked as 54th through 60th. Two more were added in May 1742: Richbell's (later Folliott's) 61st and Battereau's 62nd. In February 1744, independent companies in the West Indies were regimented to become Trelawney's 63rd, and in September of the following year some of the New Englanders who had captured Louisbourg were regimented as the 65th and 66th in order to garrison it. Of more relevance to the topic at hand, the Earl of Loudoun had in June 1745 been authorised to raise a second Highland regiment, which would become the 64th Foot but whose formation was greatly disrupted by the outbreak of the Rising. Although elements of Loudoun's Highlanders would see service at all three of the major battles of the '45, the regiment was not brought together in its entirety until after the Jacobites had been defeated.

Regular regiments of foot were organised as single battalions of 10 companies apiece, with the exception of the 1st – St Clair's, but better known as the Royals – which had two battalions. The size of the Army could be adjusted by altering the number of men per company, with regiments earmarked for active service being built up to a higher strength either through recruiting or by means of drafts from other units. In order to keep such regiments up to strength once they had gone overseas, they were also authorised to form a pair of 'additional companies' for recruiting purposes. A number of these additional companies, belonging to regiments recruiting in Scotland, were directly caught up in the events of the Rising; those in England were temporarily united to form three Provisional Battalions, for which field officers were provided by drawing upon the Marines, and assigned to garrison duties.

Distinct from all of the above was the Royal Artillery, which was responsible to the Board of Ordnance. The Master General at this time was General John Montagu, 2nd Duke of Montagu, who was also regimental colonel of the 3rd Horse and who would obtain two additional colonelcies during the course of the '45.

By the time that Prince Charles landed in Scotland, much of the regular British Army was serving overseas: four battalions of Foot Guards (one from each regiment with the field army, plus a Provisional Battalion at Ostend formed from drafts belonging to all three regiments) and 25 of foot were with the Duke of Cumberland in Flanders. Cumberland also had with him three troops of Household Cavalry, three regiments of horse including the Royal Horse Guards, and six regiments of dragoons.[2] The cavalry and Foot Guards had been on the continent since 1742, as had half of the foot: most of the remainder had seen at least one campaign. Naturally the bulk of these veterans were brought back to combat the Rising: the case of Pulteney's 13th Foot, outlined in Chapter 2, illustrates the circumstances of these units. Other infantry regiments were in overseas garrisons – four apiece at Gibraltar and Minorca, two in the West Indies, and four (including the 65th and 66th in the process of being raised) in the Americas – leaving only a handful in the British Isles. These latter were generally either newly-raised or else were engaged in recruiting up to strength either after being drawn upon for drafts or on account of having returned as cadres from the West Indies. The mounted regiments not with Cumberland, less the six regiments in Ireland which seem to have been employed primarily to find drafts for those overseas, were in England and Scotland. As with the infantry units at home, these regiments were generally less effective than those serving overseas: the sorry tale of the 13th and 14th Dragoons, as outlined in Chapter 1, exemplifies their woes.

---

2   The National Archives (TNA), SP87/17, 'State of His Majesty's British Forces in the Low Countries June the 11th 1745 N.S.' and 'State of His Majesty's British Forces in the Low Countries July the 16th 1745 N.S.'.

New-Raised Units

Whilst it was initially expected that the forces already available in Scotland under Lieutenant General Sir John Cope would be sufficient to put down the rebellious Highlanders, the swiftness of the Jacobite march south, and Cope's subsequent defeat at Prestonpans on 21 September 1745, made it clear that a much greater commitment was required. Although the major effort would be entrusted to regular regiments brought back from the war in Flanders, supplemented initially by Dutch and later by Hessian auxiliaries, numerous initiatives were also set in motion to raise new units for the duration of the emergency. These projects were carried out in a number of different ways, with varying levels of support from the establishment.

In theory, of course, this requirement could have been met through recourse to the Militia and to various existing local military and paramilitary forces. The various Trained Bands and urban watch units had dwindled until their utility for anything other than a ceremonial or policing role was negligible, as is illustrated in Chapter 4 with reference to those of Edinburgh. The situation of the English county Militia, leaving aside doubts over the its loyalties in some areas even if it could be embodied, was rather more complex, and is best summed up by the historian Frank McLynn in his study of the Jacobite invasion of England:

> Technically, as the law stood (especially after the expiration of the 1734 Militia Act), the militia could not be constituted as a legal body until the crown had repaid to the county the previous month's pay and subsistence expended by the county for the upkeep of the militia. This technicality could not be dealt with until Parliament passed the necessary statute, and it could not do this while it stood prorogued. It could not be convened until the king's return from Hanover...[3]

George did not return from Hanover until the end of August.

As McLynn also points out, the Militia was the responsibility of the Lord Lieutenants of the various counties, and Whig internal politics meant that in many counties the appointment was vacant. Even when there was a Lord Lieutenant in post, the system was so long out of use in some counties as to have become moribund: the Lord Lieutenant of Cornwall was obliged to confess that he did not know how to summon his county's contingent, whilst his counterpart in Cheshire reported that neither the Militia rolls nor its supply of arms could be found.[4] The Cumberland, Westmoreland, Northumberland, and Durham Militias were called out in September 1745, but continued legal doubts helped further undermine levels of training and commitment that were already inadequate to the purpose. Later, the Militia of some of the south-eastern counties was called out when it seemed as though a French invasion in support of the Jacobites was likely.[5] As the performance of the Cumberland

3   Frank McLynn, *The Jacobite Army in England 1745: The Final Campaign* (Edinburgh: John Donald, 1998) pp.3-4.
4   Linda Colley, *Britons: Forging the Nation 1707-1837* (New Haven: Yale University Press, 1992), pp.80-81.
5   Jonathan Oates, 'Responses in London and the Home Counties to the Jacobite Rebellion of 1745', *Southern History*, Vol.28 (2006), pp.46-73.

Militia in the defence of Carlisle demonstrated, the actual military benefits of these unit were negligible.[6]

Although the Lord Lieutenants were issued with warrants to raise forces in their counties, for an example of which see Chapter 7, most of the new units that were put into the field in England were raised and paid for either by individual magnates or by local associations. Due to the costs entailed in raising troops, many of those who had begun to do so quickly sought to pass their new projects on to the state and have them taken into the regular establishment. Writing in early October to the Duke of Devonshire, who, as both Lord Lieutenant of Derbyshire and a significant and wealthy political player in his own right, straddled the various options available, the Prime Minister Henry Pelham set out the differences between the two main categories of unit that had emerged:

> The Dukes of Bedford Rutland and Lord Gower have commissions themselves to raise Regiments, and some others are talk'd of of the same kind; the conditions are, they are att their own expences to raise these corps, and to recommend their own officers, some of which are out of the Army, the others of Gentlemen of figure in the Countys. When they are certified to be about half compleat, then an establishment is to be made for them, and they are to be paid by the Publick, these Regiments are to serve in any part of the island, to be reduced as soon as the Rebellion is over, and the officers are none of them to have half pay, excepting such as were in the army before, and then only according to the ranks they bore in other Regiments att this time. There are also other Regiments or Troops which are call'd Provincial Regiments, these I understand to be paid out of the subscription money of the several Countys, to have their Commissions from the Lords Lieutenants, and are propos'd only for the defence of the respective Countys, and of course under no obligation to stirr out of 'em.[7]

There would be in due course 15 new regiments taken onto the establishment in the way that Pelham outlined, 13 of foot and two of horse, collectively known as the Noblemen's Regiments by virtue of the status of the men who had bankrolled them. A full survey of these units, which for their short duration ranked as the 67th through 79th Foot and the 9th and 10th Horse, is provided in Chapter 3. More were envisaged: as is outlined in Chapter 7, Devonshire himself began to raise one only to be thwarted by lack of recruits, and it would seem that the Earl of Malton in Yorkshire had entertained similar plans for a time.[8] Although some of them would do good service in second-line roles, there was a strong element of jobbery about these regiments, whose officers gained all the advantages of a regular commission in return for their service and whose newly-minted colonels were therefore able to extend a great deal of patronage. This being so, it is not to be wondered that Parliament took steps to limit the number of Noblemen's Regiments.

---

6   Duffy, *Fight for a Throne*, pp.344-345.
7   Devonshire Collection Archives, Chatsworth (DCA), CS1/249.26, Pelham to Devonshire, 5 October 1745.
8   DCA, CS1/294.26, Duncannon to Hartington, 28 September 1745; see also Chapter 6 of this work for Malton's eventual contribution to the forces raised by the local defence association.

For those more concerned with the defence of their own localities, a potential downside to service in one of the Noblemen's Regiments was that, as well as being subject to full military discipline, these units were available for service anywhere in England or Scotland. Regiments raised by local means, on the other hand, were only obliged to do local service, and that under their own terms. A number of such local units therefore sprang up, gaining the collective sobriquet of Blues due to the colour generally adopted for their uniform coats. The historian Linda Colley has identified 57 local associations formed in response to the '45, but many of these do not seem to have achieved much beyond affirming their patriotism.[9] As well as the cases of Yorkshire and Derbyshire, for which see Chapters 6 and 7 respectively, the following associations are also known to have taken steps to actually raise troops: London, Devon, Durham, Lancashire, Surrey, Bristol, Chester, Liverpool, and Oxford. It is telling that the majority these locations were either directly threatened by invasion from Scotland or else, as was particularly the case with Bristol, Liverpool, and Derby, represented places that had done very well out of three decades of economic stability under the first two Georges.[10] Elsewhere, existing local organisations were revived for the purpose of raising troops, as with the Artillery Company of Norwich which resurrected the name of the Honourable Artillery Company of Norwich, originally raised in response to the events of 1715 and maintained, presumably in a ceremonial role, until as recently as 1740.[11] Name notwithstanding, the Norwich company was an infantry unit, as were those of most of the other associations, but by way of variety the Durham Association raised a small regiment of volunteer light horse, based on the model of the county's moribund Horse Militia. Political infighting, however, saw it disbanded, in favour of reverting to the Militia system, before it could be of any service beyond local patrolling.[12]

The value of the Blues units has often been written off as minimal, but this is not an entirely fair view. The majority of them did not see action, and much has been made of the ignominious withdrawal of the Derbyshire Blues when the Jacobites marched into that county. As Chapter 7 explains, the reputation of the last-named unit has not been helped by the manner in which its tale has been told; as for the others, they seem to have been no more or less effective in second-line roles than the Noblemen's Regiments, albeit somewhat limited by their localised terms of service. The Liverpool Blues, in particular, did good work covering the line of the Mersey during the Jacobite advance into England, although, much like the more famous story relating to the Derbyshire Blues, they too suffered a panic as a result of an unexpected encounter with the local livestock – albeit geese rather than cows.[13] Any such lapse was, however, more than redeemed by continued good service through to the recapture of Carlisle, notwithstanding that this required them to operate outside of their own local area. In thus cooperating effectively with the regular forces under the Duke of

9   Colley, *Britons*, pp.81, 376-377.
10   McLynn, *Jacobite Army in England*, p.5; Atkinson, 'Jenkins' Ear, The Austrian Succession War and the 'Forty-Five', p.293; Reid, 1745, p.44; John Wade, *British History Chronologically Arranged* (London: Effingham Wilson, 1839), p.429.
11   Andrew Cormack, 'The Artillery Company of the City of Norwich', *Journal of the Society of Army Historical Research*, Vol.80, No.323 (Autumn 2002), pp.181-185.
12   Carson I.A. Ritchie, 'The Durham Association Regiment, 1745', *Journal of the Society for Army Historical Research*, Vol.34, No.139 (September, 1956), pp.106-119.
13   McLynn, *Jacobite Army in England*, p.95.

Cumberland the Liverpool Blues proved themselves one of the most useful of the volunteer units.[14]

Volunteer units were also formed independently of the associations. Most famous of these is perhaps the Yorkshire Hunters, suggested with some validity to have been the precursor of the later Yeoman Cavalry, for which see Appendix to Chapter 6. In London, it is recorded that on 27 September 'Sir Gregory Page mustered a body of 500 men on Blackheath, raised and clothed at his own expense', and on 8 December 'The Lawyers met the Middle Temple-hall and agreed to form themselves into a regiment under the chief-justice Willis, of the Common-pleas, in defence of the constitution in church and state'.[15] The French invasion scare of the previous year had also seen similar initiatives in Ireland: four companies of volunteer horse were raised by John Ponsonby, First Commissioner of the Revenue, and a project for a whole regiment was begun by one Nicholas Loftus Hume, although it is unclear how close he got to his optimistic target of '1,000 gentlemen'. Ponsonby's troops, at least, were still serving at the time of the '45.[16]

To the undoubted relief of the authorities in London, Ireland remained unaffected by the Rising, and, indeed, troops were drawn upon from the Irish garrison to serve in England and Scotland. In Scotland, on the other hand, a state of civil war both increased the urgency of the response and complicated its execution. As has already been noted, the formation of Loudoun's Highlanders was badly dislocated and even in the Lowlands the swiftness of the Jacobite advance overtook such preparations as were being made, as Chapter 4 makes plain with respect to the case of Edinburgh. Lowland units were formed, however. Volunteers from the town and beyond helped to defend Stirling and its castle, whilst volunteers from Glasgow and Paisley joined in Hawley's ill-fated attempt to raise the siege.[17] In the Highlands too, considerable bodies of men were also put into the field by clans and magnates loyal to George II. In the Campbell strongholds to the west, the Argyll Militia was embodied as detailed in Chapter 5; to the north, 20 Independent Highland Companies were authorised of which 18 were actually formed.[18] In respect to the manner in which they were raised and equipped, these units had more in common with their Jacobite adversaries than with regular troops: they provided the whole of the force defeated at Inverurie on 23 December 1745, but did good work on other occasions, particularly when serving alongside elements of the regular Highland regiments.

14   For an eyewitness account of this service, see 'The Memoir of Walter Shairp: The Story of the Liverpool Regiment During the Jacobite Rebellion of 1745', in Jonathan Oates and Katrina Navickas (eds.), *Jacobites and Jacobins: Two Eighteenth-Century Perspectives* (Bristol: 4word Ltd. for The Record Society of Lancashire and Cheshire, 2006), pp.1-34.

15   Wade, *British History*, pp.429-430.

16   'R.D.', 'Ponsonby, John (1713-1789)', in Sidney Lee (ed.), *Dictionary of National Biography* (London: Smith, Elder, and Co., 1896), Vol.XLVI, p.85; Wade, *British History* p.426.

17   Jonathan Oates, *King George's Hangman: Henry Hawley and the Battle of Falkirk 1746* (Warwick: Helion, 2019), p.115.

18   Maj. I.H. Mackay Scobie, 'The Highland Independent Companies of 1745-47', *Journal of the Society for Army Historical Research*, Vol.XX, No.77 (Spring, 1941), pp.5-37; see also Peter Simpson, *The Independent Highland Companies 1603-1760* (Edinburgh: John Donald, 1996), pp.118-147, 214-220.

Foreign Auxiliaries

Lastly, although tangential to the main focus of this work, it should not be forgotten that Dutch and Hessian forces were brought over to the British Isles to help suppress the Rising. Just as with the presence of French forces along with the Jacobite army, the presence of these troops serves to reiterate the fact that the '45 was only part of a wider European war. In both cases, however, political issues limited the utility of these troops. With the Dutch, the problem stemmed from the troops in question being paroled prisoners of war and forbidden thereby from fighting the French; the arrival of the first French support for the Jacobites necessitated their withdrawal. The Hessians, on the other hand, were commanded by Prince Frederick of Hesse-Cassel whose sympathies were inclined towards his enemies and whose troops, though veterans, were as a result side-lined into a role away from the main army.[19]

---

19   An outline order of battle for both foreign contingents is included in Appendix I of this work. For more on the Hessians, see Christopher Duffy, *The Best of Enemies: Germans Against Jacobites, 1746* (London: Bitter Books, 2013). With respect to the Dutch, a full study of their service in the British Isles remains to be written, but for details of the units involved see Marc Geerdink-Schaftenaar, *For Orange and the States: The Army of the Dutch Republic 1713-1772* (Warwick: Helion, 2018), Part I: Infantry.

1

'These are only Cope's Dragoons': The 13th and 14th Dragoons

Jonathan D. Oates

The two dragoon regiments stationed in Scotland at the onset of the Jacobite Rising of 1745 were the 13th and 14th regiments, which, as Munden's and Dormer's Dragoons respectively, were both established in July 1715 to meet the danger of the Jacobite threat of that year. They had seen service at the Battle of Preston under Major General Charles Wills (1666-1741) on 12-14 November 1715. However, with the reductions to the English military establishment made in 1718 they were sent to Ireland and later to Scotland. They had seen no active military service in the following three decades and so very few men in either regiment had any experience of battle. In 1745 their respective colonels were James Gardiner and Lieutenant General Archibald Hamilton. They were present at both the Battle of Prestonpans (21 September 1745) and at the Battle of Falkirk (17 January 1746). Their record both before and at the former was ignominious; at the latter scarcely better, and they saw no significant active service for the remainder of the Jacobite campaign. This chapter will explore the officers and men of these two regiments and examine their conduct during the '45, using a variety of contemporary published and manuscript sources to do so.

The two regiments together numbered about 600 men in all when the Rising broke out, so were recruited up to their full established strength.[1] We first need to discover who served therein. It is relatively easy to discover who the officers were, for they are listed in the relevant manuscript Army Lists, which show their names and lengths of service. Newspapers and contemporary histories usually refer to them as well if they became casualties in battle, which is not always the case with the rank and file.

---

1   Anon., *The Report of the Proceedings and Opinions of the Board of General officers in the examination into the Conduct, behaviour and Proceedings of Lieutenant General Sir John Cope* (Dublin: George Faulkner, 1749), p.42.

Table 1: Gardiner's 13th Dragoons, Officers[2]

Name	Rank	Date of first commission	Date of present commission	Remarks
Gardiner, James	Colonel	1702	1743	Killed at Prestonpans
Whitney, Shugborough	Lieutenant Colonel	1704	1739	Wounded at Prestonpans; killed at Falkirk
Hungerford, George	Major	1716	1739	
Peterson, Ludovick	Captain	1708	1734	
West, John	Captain	1724	1739	
Downes, Richard	Captain	1720	1739	
Toovey, John	Captain	1722	1741	Absent at Prestonpans; ADC to Hawley
Crofton, William	Captain		1733	Wounded at Prestonpans
Ross, Andrew	Captain-Lieutenant	1709	1741	
Johnson, James	Lieutenant	1736	1741	
West, Charles	Lieutenant	1734	1739	
Vezoy, Edward	Lieutenant	1734	1741	
Turner, Francis	Lieutenant	1733	1739	
French, John	Cornet		1741	
Crow, Thomas	Cornet		1739	Prisoner after Prestonpans
Bland, John	Cornet		1741	
Wills, John	Cornet		1734	
Dalzell, Phillip	Cornet		1739	
Alcock, John	Cornet		1741	Prisoner at Prestonpans
Burroughs	Cornet			Wounded at Prestonpans; made prisoner
West	Quartermaster			Made prisoner at Prestonpans
Young	Quartermaster			Made prisoner at Prestonpans

Gardiner and Whitney had just over four decades of military service each. Gardiner had been a lieutenant in Portmore's Dragoons, then a captain in Stanhope's Dragoons, and a major in Stair's in 1727. Whitney had begun his military career as an ensign in Derby's Foot, becoming a lieutenant in 1707 and then a captain in Irwin's Foot by 1709. By 1728 he was a dragoon major. The captains had seen between 21-37 years each, but only between 4-6 in their present ranks. The lieutenants had served between 4-22 years, but only between 4-12 as lieutenants. The cornets had seen 4-11 years of service each. The two senior officers and Captains Ross and Peterson had all served in the War of the Spanish Succession, albeit in different regiments, and presumably all four had seen action at the Battle of Preston in 1715 –Gardiner himself had certainly done so. Most had served long apprenticeships before rising to captain or above.

We now turn to the rank and file. It is much more difficult to ascertain to ascertain their identities than is the case for the officers, but are not all unknown to history. Pension records

2   TNA, WO64/10; F. Douglas, *History of the Rebellion in 1745 and 1746* (Aberdeen: F. Douglas and W. Murray, 1755), p.26.

provide some of the information for the men below; selected casualty listings provide other names.

Table 2: Gardiner's 13th Dragoons, Rank and File[3]

Name	Rank	Age	Length of service	Parish of origin	Former occupation	Remarks
MacClennan, James	Sergeant	42	19	Killeshandra, Cavan	Farmer	
Moor, John	Private	37	4	Kildonnan, Cavan	Farmer	
Crosby, Michael	Private	25	8	Dumore	Bricklayer	Disabled in left hand at Falkirk
Cochran, Thomas	Private	48	4.5	Coleraine	Labourer	Lost use of left arm by fall from horse at Falkirk
Davis, Luke	Private	20	2.5	Randalstown, Antrim	Farmer	Wounded and disabled in left head and thigh at Prestonpans and Falkirk
Killey, Thomas	Private	20	3.5	Newtownlandry, Londonderry	Labourer	Wounded in right shoulder at Falkirk
Craig, John	Private	29	7.5	Strokestown, Roscommon	Miller	Disabled in left heel at Falkirk
Walker, Jeremiah	Private	29	8	Donegal	Labourer	
McKenzie, John	Private	48	22	Kilrea, Antrim	Weaver	
Scott, Matthew	Private	34	12	Ruffiland, Down	Weaver	
Johnston, John	Private	52	23	Downpatrick	Pedlar	
Montgomery, Alexander	Private	41	11	Bimbuy, Tyrone	Labourer	
Tinley, William	Private	22	1	Belfast	Farmer	
Reed, Joseph	Private	47	19	Killimor	Farmer	
Rankin, James	Private	31	11	Lurgan, Armagh	Weaver	
Dobey, Hugh	Private	22	3	Ardee, Louth	Labourer	
Crane, Matthew	Private	54	22	Londonderry	Farmer	
Brereton, John	Private	26	8	Carbury, Kildare	Labourer	Shot in groin at Falkirk
Hyde, James	Private	50	23	Portadown, Armagh	Weaver	
Rob, James	Private	55	29	Armagh	Weaver	
Scott, Isadiah	Private	23	1.5	Cothhill, Monaghan	Pedlar	
Kilby, George	Private	41	21	Streete, Westmeath	Farmer	
Walsh, Robert	Private	41	18	Inniskillen	Farmer's son	
Oliver, James	Private	45	19	Killimor, Monaghan	Farmer	

3   TNA, WO116/4; W.B. Blaikie (ed.), 'Origins of the Forty Five', *Scottish Historical Society*, series 2, vol.2, (1916), p.433; RA, CP19/58.

Name	Rank	Age	Length of service	Parish of origin	Former occupation	Remarks
Geen, John	Private	48	22	Killimor, Monaghan	Farmer's son	
Farelle, Lawrence	Private	26	3	Roscommon	Farmer	Wounded in head and lost finger at Falkirk
Driver, Matthew	Private	47	20	Downpatrick	Labourer	
McCullen, James	Private	33	5	Disgrade, Tyrone	Labourer	
Johnston, Robert	Private	38	8	Unknown	Unknown	
Moses, Thomas	Private	33	13	Clonuff, Down	Farmer	Shot through body at Falkirk
Parry, John	Private	46	16	Longford, Ireland	Perriwig maker	
Trumble, William	Private	47	17	Inniskillen	Farmer	
Robinson, Andrew	Private	44	22	Clongish, Longford,	Farmer	
Charles, George	Private	51	20	Tavistock	Servant	
Gilmor, Thomas	Private	45	18	Newry, Down	Labourer	
Hunt, Robert	Private	48	28	Pettern, Malmesbury	Butcher	
Robinson	Private	Unknown	Unknown	Fisheraw	Unknown	Killed at Falkirk; married; 2 children
Ormsby	Private	Unknown	Unknown	Ireland	Unknown	Killed at Falkirk; married; 3 children
McQuay	Private	Unknown	Unknown	Haddington	Unknown	Killed at Falkirk; married; 2 children
Montgomery	Private	Unknown	Unknown	Kelso	Unknown	Killed at Falkirk; married; 2 children
Lewisly	Private	Unknown	Unknown	Kelso	Unknown	Killed at Falkirk; married; 2 children
Vincent	Private	Unknown	Unknown	Edinburgh	Unknown	Killed at Falkirk; married; 3 children
Nickle	Private	Unknown	Unknown	Stirling	Unknown	Killed at Falkirk; married; 1 child

Of the sample of 38 troopers that we know about (a little more than 10 percent of the whole), we can see the following results. There were 32 Irishmen (84 percent), five Scots (13 percent) and an Englishman from Devonshire (3 percent). Of their occupations, a dozen were farmers (31.6 percent), nine were labourers (23.7 percent), five were weavers (13.2 percent); there were two pedlars, two farmer's sons and a butcher, a servant, a wigmaker, a miller and a bricklayer. Their ages ranged from 22 to 55, with a mean average of 40, though this result is skewed by the number of men who appear in the sample as a result of claiming pensions and who thus were typically older men. Their lengths of service in the Army ranged from one year to 29, with a mean average of seven and a half years. However, none would have seen any active military service, as none had enlisted before 1716.

Table 3: Hamilton's 14th Dragoons, Officers[4]

Name	Rank	Date first commission	Date present commission	Remarks
Hamilton, Archibald	Colonel	1688	1737	Absentee
Wright, William	Lieutenant Colonel	1700	1737	Wounded and made prisoner at Prestonpans
Bowles, Richard	Major	1720	1742	Wounded and made prisoner at Prestonpans
Clark, James	Captain		1738	
Paterson, Joseph	Captain		1742	
Norris, James	Captain	1705?	1733	
Ellis, Thomas	Captain-Lieutenant	1707	1742	
Smith, Peter	Lieutenant	1724	1742	
Hamilton, William	Lieutenant	1700?	1720	
Baillie, James	Lieutenant	1721	1739	
Ross, William	Lieutenant	1707	1729	
Knapton, Alexander	Lieutenant	1700?	1733	
Forth, Arthur	Cornet	1739		
Nash, George	Cornet	1739		Wounded at Prestonpans
Monck, William	Cornet	1742		
Mallone, Henry	Cornet	1739		
Maine, John	Cornet	1734		
Smith, Trevor	Cornet	1734		
Jacob	Cornet			Prisoner after Prestonpans
Nash	Quartermaster			Prisoner after Prestonpans
Trotter	Surgeon			Prisoner after Prestonpans

The officers had diverse ranges of experience. Wright was a veteran of 45 years of military service; Bowles had 25 but only three in his current rank. The captains had between three and 40 years of experience each, with between three and 12 years as captains. The lieutenants had between three and 45 years of experience as officers and between three and 25 as lieutenants. Finally, the cornets had between 3-11 years of experience. It is probable, therefore, that Wright, two of his captains and one of his lieutenants had all served in the War of Spanish Succession, albeit in different regiments. After 1713, Knapton had been a lieutenant in the short-lived regiment of Molesworth's Dragoons, from 1715-1718. Wright had served as an infantry officer, as captain and major Otway's 35th Foot, until at least 1724.

---

4   TNA, WO, 64/10, Army List, 1745; Douglas, *History*, p.26.

Table 4: Hamilton's 14th Dragoons, Rank and File[5]

Name	Rank	Age	Length of service	Parish of origin	Former occupation	Remarks
Armstrong, John	Private	23	6	Menteith	Farmer	
Keandill, Thomas	Private	22	3	Lisnaskea, Fermanagh	Confectioner	Disabled in left arm at Falkirk
Caufield, James	Private	39	4	Stradbally, Queen's County	Cooper	Disabled by several wounds at Falkirk
McGlaudrey, Robert	Private	45	7	Cookehill, Cavan	Revenue Collector	Disabled in both hands and lost his left eye at Falkirk
Barnet, Patrick	Private	28	3	Dunlavin, Wicklow	Shoemaker	Cut across the nose and lost his left eye at Falkirk
Fraser, Patrick	Private	21	3	Dublin	Draper	Lost his right arm and two fingers in the left hand at Falkirk
Kerney, John	Private	31	5	Armagh	Weaver	Disabled in the hands, stabbed in the back at Falkirk
McCrea, John	Private	28	7	Cookstown, Tyrone	Farmer	Disabled in right hand, cut under the nose at Falkirk
Murray, John	Private	26	7	Armagh	Maltster	Disabled in right shoulder and other parts at Falkirk
McMannus, Henry	Private	Unknown	Unknown	Unknown	Unknown	Joined Jacobites; hanged on 24 January 1746
Johnstone, Peter	Private	51	27	Clayton, Yorkshire	Brazier	
Townley, Samuel	Unknown	41	3	Newry, Ireland	Weaver	Lost left hand at Falkirk
Holiday, Robert	Unknown	41	20	Belturbet, Cavan	Farmer	
Barsell, Edward	Sergeant	46	29	Welford, Gloucestershire	Cooper	
Kirkland, John	Unknown	29	7	Tartaragha, Armagh	Weaver	
Bishop, Ambrose	Unknown	33	4	Farlow, Waterford	Labourer	
Irwin, Francis	Corporal	40	21	Ballyshannan, Donegal	Farmer	
Stewart, James	Unknown	40	19	Trim, Fermanagh	Labourer	

5   TNA, WO116/4; Royal Archives (RA), Cumberland Papers, 19/58, Albermarle to Faulkner, 22 November 1746; Blaikie, 'Origins', p.433.

Name	Rank	Age	Length of service	Parish of origin	Former occupation	Remarks
Farrell, Thomas	Unknown	33	10	Annagh	Unknown	
Brunker, Richard	Drummer	45	19	Stepney	Silk Weaver	
Armstrong, John	Unknown	22	5	Carrymarble, Sherries	Farmer	
Nelson, James	Unknown	40	19	Clones, Monaghan	Farmer	
Willey, Alexander	Drummer	44	23	Coleraine	Shopkeeper	
Overton, Thomas	Unknown	57	34	Warwick	Bricklayer	Wounded in arms at Falkirk
Smith, Henry	Unknown	39	19	Inniskillen	Farmer	Disabled by wounds at Prestonpans
Gibbins	Private	Unknown	Unknown	Unknown	Unknown	Killed at Falkirk; married
Smith	Private	Unknown	Unknown	Unknown	Unknown	Killed at Falkirk; married
McKenny	Private	Unknown	Unknown	Unknown	Unknown	Killed at Falkirk; married
Blood	Private	Unknown	Unknown	Unknown	Unknown	Killed at Falkirk; married
Wilson	Private	Unknown	Unknown	Unknown	Unknown	Killed at Falkirk; married
Shaw	Private	Unknown	Unknown	Unknown	Unknown	Killed at Falkirk; married
Moore	Private	Unknown	Unknown	Unknown	Unknown	Killed at Falkirk; married
Cumpson	Private	Unknown	Unknown	Unknown	Unknown	Killed at Falkirk; married
Reilly	Private	Unknown	Unknown	Unknown	Unknown	Killed at Falkirk; married
Scott	Private	Unknown	Unknown	Unknown	Unknown	Killed at Falkirk; married
Wilson	Private	Unknown	Unknown	Unknown	Unknown	Killed at Falkirk; married
McCann	Private	Unknown	Unknown	Unknown	Unknown	Killed at Falkirk; married

The men whose details we know of, 26 in all or around 10 percent of the whole, form too small a sample be taken as being completely representative. Bearing that caveat in mind, 19 of these men, or 73 percent, were Irish, with two Yorkshiremen (7.7 percent) and two Scots (7.7 percent), with a man from Warwickshire, one from Gloucestershire and an East Ender. They were from diverse backgrounds; seven, (26.9 percent) had been farmers, four (15.4 percent) had been weavers, three (11.6 percent) had been coopers and two labourers (7.7 percent). There was one man from each of the following professions too; a shopkeeper, a bricklayer, a shoemaker, a draper, a revenue collector, a confectioner, a maltster and a brazier. Their ages ranged from 21 to 57 years, with a mean average of 32.7. Their lengths of military service were from three years to 34, with a mean average of 11.5. At least a dozen men were married. Only one man had seen any active military service, as he had enlisted in the army in 1711 and so may well have served in the Jacobite campaign of 1715; quite possibly he would have been at the Battle of Preston if the entirety of his service was spent in the same regiment.

Some of these men were probably Catholic, the majority Christian denomination in Ireland, though recruitment of Catholics was frowned upon. This may have led some to have been sympathetic towards the Jacobite cause, but this is a matter we cannot be sure about; we know that at least one man from the regiment joined the Jacobite army, but he may not have been alone. Fears about Irishmen deserting were unfounded.

To conclude, regarding the officers and men. These were not, in the main, newly recruited novice soldiers as is often suggested.[6] However, only a very small number had seen any active service at all. The soldiering they would have experienced in Ireland and Scotland would have been policing roles, dealing with smugglers, rioters and so on, not against any formed military foe. They were not, therefore, adequately prepared to deal with a full scale war against an irregular or regular enemy.

These two regiments of dragoons formed the mounted contingent of Sir John Cope's forces in Scotland when Charles Edward Stuart arrived in July 1745 to reclaim the throne of his father. They were all based in the Scottish Lowlands, almost certainly for reasons of the ease of supply of food for horses and men. On 2 July, Gardiner's was stationed at Stirling, Linlithgow, Musselburgh, Kelso and Coldstream. Hamilton's was at Dunse and Haddington and adjacent places. Cope, on hearing the news of the Rising, and receiving orders to deal with the threat, initially made preparations for the two regiments to join his force which would march through the Highlands to nip the 'rebellion' in the bud. This was on 3 August.[7] However, as contemporary historian John Home wrote, 'cavalry being judged unserviceable in so rough a country, where it was not easy to subsist them', they remained at Stirling whilst Cope's infantry and artillery marched northwards.[8]

On 19 August, Hamilton's was ordered to be stationed at Canongate and Edinburgh; Gardiner's were to remain at Edinburgh.[9] The men of Hamilton's found themselves moving around the capital; on 31 August being at St Anne's Yard, Edinburgh, then to Beardson's Park, north of the castle on 4 September. Two days later they were stationed on the Leith Links.[10] Meanwhile, with Cope's main force failing to confront the Jacobite forces in the Highlands and being forced to march to Aberdeen and Inverness, in search of shipping back to Edinburgh, the Jacobite army had a free run into the Lowlands.

As in 1715, Stirling was the key to the Lowlands. Having remained a few days at Perth, the Jacobites then marched towards Stirling. However, unlike in 1715, there was only Colonel Gardiner and his dragoons there to stop them. It was 13 September. Apparently the Jacobites

---

6   See, for example, Stuart Reid, *1745: A Military History of the Last Jacobite Rising* (Spellmount: Staplehurst, 1996), pp.12-13.

7   Anon, *Proceedings*, pp.5-6.

8   John Home, *The History of the Rebellion in the Year 1745* (London: A. Strahan, 1802), p.57.

9   Anon, *Proceedings*, p.16.

10   Douglas, *History*, pp.9-10.

heard that the regiment 'had threaten'd to cut us all to pieces if we durst attempt to cross the Forth'. The Jacobites expected to fight there, having identified a ford at Balquhan.[11]

A Jacobite advance guard of 300 men pushed forward on the night of 13 September. Both sides exchanged fire, but the dragoons 'galloped away in great hurry' and arrived at Falkirk that night. John Murray of Broughton, Charles' secretary, was clear that Charles thought that the ford could have been held against them:

> Att passing the river, he expressed a good deal of surprise to find that he had mett with no opposition, and demanded what for officers they had got in Brittain, who were capable of abandoning so advantageous a post.

There was a Jacobite misconception that they were facing two regiments of dragoons there, as Broughton wrote:

> had the two regiments of dragoons first cut the banks of the River, and then entrenched themselves with two or three pieces of cannon, they could have made it very difficult for him to pass, and in all events could have had their horses so near as to have made a safe retreat had they been obliged to abandon the post, and must have cost the Chevalier a good many men.[12]

Andrew Henderson, an Edinburgh schoolmaster, later wrote, 'had they [Hamilton's] been with him [Gardiner] at Stirling, he could have stopped the enemy's passage'.[13]

Gardiner's Dragoons retreated towards Edinburgh. The regiment stationed at Corstorphine, to the west of Edinburgh, along with the Edinburgh City Guard and the city volunteers, on 15 September. Edinburgh's Lord Provost ordered Lieutenant General Joshua Guest, the castle's governor, to have Hamilton's Dragoons join them. At noon they marched through the city and the sight of them impressed the onlookers, 'the horse and men tho' raw and young looked extremely well'.[14] John Marchant, a contemporary historian, wrote likewise, 'they galloped thro' the city in high spirits, brandishing their swords and huzzaing'.[15] Brigadier General Thomas Fowke (c.1690-1765), who was in command of the two regiments, was less pleased with what he saw:

> I found many of the horses' backs not fit to receive the Riders, many of the men's and some of the officers' legs so swelled, that they could not wear boots, and those who really were to be depended upon, in a manner overcome for want of sleep.[16]

---

11 John Marchant, *History of the Present Rebellion* (London: R. Walker, 1746), p.88.
12 R.F. Bell (ed.), 'Memorials of John Murray of Broughton, 1740-1747', *Scottish Historical Society*, series 1 (1897), p.191.
13 Andrew Henderson, *History of the Rebellion* (London: R. Griffiths, 1748), p.11.
14 Home, *History*, p.88; Douglas, *History*, p.11.
15 Marchant, *History*, p.94
16 Anon., *Proceedings*, p.70.

The Jacobite advance guard met their opposite numbers in the early afternoon at Corstorphine on 16 September. The Jacobite horsemen rode forward and fired their pistols at the dragoons, 'who, without returning some shot, wheeled about and rode off, carrying their fears to the main body'.[17]

Meanwhile, there was a council of war held by the dragoon officers, with Fowke advocating an advance if Guest agreed and if the men were in a fit condition to do so. Fowke later admitted, 'both the men and horses were in a great want of everything'. Gardiner was pessimistic, stating that his regiment 'being harassed and fatigued for 11 days and 11 nights, little or no provisions for the men, no forage for the horses… if they stayed another night on that Ground, it was to be feared His Majesty would lose two regiments of dragoons'. There was a unanimous decision to retreat. It was also noted that the terrain was unsuitable, 'full of defiles inclosed by stone walls and quite unfit for dragoons to act upon'.[18]

This took place at about three in the afternoon. According to some sources this was a panic-stricken rout. Lord Elcho, a Jacobite officer, wrote, 'They gave out they were going to fight the Highlanders next day', but were 'struck with such a panick, that they wheel'd about and galloped away in the greatest confusion'.[19] Even Fowke admitted 'The Alarm went among the men from right to left to bridle up, which occasioned a great confusion among them'.[20] Mr Douglas, a contemporary historian, wrote that they left their baggage and tents and 'Their precipitant flight occasioned a general consternation in the city'.[21] Yet Captain Clark later said, 'The Retreat from Coltbridge to Prestonpans was regularly performed', but he claimed that the panic began at the latter, with some dragoons riding off to North Berwick and Dunbar.[22]

The two regiments arrived at Leith and found that the quartermasters had not assembled provisions and forage there. On learning that Cope was expected at Dunbar any day, having taken ship from the Highlands after inconclusive marches there, they marched there via Musselburgh and Haddington. They met Cope and his infantry disembarking on 17 September. On the march westwards towards Edinburgh, Cope did much to encourage his troops, as Lieutenant Colonel Charles Whitefoord of Cochrane's 5th Marines, who acted as an adjutant to Cope, noted:

> all along the march, by riding through the ranks and encouraging the men, you rais'd their spirits to such a degree that all express'd the strongest desire for action. Even the dragoons breathed nothing but revenge and threaten'd the rebels with destruction.[23]

17   Home, *History*, p.88.
18   Anon., *Proceedings*, pp.71, 75.
19   Lord Elcho, *Short Account of the Affairs of Scotland, 1744-1746* (Edinburgh: David Douglas, 1907), pp.254-255.
20   Anon., *Proceedings*, p.77.
21   Douglas, *History*, p.12.
22   Anon., *Proceedings*, p.50.
23   W.A.S. Hewins, *The Whitefoord Papers* (Oxford: Clarendon, 1898), p.93.

Alexander Carlyle, son of a local minister, noted that officers had mixed views about the likelihood of success, with Colonel Gardiner, who 'looked pale and dejected, which I attributed to his Bad Health and the Fatigue he had lately undergone', replying when asked about victory, 'That he hop'd it might be so' and a cornet who was a kinsman of his 'spake of victory as a thing certain if God were on our side'.[24]

Gardiner was also concerned about the troops under his command, confiding on the eve of battle that he believed the men had not recovered from their panic after having fled the enemy only several days ago, and 'I have not above 10 men in my regiment whom I am certain will follow me. But we must give battle now and God's will be done'.[25] The anonymous Edinburgh critic noted, of the cavalry, 'two dastardly Irish regiments of dragoons. These poltrown squadrons'.[26]

On 20 September the two armies encountered each other, though a morass lay between them. There was some manoeuvring on that day. During the night of 20 September, Cope sent cavalry patrols out to keep a watch for the Jacobites, who had found a route through the marsh. A cornet and 30 dragoons were sent to Seton, with a lieutenant and 30 men to support them. A captain and a quartermaster were to stand at the entry road to the morass, with 50 dragoons in support. Cope later stated, 'Here, to do the dragoons justice, they were very alert, and their patrols night good intelligence the whole night of every motion the Rebels made'.[27]

Cope's cavalry was posted on each wing of the army. On the left were two squadron of Hamilton's Dragoons, about 125 men, and on the right were a like number of two squadrons of Gardiner's. In the second line were, on the left, one squadron of Hamilton's, about 100 men and on the right one of Gardiner's, another 100 men. There were also dragoon patrols, numbering a further 118 men.[28]

At daybreak the Jacobites were now to the east of Cope's line, and Cope had his men wheel to face them. This meant that Gardiner's now had the right flank and Hamilton's the left. An officer noted, of Cope, 'the diligence and activity which the general behaved himself. He first order'd the right to form, and then gallop'd to the left, and brought the dragoons up to their ground: from thence I saw him hasten back along the front of our line, to the right, upon his observing that the rebels were advancing to attack it'.[29] Cope himself later wrote, 'I returned again the same way to the right, encouraging the men as I went along the line, to do their duty'.[30] When he reached the left he noticed that Hamilton's Dragoons had not drawn their swords. He became 'very angry' and ordered them to do so.[31] Fowke reinforced Cope's message, 'I took the opportunity of assuring the squadrons, that I had not the least doubt, but that their Behaviour would that do us honour, and that our success

---

24 James Kinsley (ed.), *Anecdotes and Characters of the Times* (Oxford: Oxford University Press, 1973), pp.68-69.
25 Kinsley (ed.) *Anecdotes*, p.68.
26 Anon., *The Woodhouselee Ms: A Narrative of Events in Edinburgh and district during the Jacobite Occupation* (Edinburgh: W. and R. Chambers, 1907), p.29.
27 Anon., *Proceedings*, p.39.
28 Douglas, *History*, pp.24, 27-28.
29 *Gentleman's Magazine*, 15, (1745), p.638.
30 Anon., *Proceedings*, p.40.
31 James Allardyce, (ed.), *Historical Papers relating to the Jacobite Period, 1699-1750* (Aberdeen: Spalding Club, 1895), Vol.I, p.281.

would in a great measure, be owing to their conduct'. Cope believed that 'the Dragoons were a great part of our strength, and of whom the received notion was that the Highlanders were afraid'.[32] Gardiner addressed his dragoons, 'to engage them to exert themselves courageously in the service of their country'. Apparently, 'They seemed most affected with the address and expressed a very ardent desire of attacking the enemy immediately'.[33]

There were some difficulties in ordering the little army. The infantry outguards were unable to join their own units so formed up to the right of Lee's Foot. This meant that Gardiner's two dragoon squadrons did not have enough room to form up, so Gardiner's own squadron had to form up behind Whitney's. Furthermore, the artillery guard was now before Whitney's squadron, thus blocking their movement forwards.[34] Meanwhile, on the left, once the Jacobites advanced, Hamilton's Dragoons apparently 'made a very regular fire'. The Jacobites were undeterred, cheered and fired back, 'which was very brisk' and 'the dragoons were immediately thrown into disorder'.[35]

The fact that of all these cavalrymen only one dragoon – former farmer of Inniskillen, 41 year old Henry Smith (and with 21 years of soldiering behind him one of the most experienced soldiers in the battle) from Hamilton's – later claimed a wound pension from injuries inflicted at the battle suggests that the cavalry played only a very minor role in it.[36] The Jacobites then made 'an irregular fire, which killed some dragoons and horses' and these fatalities included a corporal being shot dead on the spot. One commentator wrote that 'Hamilton's dragoons never engaged, but galloped off without stricking a stroke'.[37] Captain Clark, in charge of the reserve squadron, later recalled calling the men to stand firm, but without avail. He then hoped that his own squadron would charge the Jacobites, but 'this squadron immediately quitted their officers and fled'.[38]

Wightman, however, wrote that they routed 'without firing, or being fired upon, and without drawing a sword'. In fact, their manoeuvre disordered the detachments of Loudoun's 64th Highlanders, too.[39] Sir John MacDonald, a Jacobite officer, referred to 'the cavalry flying before the Highlanders on the plain like a flock of sheep which after having run away, gathers together and then begins to run again when seized by a fresh fear'.[40]

On the right, Whitney saw a column of Jacobites moving to attack Gardiner's Dragoons when Lord Loudoun approached him and suggesting it would be advantageous if he wheeled his squadron to the right and took the enemy in the flank. Whitney concurred and the manoeuvre 'was done with all the calmness, silence & Resolution that I could wish from brave men'. The squadron was a mere 20 yards from the Jacobite flank and as Whitney

---

32   Anon., *Proceedings*, pp.72, 63.
33   Philip Doddridge, *Some Remarkable Passages in the Life of the Hon. Colonel James Gardiner* (Dublin: printed for the booksellers, 1770), p.173.
34   Home, *History*, p.117.
35   Blaikie, 'Origins', p.408.
36   TNA, WO116/4, Royal Hospital, Chelsea: Disability and Royal Artillery Out-Pensions, Admission Books, 1746 Feb. 14-1754 Dec. 18.
37   National Records of Scotland (NRS), GD26/9/486, Unknown to Mackie, undated; Anon., *Proceedings*, pp.57-58.
38   Anon., *Proceedings*, p.58.
39   Duncan Forbes, *Culloden Papers* (London: T. Cadell and W. Davies, 1815), p.224.
40   A. and H. Tayler, *1745 and After* (London: Thomas Nelson and Sons, 1938), p.82n.

recalled, 'I gave the word of command to my squadron to charge into the middle of them'. It was at this crucial moment that a musket ball shattered Whitney's left arm, 'otherwise I thought I had the fairest opportunity of doing a notable piece of service'.[41]

Whitney retired to the rear of his squadron but not before he ordered Lieutenant West to lead the charge. This officer 'came with great Alacrity to the head of the standard, but having a wild, unruly horse he fell a plunging & never ceased till she threw the lieutenant on his back on the ground, by which means a second occasion of doing good service was lost'.[42]

Gardiner's Dragoons fled by Preston, except for perhaps 15 men.[43] Jacobite firing had been 'very irregular', though one man thought that they had 'receiv'd a terrible fire' which had struck panic into men presumably unused to gunfire, and the colonel's squadron fled, leaving Gardiner to vainly call them to stand. Fowke also 'endeavoured for Gardiner to rally ye dragoons'.[44] According to Henderson, the cavalry horses were young and became 'affrighted at such a noise in the morning, fell a capering, fled off at once'. Some riders were dismounted in the process. Apparently these riderless horses ran through the Jacobites towards Dunbar.[45] The Jacobite infantry had been encouraged to attack the cavalry by aiming for the horses' noses, who would then wheel about with their wounded faces so that a few so afflicted would throw a whole squadron into disorder. Scythe-armed men could cut a horse in two with their lethal weapons.[46] The dragoons' flight also had the effect of throwing the infantry into 'ye utmost disorder'.[47]

Seeing the Jacobites were attacking, Cope rode over but by now the cavalry and artillery guard were in flight. He 'endeavoured to get them to order but it would not do'. The infantry could not be rallied either.[48] Attempts were made to rally the men. Cope wrote, 'Seeing the dragoons go off in this manner, I went to the Foot, to try by their means to retrieve the affair...I endeavoured all I could to rally them, but to no avail'.[49]

Some dragoons, who were being fired upon, fled through the village of Preston. Gardiner's Dragoons fled through the defiles in the park walls on the right whilst Hamilton's took those on the left. At the west end of Preston, Cope, Loudoun, and Home stopped the dragoons' flight and tried to have them return to the field. Cope hoped that they could now charge the disordered enemy who were in pursuit of fleeing infantrymen.[50] He later stated 'I did all I could to get them to rally, but there was no prevailing on them to turn their faces to the Enemy'.[51] When the cavalry were alongside Lord Grange's Park, some Jacobite musketry came their way and so they retired again.[52] According to Carlyle, two men were shot dead

41   RA, CP6/111, Whitney to Lascelles, 11 October 1745.
42   RA, CP6/111, Whitney to Lascelles, 11 October 1745.
43   Murray, 'Memorials', p.203; Doddridge, *Some Remarkable Passages*, p.177.
44   Douglas, *History*, p.22
45   NRS, GD26/9/486, Unknown to Mackie, undated.
46   Henderson, *History*, p.30.
47   James Johnstone, *A Memoir of the Forty Five* (London: Folio Society, 1858) p.37.
48   RA, CP9/152, Lascelles' Narrative, 26 January 1746; NRS, GD26/9/486, Unknown to Mackie, undated.
49   Allardyce, *Historical Papers*, p.281.
50   Anon., *Proceedings*, p.41.
51   Anon., *Proceedings*, p.42.
52   James Ray, *History of the Rebellion* (Edinburgh, Unknown Publisher, 1754), p.36.

here.[53] Whitney 'and some officers of distinction made to yt narrow lane near Gardiner's house and appos ymselves sword in hand threatened to kill those dragoons who would not return, but these officers were carry'd off by ye violent press of men and horses'.[54]

Finding he could not rally his men, Cope at the head of his dragoons, now 450 strong and in an orderly body, and some volunteers, took the road to Carberry Hill. About 15 infantrymen joined them. The Jacobites lacked the cavalry and the time to pursue. The defeated men rode to Lauder and then to Berwick on the following day.[55]

Jacobite Sir John MacDonald wanted to stop the escape of some of the dragoons and found an officer with 50 Athollmen. They initially agreed to his suggestion, but then desisted because they thought that they had too few men. Once the bulk of dragoons had passed, MacDonald then suggested that now they might seize a few men and their horses. MacDonald's servant captured one horse but that was all.[56] Some of those in flight were fired upon. Captain John Maclean, of the Jacobite army, wrote 'We met some of them that was making their escape and fired our pieces at them'.[57]

Notwithstanding that the majority of the dragoons fled, there were acts of resistance. Most famously there were the actions of Gardiner, who, according to one account, having tried and failed to rally his dragoons and seeing the officers of a nearby infantry unit fall:

> immediately quitted his horse, snatch'd up a half pike and took it upon him the command of the Foot, at whose head he fought, until he was brought down by three wounds, one in his shoulder with a ball, another in his forehead by a broad sword, and the third, which was the mortal stroke, in the hinder part of his head by a Lochaber axe: this would was given him by a Highlander, who came behind him, when he was fetching a stroke at an officer. With whom he was engaged.[58]

Some from both sides saw his death as being heroic for he could have taken the opportunity to escape.[59] Murray of Broughton was unsympathetic, claiming that Gardiner's 'obstinacy occasion'd his own fall'.[60] Gardiner was buried three days later in the churchyard at Trannet, where eight of his children were already interred (his widow and a surviving daughter were currently at Stirling Castle). The nearby Bankton House was his home.[61]

The dragoons' casualties were relatively light because – unlike the less mobile infantry – most rode away before they could be injured, killed or captured.

53 Kinsley, *Anecdotes*, p.74.
54 NRS, GD26/9/486, Unknown to Mackie, undated.
55 Blaikie, 'Origins', p.408; Henderson, *History*, p.30.
56 Tayler, *1745*, p.82n.
57 Iain Brown and Hugh Cheape, *Witness to Rebellion: John Mclean's Journal of the Forty Five and the Penicuik Drawings* (East Linton: Tuckwell Press, 1996), p.22.
58 *Newcastle Courant*, 19 October 1745.
59 Ray, *History*, p.39.
60 Murray, 'Memorials', p.204.
61 Ray, *History*, p.39.

Table 5: Prestonpans Casualties, Gardiner's 13th Dragoons

Type	Field Officer	Captain	Lieutenant	Cornet	Other Officer	Rank and File	Total
Killed	1	0	0	0	0	Unknown	Unknown
Wounded	1	1	0	1	0	Unknown	Unknown
Prisoner	0	0	0	2	2	52	56
Total	2	1	0	2 (one wounded and made prisoner)	2	At least 52	At least 59

Table 6: Prestonpans Casualties, Hamilton's 14th Dragoons

Type	Field Officer	Captain	Lieutenant	Cornet	Other Officer	Rank and File	Total
Killed	0	0	0	0	0	Unknown	Unknown
Wounded	2	0	0	1	0	Unknown	Unknown
Prisoner	2	0	0	1	2	62	67
Total	2 (same men wounded and made prisoner)	0	0	2	2	At least 62	At least 68

There was no list made of rank and file killed, but 52 men of Gardiner's and 62 of Hamilton's were taken prisoner. Many of these prisoners were also wounded.[62] Horses were also slain, even after their riders had fled or being killed. According to Elcho, horses as well as men had fought, presumably by kicking or biting the Jacobites.[63] Of the dragoon prisoners, as we shall see, at least five joined the Jacobite army.

Cope wrote to Thomas Pelham-Holles, Duke of Newcastle, principal Secretary of State, on the evening of the battle and on the day thereafter at Berwick to explain his defeat, 'I cannot reproach myself, the manner in which the army came on, which was quicker than can be described (of which the men have been long warned) possibly was the cause of our men behaving amiss'. He added on the next day, 'to the ill behaviour of some of the dragoons, in consequence of which the whole line took a pannick'.[64]

Condemnation by the officers of the rank and file (who had few advocates) was universal. Robert Craigie, Lord Advocate, wrote, 'The officers in general condemn the soldiers and in a particular manner the dragoons who they say did not strike one blow before they fled... We think this accounts for the defeat', not the bravery of their enemies nor their numbers.[65] Yet according to Philip Doddridge, Gardiner's contemporary biographer, the officers of Gardiner's were blamed, for in a letter to the colonel's widow, 'it is said that the King has resolved to try all ye officers of it for their late conduct', though this never happened.[66]

The two dragoon regiments went with Cope to Berwick and became part of Field Marshal George Wade's command. The colonelcy of Gardiner's late regiment was transferred to

---

62   Elcho, *Short Account*, p.275; Home, *History*, p.120; *Gentleman's Magazine*, 15, p.518.
63   Elcho, *Short Account*, p.274.
64   TNA, SP36/68, f.209r, Cope to Newcastle, 21 September 1745; TNA, SP36/68, f.239b, Cope to Newcastle, 22 September 1745.
65   TNA, SP54/26/35, Craigie to Unknown 23 September 1745.
66   NRS, GD498/1/26, Doddridge to Lady Gardiner, 26 October 1745.

Colonel Francis Ligonier, who had served as a soldier since 1711 and was younger brother of Lieutenant General John Ligonier, and so was termed Ligonier's Dragoons hereafter. As with the aftermath of the Edinburgh retreat, the dragoons now appeared as fire eaters, according to a letter from Berwick, 'The Dragoons, &c that escaped from the late battle of Prestonpans, seem resolved to retrieve their honour at the loss of their lives'.[67] Following the advance of the Jacobite army into England, they arrived with two infantry battalions at Edinburgh on 14 November, under the command of Lieutenant General Roger Handasyd and helped to regain governmental control of much of the Lowlands whilst the main Jacobite army was in England in November and December 1745. Their duties seem to have been routine; part of Ligonier's helped escort prisoners from Leith to Edinburgh on 6 December, but on 23 December both regiments were ordered to Edinburgh to safeguard the city from the Jacobite army which had returned from England.[68]

Wade was replaced by Lieutenant General Henry Hawley (1685-1759) at the year's end and so the two regiments now came under his command. Hawley was not entirely happy with some of his men. Ligonier's (which had been his own regiment from 1730-1740) and Hamilton's were deemed by him 'the Remains of the two Irish regiments here, which I can't much depend upon', but he had little choice.[69] On Monday 6 January 1746, Hawley arrived in Edinburgh. On the way there, he was met, ironically enough, at Prestonpans by both regiments of dragoons, 'but he upbraided them with their Cowardice, and desired them to put up their swords at that time, and see to use them better in the Hour of Action'.[70] Ligonier's regiment was now 253 strong and Hamilton's 266.[71] At Prestonpans, both regiments had been divided into three squadrons, but, at the time of Falkirk, they had been reduced to two, presumably because of the losses taken at Prestonpans.[72] Hawley remained unimpressed with the cavalry, writing that they were 'the debris of two Irishe regiments of dragoons, very weak and all the rest intimidates and cowed since the battle of Prestonpans'.[73]

The regiments next saw service at Falkirk on 17 January along with Cobham's 10th Dragoons. Upon receiving news of the approach of the Jacobite forces, the three regiments had formed up in front of the camp 'in a moment'. Hawley told Captain John Masterton, a staff officer, to have them 'march immediately to him which was on a hill and ordered Major General Huske to follow with the Foot in two lines'. This having been accomplished, Hawley's next instructions for Masterton was

> to go to Lieutenant Colonel Shugborough Whitney, once major and then lieutenant colonel in Hawley's dragoons (who was on the left of the whole as all our dragoons were in two lines) to desire him to file more to the left than the rebels might not

67   *York Courant*, 15 October 1745.
68   Henderson, *History*, pp.81, 86.
69   RA, CP8/168, Hawley to Newcastle, 31 December 1745.
70   Henderson, *History*, p.88.
71   TNA, SP54/27/32C, List of Hawley's forces, 10 January 1746; TNA, SP54/27/38B, Casualty return, 17 January 1746.
72   Anon., *Proceedings*, p.37
73   RA, Hawley Toovey Papers, 7411-101-11, Hawley's Autobiography, p.24.

outflank us and make room for the Foot to march up the hill, upon wch ye sd colonel told me he could march no further for they were a morass on his left.[74]

Captain James Stewart MacKenzie, a staff officer, later wrote that 'the General imagined the enemy was more afraid of Horse than Foot'.[75]

The dragoons were formed up as seven squadrons on the left of the main army, for a ravine to the army's right prevented them from forming up on both flanks as they had done at Prestonpans. Once Hawley had seen to his infantry, he returned to find Colonel Ligonier at the head of the dragoons. Hawley ordered him to go to the left of the dragoons at the head of Cobham's there, with Whitney at the front of the adjacent squadron.[76] The three regiments of dragoons made feints towards the Jacobite right (composed of about 1,600 infantry in the first line), trying to entice them into firing at long range so that they could charge safely home against troops who were reloading and could not fire a second time.[77] The dragoon regiments were 'a good way before' their own infantry. Lord George Murray, commander of the Jacobite right, realised their plan and then he and Colonel John Roy Stuart 'made a very quick motion till he gained a morass, by which he saved being flanked'.[78] Once again the dragoon regiments attempted to unnerve the regiments opposite them. Elcho recorded their next move that they, 'at last came down in a line at full trot & attacked them sword in hand'.[79]

However, as Hawley noted, the cavalry charge was uneven. Cobham's three squadrons and Ligonier's two 'went on very handsomely', but 'Hamilton's who were in the centre, never stirred'.[80] However, this must be incorrect for at least 10 men of Hamilton's were wounded and a dozen were killed, some in hand to hand combat. Jacobite John Daniel was initially overawed by the sight, later writing:

> Here I must acknowledge, that when I saw this moving cloud of horse, regularly disciplined, in full trot upon us down the summit, I doubted not but that they would have ridden over us without opposition (I mean the front line) and bear us down without difficulty in their impetuous progress.[81]

Elcho recorded that, in response, 'The Highlanders march'd up to them very slowly, with their pieces presented, every man taking his aim, and when the dragoons came within half pistol shot of them, gave them a full discharge, which kill'd a great many of them'. Elcho claimed 400 were killed but this is a huge exaggeration; about 118 of the dragoons became casualties but only a fraction of these were fatal.[82]

---

74   TNA, SP54/27/55B, Masterton to Unknown, 21 January 1746.
75   HMC 14th Report, IX, p.139.
76   James Maxwell, *Narrative of the Expedition of Prince Charles* (Edinburgh: T. Constable, 1841), p.100.
77   RA, HT 7411-101-11, Hawley's Autobiography, p.25.
78   Blaikie, 'Origins', p.411.
79   Elcho, *Short Account*, p.375.
80   RA, HT 7411-101-11, Hawley's Autobiography, p.25.
81   Blaikie, 'Origins', p.195.
82   Elcho, *Short Account*, p.375.

James Johnstone, a Jacobite officer, wrote that there was then hand to hand fighting:

> The cavalry…rushed upon the Highlanders at a hard trot, breaking their ranks, throwing down everything before them and trampling the Highlanders under the feet of their horses, the most singular and extraordinary combat immediately occurred. The Highlanders, stretched on the ground, thrust their dirks into the bellies of their horses. Some seized the riders by their clothes, dragged them down and stabbed them with their dirks, several again used their pistols, but few had sufficient space to use their swords.

MacDonald of Clanranald found himself trapped under a dead horse and was unable to extricate himself. He saw a Highlander struggling with a dismounted dragoon. The former was triumphant and then aided Clanranald. Johnstone concluded, 'The resistance of the Highlanders was so incredibly obstinate that the English, after having been for some time engaged pell-mell with them in their ranks, were at length repulsed and forced to retire'.[83]

Among the dead was Whitney, who had escaped the debacle of Prestonpans despite being wounded, and of whom Hawley later wrote, 'poor Whitney had devoted his life to redeem the character of his men and I saw him lose it, just by me, a gallant good man, and he the only one I would have recommended [for promotion]'.[84] Others received severe wounds; John Kirkland, a 30 year old trooper from Hamilton was 'disabled by several stabs and bruises'; John Kerny of the same regiment was 'disabled in both hands, stabb'd in the back'. Others in that regiment received severe wounds to the hands and fingers, suggestive of fierce hand to hand fighting. Patrick Barnet was 'cut across the nose'.[85]

The dragoons who remained alive, fled, 'who in their flight run down all along the Princes first line and got the fire of the whole line'. This was because their own infantry had by now advanced close to them and so they could not go straight back without breaking their own lines. Captain Masterton was shocked, 'for such pannick God keep me from ever seeing again that our forces was in'. Hawley tried to rally them. He drew his pistol, 'but threats and fair words would not do for they never stopped till they got to camp wch was a good mile distant'. He was almost run over by the fleeing horsemen.[86] Hawley himself later wrote: 'The Lieutenant General in trying to stop the dragoons was beat downe, him and his horse, by them twice and bothe times was very near being killed or taken by the Highlanders…He was at last forced along with the crowde to the bottom of the hill'.[87]

The Jacobites clearly did not have a high opinion of the dragoons, for Colonel John Roy Stuart cried 'Gentleman, keep your ground, these are only Cope's Dragoons'.[88] However, there is a story about a duel between one of the dragoons and Donald Macleod of Berneray (1692-1781), presumably after the charge had been repelled. Apparently, the latter:

83   Johnstone, *Memoir*, p.87.
84   TNA, SP54/27/38a, Hawley to Unknown, 21 January 1746.
85   TNA, WO116/4.
86   TNA, SP54/27/55b, Masterton to Unknown 21 January 1746.
87   RA, HT 7411-101-11, Hawley's Autobiography, p.25.
88   Henderson, *History*, p.94.

engaged at a distance from the rest with an Irish dragoon. They were both skilful swordsmen and the contest was not easily decided: the dragoon at last had the advantage, and the Highlander called for quarter; but quarter was refused him; and the fight continued until he was reduced to defend himself upon his knee. At that instant one of the Macleods came to his rescue; who, as is said, offered quarter to the dragoon, but he thought himself obliged to reject what he had before refused, and, as battle gives little time to deliberate, was immediately killed.[89]

Table 7: Falkirk Casualties, Ligonier's 13th Dragoons

Type	Field Officer	Captain	Lieutenant	Cornet	Other officer	Rank and File	Total
Killed	1	0	0	0	0	2	3
Wounded	0	0	0	0	0	16	16
Missing/Prisoner	0	0	2	2	0	29	33
Total	1	0	2	2	0	47	52

Table 8: Falkirk Casualties, Hamilton's 14th Dragoons

Type	Field Officer	Captain	Lieutenant	Cornet	Other officer	Rank and File	Total
Killed	0	0	0	0	0	0	0
Wounded	1	0	1	0	0	4	6
Missing/Prisoner	0	0	0	1	2	59	62
Total	1	0	1	1	2	63	68

It should be noted that the numbers for those missing include additional dead. As noted above in the list of men whose identities are known, seven of Ligonier's were killed and 12 of Hamilton's and those were just the married men, so the total number of fatalities must clearly be higher; by how much we cannot know. Hamilton's Dragoons, which took the heaviest casualties of any of Hawley's mounted regiments, also lost 79 horses, presumably some being killed, others taken, and some running off.[90]

Colonel Ligonier died ten days after the battle, not by wounds, but because he had been unwell prior to the fighting but could not be persuaded not to lead his men. Despite being bled and blistered beforehand, he was drenched to the skin by the rain on the day of the action, contracted a cold and quinsy and died.[91] He was replaced as colonel by Peter Naison on 3 March 1746, the regiment thus undergoing it's second name-change of the campaign.

Shortly after the battle, the Duke of Cumberland, the army's new commander, wrote to Hawley thus, 'As to the Behaviour of the Irish Dragoons, I am not surprised. For, escaping the first time, made them like safe methods. But I hope that the orders the Duke of Newcastle sends you this Post will hinder such Proceedings for the future. Officers should especially be made examples of'.[92] Hawley put the outcome of the battle down to the behaviour of those

---

89 Ronald Black (ed.), *To The Hebrides: Samuel Johnson's Journey to the Western Islands and James Boswell's Journal of a Tour* (Edinburgh: Birlinn, 2011), p.207.
90 Blaikie, 'Origins', p.433; RA, CP16/223, Horses lost to Hamilton's Dragoons, undated.
91 Blaikie, 'Origins', p.177n.
92 RA, CP9/141, Cumberland to Hawley, 23 January 1746.

under him. He made no distinction between officers and men in this, writing on 20 January to Newcastle, regarding 'the genll good behaviour of the officers, except a few, who require some scrutiny'.[93]

Hawley held court martials on those deemed to have misbehaved during the battle. In this he had been sanctioned by Newcastle. Brigadier General Munden was to be president of the court martials.[94] Hawley asked Cumberland for instructions, 'may I beg to aske shall they all be hanged, there's one of Hamilton's hanged for deserting to the rebels… theres some dragoons tried yet for the same crime and worse, I have acquainted the Duke of Newcastle… re officers'.[95]

The dragoon found guilty of desertion was Henry Macmannus of Hamilton's, an Irishman who had joined the Jacobites after having been made prisoner at Prestonpans.[96] He was hanged with three other men at noon on 24 January and remained on the Grassmarket gibbet in Edinburgh for 24 hours. Two captains, one lieutenant and six privates of Hamilton's were found guilty and sentenced to death by shooting, to take place on 27 January. However, they were reprieved. Two men, though, were 'punished by severe whipping' for 'running in here before they stopt'; they were to have been shot. Other dragoons had been tried for the same offence.[97] In ordering these trials, Hawley had been well within his rights. Army commanders had been given permission to hold courts martial where necessary and desertion in war time was a capital offence under the Articles of War. It had already occurred during the campaign and was to recur. For example, when Cumberland had taken Carlisle on 31 December 1745, four men who had deserted from the dragoons following the Prestonpans battle had been apprehended and were hanged there and then (Sir John Ligonier wrote 'I wish the vermin at Carlisle hang'd').[98]

However, Hawley retained his impression on the worth of the cavalry, writing 'as for the dragoons, I have done wt them' and later that 'the men are so bad and so cowed' that he did not know what to do with Ligonier's and Hamilton's.[99] Apparently 31 dragoons had been tried and Hawley foresaw that 32 men would be shot and another 47 hanged for cowardice and desertion respectively.[100] Yet all were pardoned on Cumberland's arrival. The Duke wrote:

As Hawley communicated to me copies of the infamous sentence that are passed on our cowardly officers, I thought it better to pardon the private men, to give a sort of mark of favour to the corps. If I might venture to give my opinions of the officers, I wish the King to supercede them all, since they are not hanged.[101]

93   TNA, SP54/27/34, Hawley to Newcastle, 20 January 1746.
94   TNA, SP54/27, 35, Hawley to Newcastle, 20 January 1746.
95   TNA, SP54/27/48, Hawley to Cumberland, 29 January 1746.
96   Douglas, *History*, p.128.
97   TNA, SP54/27/187.
98   Douglas, *History*, pp.98, 266.
99   TNA, SP54/27/35, Hawley to Newcastle, 20 January 1746; TNA, SP54/27/38a, Hawley to Unknown., 21 January 1746; TNA, SP54/27/41, Hawley to Newcastle, 24 January 1746.
100 TNA, SP54/27/35, Hawley to Newcastle, 20 January 1746; TNA, SP54/27/48, Hawley to Cumberland, 29 January 1746.
101 TNA, SP54/27/35, Hawley to Newcastle, 20 January 1746; TNA, SP54/27/55a, Cumberland to Newcastle, 30 January 1746.

Hawley was probably also influenced towards moderation by a letter of Lord Milton who suggested that 'I therefore submit to your consideration that it may not be for the general good, that the execution of these private men be delayed at least for some little time'.[102]

Falkirk was the last action which the two regiments of dragoons took part in. As Cumberland marched his army towards Stirling on 1 February, he had the two regiments 'patrole along the roads leading westward' to stop anyone leaving the city to give advance notice of the army's advance to the Jacobite army.[103] After that, the two regiments did not join the main force of the army as it advanced northwards towards the Jacobite army, but remained at Bannockburn, near Stirling.[104] The remnants of the two regiments, along with St George's 8th Dragoons, took part in the attempted relief of Blair Castle in April 1746 as part of Major General the Earl of Crawford's command.[105] The last action of Hamilton's Dragoons in the '45 is noted as having being involved in the final stamping out of the dispersed Jacobite forces after Culloden. In early July some of them attacked a party of Jacobites in the Braes of Angus, who were in search of provisions. Some of the latter were killed and seven, including an officer, were captured and taken to Dundee.[106]

Despite popular belief that these two regiments of dragoons were manned by raw recruits, we have seen that, as far as the known officers and men go, this was far from the case. Yet it is true that the vast majority had never seen active service of any sort in a shooting war. It cannot be denied, though, that they performed poorly at both battles in which they were present. However, on the second occasion they did at least charge the enemy, which had not been the case at Prestonpans. At Falkirk, though, they were very much out on a limb, unsupported by friendly infantry or artillery and against an enemy which was unbroken and well-armed with muskets ready for their first volley of the action. The subsequent repulse was not their fault. Had they been retained as an active part of the army led by the Duke of Cumberland, they may well have performed creditably at the Battle of Culloden, as fellow dragoons of Cobham's did – and Cobham's had been repulsed at Falkirk, too. Yet by January 1746 they had fled on two occasions and that was felt to be two too many.

102 Home, *History*, p.351.
103 Henderson, *Life*, p.226.
104 Douglas, *History*, p.152.
105 Christopher Duffy, *The Best of Enemies: Germans against Jacobites: 1746* (London: Bitter Books, 2013), pp.106, 126.
106 Douglas, *History*, pp.246-247.

2

Major General Pulteney's 13th Regiment of Foot and the Regular British Infantry

Mark Price

Introduction

The following is based primarily around contemporary newspaper reports, arranged in a chronological order, supplemented by letters and other archival material. All of these sources could be considered 'pro-Government' and no effort has been made to correct for any bias in the narrative or reporting of events. Incidents and events reported in relation to the army as a whole are assumed to have been applicable to Pulteney's Regiment where the latter is not mentioned directly. The spelling of place names has been updated where it is thought that this would be of benefit when following the route of the army using modern maps and to help locate the events described within the current landscape.

The narrative covers the period from September 1745 when Pulteney's Regiment transferred from Flanders to England through to August 1746 when the regiment shipped from Scotland to return to Flanders. In focussing on Pulteney's we trace the progress of the army which operated in the east of the country under Field Marshal Wade then follow it as part of forces unified firstly under the command of Lieutenant General Henry Hawley and subsequently HRH the Duke of Cumberland.

A Brief History of Pulteney's Regiment in the Preceding Years

The regiment, then known as Brigadier Middleton's Regiment, served as part of the garrison at Edinburgh during the period 1735 to 1739. Following the death of Middleton in May 1739 Henry Pulteney Esq. was appointed colonel of the regiment in July 1739. Henry Pulteney was serving as a major in the Coldstream Guards prior to this appointment.

As the situation on the continent worsened Pulteney's Regiment was one of the units stationed at the Camp on Lexden Heath in 1741. These units were retained in readiness to proceed to the continent in case of war. In 1742 the unit was ordered to Flanders as part of a 17,000 strong force under the command of the Earl of Stair. In 1743 the regiment took part in the Battle of Dettingen and, after a relatively quiet year of campaigning in 1744, they were involved in the bloody Battle of Fontenoy in May 1745 where the regiment suffered 38 killed, 44 wounded and 10 missing. By September 1745 the regiment was to be found at Vilvoorde near Brussels.

Assembly at Doncaster and the March to Newcastle

On Friday 13 September the seven regiments of foot, including Pulteney's, along with three battalions of Foot Guards, left the Camp at Vilvoorde and made long marches to Willemstad where they arrived on Thursday 19 September. During this march they had no quarters assigned to them, but instead pitched their tents each night. Once at Willemstad the troops embarked ready to return to England.[1] These particular regiments had been chosen as picked battalions whose losses after the Battle of Fontenoy had largely been replaced by drafts, in total they numbered 245 officers and 7,269 other ranks.[2]

On the afternoon of Sunday 22 September, the troops arrived at Gravesend and that evening they began to disembark from the transports, which continued through to the next day. Once disembarked the troops immediately began to march northwards, some by the Highgate Road and others by way of Enfield.[3]

During the same period the additional (recruiting) companies based in England from Pulteney's, along with those belonging to Barrell's, Sowle's, Bragg's, Douglas' and Cholmondely's Regiments, were combined into a Provisional Battalion under Colonel Duncombe. This battalion was then used to guard prisoners of war at Plymouth where they remained until at least January 1746.[4] Joseph Johnston, a soldier of Pulteney's, was later recorded as having 'Lost the use of his left arm in Guarding the French Prisoners at Plymouth'.[5]

On Thursday 26 September Field Marshal Wade was appointed commander in chief of the forces gathered to fight against the rebels.[6] He set out for Doncaster on Sunday 6 October ready to take command of the forces assembling in the north.[7] As the foot marched north it was reported that in all the country towns and villages through which the troops passed they had been received with affection and furnished with all kinds of refreshments.[8] By 9 October the regiments were starting to arrive at the camp at Wheatley Hills (a mile and half south east of Doncaster), with all the remaining forces expected to arrive within a few days' time. Officers made busy buying horses and putting right the defects and deficiencies

---

1   *Derby Mercury*, Friday 27 September 1745 to Friday 4 October 1745.
2   C.T. Atkinson, 'Jenkins' Ear, The Austrian Succession War and the 'Forty-Five: Gleanings from Sources in the Public Record Office', *Journal of the Society for Army Historical Research*, Vol.22, No. 91 (Autumn 1944), p.291.
3   *Derby Mercury*, Friday 20 September 1745 to Friday 27 September 1745.
4   Atkinson, 'Jenkins' Ear, The Austrian Succession War and the 'Forty-Five', pp.291-292.
5   The National Archives (TNA), WO 116/4, Royal Hospital, Chelsea: Disability and Royal Artillery Out-Pensions, Admission Books.
6   *Caledonian Mercury*, Wednesday 2 October 1745.
7   *The Gentleman's Magazine*, 1745, p.554.
8   *Newcastle Courant*, Saturday 5 October 1745 to Saturday 12 October 1745.

in their camp equipage that had arisen in the previous six months campaigning and during long march north.[9] Pulteney's Regiment was now being resupplied with tents that had been previously issued to the Dutch and Swiss troops.[10]

On arrival at Doncaster Field Marshal Wade proceeded to review the forces he could muster,[11] again on Friday 18 October the British forces were reviewed prior to their proposed march north.[12] However, the next day Wade was forced to postpone his march towards Newcastle-upon-Tyne by one day due to a lack of bread, forage and money.[13]

Finally on Monday 21 October the troops were all set to march without fail;[14] it was proposed to march about 10 miles per day till they reached Newcastle.[15] It was said to be a fine sight to see what good order they marched off in and the soldiers are reported as having expressed an earnest desire to fight the rebels before they could retreat into the highlands.[16] They broke camp and set off arriving that afternoon at the south end of Ferrybridge where they pitched their tents on the east and west of the road contiguous with the town.[17] Meanwhile the purveyors of Wade's army had moved ahead to Darlington where they employed all the town's bakers to get bread ready for the troops.[18]

On Tuesday the army marched from Ferrybridge to Wetherby, the troops were said to be tolerably well but a little disordered.[19] The march continued northward with little to report and by Friday 25 October the foot were at Northallerton where they halted to be mustered.[20]

From Northallerton the troops marched to Darlington;[21] even at this stage of the march numbers in the army were said to be diminishing daily due to sickness caused by the severity of the weather.[22] It was around this time that Squire Thornton of Cattal, near Boroughbridge, with his newly raised independent company of Yorkshire Blues was attached to Pulteney's Regiment.[23]

As the troops approached Newcastle the march still seemed to be progressing in an orderly manner and it was made sure the men were provided with wood, straw and the like. The greatest difficulty on the march had been moving the artillery due to the poor state of the roads.[24]

On Monday 28 October Field Marshal Wade arrived at Newcastle attended by several other officers.[25] Following behind the next day came the men of Pulteney's Regiment

---

9   *Stamford Mercury*, Thursday 17 October 1745.
10 University of Nottingham Manuscripts and Special Collections (UNMSC), Ne C 1690, Wade to Pelham, Camp near Doncaster, 16 October 1745.
11 *Caledonian Mercury*, Monday 7 October 1745.
12 *Derby Mercury*, Friday 11 October 1745 to Friday 18 October 1745.
13 TNA, SP 36/72/43 Letters & Papers Marshal Wade, at camp near Doncaster, 25-31 October 1745.
14 *Derby Mercury*, Friday 18 October 1745 to Friday 25 October 1745.
15 *Newcastle Courant*, Saturday 19 October 1745 to Saturday 26 October 1745.
16 *Stamford Mercury*, Thursday 31 October 1745.
17 *Derby Mercury*, Friday 25 October 1745 to Friday 1 November 1745.
18 *Derby Mercury*, Friday 25 October 1745 to Friday 1 November 1745.
19 UNMSC, Ne C 1673, Wentworth to Pelham, Wetherby, 22 October 1745.
20 *Stamford Mercury*, Thursday 31 October 1745,
21 *Gentleman's Magazine*, 1745, p557.
22 TNA, SP 36/72/287 Letters & Papers, Wade to Newcastle, Darlington 25-31 October 1745
23 *Stamford Mercury*, Thursday 31 October 1745; see also Chapter 6 of this work.
24 UNMSC, Ne C 1673, Wentworth to Pelham, Wetherby, 22 October 1745.
25 *Newcastle Courant*, Saturday 26 October to Saturday 2 November 1745.

who marched along and encamped on the Town Moor with the other English and Dutch Regiments;[26] once the soldiers had pitched camp many thousands of people from the surrounding country went to see them.[27] Squire Thornton's troops, despite being attached to Pulteney's Regiment, appear not to have reached Newcastle until Thursday.[28] For the security of the camp the army detached several hundred men every night, who were posted some miles distant from the camp to prevent it from being surprised.[29]

The winter weather continued to worsen and there were concerns that the Flanders regiments were growing sickly; both due to a lack of the necessary refreshments and from having to lie on the bare ground. There was also the worry that the soldiers in their fatigued and sickly state may have had to face rebels who were still fresh and full of vigour.[30] Though the army at Newcastle was large on paper, in reality its numbers were reduced by much sickness and incapacity amongst the soldiers. There was also said to be a lack of 'bat horses' (baggage horses for carrying regimental equipment) which was creating difficulties. The troops were still in need of various items including watch coats and some senior commanders worried about the morale and capabilities of soldiers who had become 'a poor creature that lies on the wet ground, poorly fed and poorly cloathed and nothing to cover him and keep him warm'.[31] To ease the supply problems affecting Wade's forces the government contracted for 800 wagons for four months to carry provisions to the army.[32]

As well as the health of the troops, there was a worry that if Field Marshal Wade himself was to become incapacitated command would fall upon Count Nassau and, following that, on Lieutenant General Schwartzenberg with the prospect that English troops could be commanded by foreigners in their own country![33] Notwithstanding these issues, drill and training carried on with each regiment going through their exercise and firings with great dexterity and to the entire satisfaction of their commanders and the general applause of a great many spectators.[34]

Having now reached Newcastle there was uncertainty as to what to do next and as would be the case at many points in the coming weeks the intentions of the rebels were unclear. A planned march from Berwick was countermanded on 5 November.[35] Then on 7 November a council of war was held at Field Marshal Wade's quarters;[36] here it was decided the army would stay at Newcastle until the designs of the rebels could be more certainly known.[37]

The following day, Friday 8 November, Count Maurice of Nassau (commanding the Dutch forces) and Field Marshal Wade accompanied by a great number of other general officers reviewed the forces encamped on the Town Moor, the army was drawn up in order of battle,

26 *Newcastle Courant*, Saturday 26 October to Saturday 2 November 1745.
27 *Derby Mercury*, Friday 1 November 1745 to Friday 8 November 1745.
28 *Derby Mercury*, Friday 1 November 1745 to Friday 8 November 1745.
29 *Newcastle Courant*, Saturday 2 November 1745 to Saturday 9 November 1745.
30 UNMSC, Ne C 1675/1, Wentworth to Pelham, Newcastle-upon-Tyne, 3 November 1745.
31 UNMSC, Ne C 1701/1-2, Tyrawley to Pelham, Newcastle-upon-Tyne, 5 November 1745.
32 *Stamford Mercury*, Thursday 14 November 1745.
33 UNMSC, Ne C 1700, Tyrawley to Pelham, Newcastle-upon-Tyne, 3 November 1745.
34 *Newcastle Courant*, Saturday 2 November 1745 to Saturday 9 November 1745.
35 *The Gentleman's Magazine*, 1745, p.602.
36 TNA, SP 36/73/1/119, Copy of letter from Wade to Newcastle, 7 November 1745.
37 *The Gentleman's Magazine*, 1745, p.603.

consisting of two grand lines, each three men deep and nearly two miles long, with their officers standing at the head of each regiment and the Train of Artillery properly disposed, the whole 'made the most grand and delightful appearance'.[38] Despite the spectacle some senior officers privately complained that it was still not clear whether the army should be marching south or north.[39]

Sickness continued to afflict the army which was now reported to be comprise only 10,128 effective men rather than the 13,000 expected. The numbers were expected to reduce further, yet requests to issue the men greatcoats and brandy were not acted on.[40] Even as the army prepared to leave Newcastle there were concerns about the lack of preparation for the march that was about to take place.[41]

A further council of war on Monday 11 November decided on marching south, but after reconsidering evidence of the rebels 'hovering' around Carlisle that march was postponed.[42] On Tuesday 12 November it was decided decisively that while the rebels remained near Carlisle Field Marshal Wade should keep his forces where they were.[43] Finally, on Friday 15th, it was determined in a further council of war to march via Hexham to the relief of Carlisle, starting on the Saturday morning.[44]

Before this march, returns of sick at Newcastle showed the army to have a fit strength at 11,328. This being largely due to the 'severe season' and illness in the ranks.[45] According to some, the affairs of the army had now come 'near to a crisis' and the greatest difficulty to be faced on the planned march would be the weather since the ground was covered in snow. It was expected there would be no problems in subsisting on the march to Hexham but it was observed that beyond that the country between Hexham and Carlisle was 'quite ruined'. It was suggested that an allowance of beef and brandy might help to encourage the men on the march.[46]

At 10 o'clock in the morning on Saturday 16 November the army set off heading for Ovingham.[47] It was 8 o'clock that night before they reached their destination, many of the soldiers dropping behind, due to the badness of the roads and excessive fatigue.[48] The snow was extremely deep in several places and it was a day of severe hail and frost. It was reportedly taking up to three or four hours for the troops to march a mile, the pioneers having to fill up ditches along the way to make a passage for the artillery and baggage. In those few tents which could be pitched, the men lay one upon another, greatly fatigued after their march.[49]

The next day the troops set off for Hexham, the first column arrived about four in the afternoon, but the rear did not arrive till near midnight. They encamped on a moor half a

38   *Stamford Mercury*, Thursday 14 November 1745.
39   UNMSC, Ne C 1676, Wentworth to Pelham, Newcastle-upon-Tyne, 8 November 1745.
40   UNMSC, Ne C 1702/1-2, Tyrawley to Pelham, Newcastle-upon-Tyne, 10 November 1745.
41   UNMSC, Ne C 1703, Tyrawley to Pelham, Newcastle-upon-Tyne, 11 November 1745.
42   UNMSC, Ne C 1678, Wentworth to Pelham, Newcastle-upon-Tyne, 11 November 1745.
43   TNA SP 36/73/3/3 Letters & Papers Folios 3-4, Wade to Newcastle, 12 November 1745.
44   *The Gentleman's Magazine*, 1745, p.604.
45   TNA SP 36/73/3/59 Letters & Papers Folio 63, Returns of sick at Newcastle.
46   UNMSC, Ne C 1678, Wentworth to Pelham, Newcastle-upon-Tyne, 11 November 1745.
47   *The Gentleman's* Magazine, 1745, p.605.
48   Samuel Boyse, *An Impartial History of the Late Rebellion in 1745* (Dublin: Edward and John Exshaw, C. Wynne, and O. Nelson, 1748), p.94.
49   John Metcalf, *The Life of John Metcalf* (York: E. & R. Peck, 1795), p.83.

mile from Hexham, here the inhabitants had taken care to provide a quantity of straw and made good fires all over the ground for the troops.[50] By this time the town and castle of Carlisle had already surrendered to the Jacobites, and, the roads to Carlisle being judged impassable due to the great quantity of snow that had fallen, it was resolved to immediately march back to Newcastle.[51] However, the weather and the condition of the troops forced them to remain at Hexham for a further three days.

The state of the army was said to be 'as bad as bad can well be'. They had marched from Newcastle in the worst weather conditions experienced, including violent snow storms and hail; few of the tents could be pitched due to the hardness of the ground, and heavy snow had been followed by a quick thaw which had brought about more sickness in the troops.[52]

Table 1: The Stages of the March of Pulteney's Regiment from Vilvoorde to Hexham

Route		Approximate Distance*	Date*	Days March*	Miles per Day*
Vilvoorde	}	58 miles	13 September	6	9¾
Willemstad			19 September		
Gravesend	}	175 miles	23 September	14	12½
Doncaster			9 October		
Doncaster	}	16½ miles	21 October	1	16½
Ferrybridge			21 October		
Ferrybridge	}	17 miles	22 October	1	17
Wetherby			22 October		
Wetherby	}	12½ miles	23 October	1	12½
Boroughbridge			23 October		
Boroughbridge	}	21 miles	25 October	1	21
Northallerton			25 October		
Northallerton	}	16 miles	26 October	1	16
Darlington			26 October		
Darlington	}	12½ miles	27 October	1	12½
Ferryhill			27 October		
Ferryhill	}	13 miles	28 October	1	13
Chester-le-Street			28 October		
Chester-le-Street	}	9 miles	29 October	1	9
Newcastle			29 October		
Newcastle	}	11½ miles	16 November	1	11½
Ovingham			16 November		
Ovingham	}	11 miles	17 November	1	11
Hexham			17 November		

*These dates and distances are approximate and for the longer marches an allowance has been made for rest days. The total distance marched was approximately 373 miles, which was covered in 30 days of marching over a period of 65 days total, with an average rate of march of 12½ miles per day when the troops were not halted.

---

50   Boyse, *Impartial History*, p.94.
51   *The Gentleman's Magazine*, 1745, p.605.
52   UNMSC, Ne C 1680, Wentworth to Pelham, Hexham, 19 November 1745.

The March South from Newcastle to Wakefield

The army had arrived back at Newcastle on 22 November, here the forces hoped to find the good quarters necessary to refresh themselves after so ruinous a march,[53] the army being fatigued and half-starved by this time.[54] The foot of the returning army were in fact lodged in public halls, glass houses, malt houses, corn lofts and any other empty buildings available.[55]

On 23 November news of the rebels' march south from Carlisle was confirmed and a council of war was held at Newcastle where it was determined that Field Marshal Wade's army would march towards them.[56] However the reality was that Wade's army was still 'in a bad condition' and unable to follow the rebels,[57] despite a recent issue of brandy which was said to have had a beneficial effect![58] In addition it was becoming difficult to find supplies, and so the march south had to be delayed.

On the morning of Tuesday 26 November the troops finally marched south from Newcastle by way of the western road,[59] advancing by slow marches to Piercebridge.[60] Here the army halted for a short while to await a delivery of bread,[61] and it was decided that from then on the army would march as a single body in order to ease the burden on the towns they were to pass through.[62]

The next stage of the march would take the army back to Wetherby; the English foot were said to still show much ardour despite being somewhat weakened by sickness. The country people were very kind to the English troops inviting them into their houses and treating them without suffering them to pay. Once at Wetherby the foot encamped and the cavalry cantoned in the villages on the right and left of their line.[63]

The army halted at Wetherby for a day on 5 December when they received bread from Leeds and a supply of shoes, stockings and flannel waistcoats from London. These flannel waistcoats were a gift from the Quakers who supplied 10,000 waistcoats for the army; these were described as 'woollen waistcoats to double over the breast and belly long enough to be under their waistbands and to be worn under their own cloathing'.[64] The provision of such garments for use in the severe winter weather might have been expected to receive universal approval but some suggested that beef or brandy might have been more useful;[65] others thought the garments may have been positively harmful:

53   Boyes, *Impartial History*, p.101.
54   TNA, SP 36/74/2/61 Letters & Papers Folios 61-62, Wade to Newcastle, 23 November 1745.
55   *Derby Mercury*, Friday 22 November 1745 to Friday 29 November.
56   TNA, SP 36/74/2/61, Letters & Papers Folio 66. Proceedings of Council of War at Newcastle.
57   TNA, SP 36/74/2/105, Herbert to Newcastle, Shrewsbury, 24 November 1745.
58   UNMSC, Ne C 1681, Wentworth to Pelham, Newcastle-upon-Tyne, 22 November 1745.
59   *Newcastle Courant*, Saturday 23 November 1745 to Saturday 30 November.
60   Boyes, *Impartial History*, p.106.
61   UNMSC, Ne C 1682, Wentworth to Pelham, Piercebridge, 29 November 1745. *Newcastle Courant*, Saturday 23 November 1745 to Saturday 30 November.
62   TNA, SP 36/75/1/79 Letters & Papers Folios 79-84, Wade to Newcastle, 28 November 1745.
63   *Caledonian Mercury*, Tuesday 10 December 1745.
64   *The Gentleman's Magazine*, 1745, p.622.
65   UNMSC, Ne C 1682, Wentworth to Pelham, Piercebridge, 29 November 1745.

Our soldiers had here the Quakers gift of Flannel Waistcoats delivered to them which I believe did more harm than good for they ought to have wore them only when they lay in camp and stood Centinels, but they wore them indifferently at all times, as on the march which made them excessive hot and sweat; then they would frequently pull them off so get cold.[66]

Once re-equipped and resupplied, the soldiers marched to Ferrybridge where they again halted. The original intention was to continue the march south to Doncaster but there was a growing realisation that the rebels were able to greatly outmarch the Government armies.[67]

Although the army was ordered to march for Doncaster on the morning of 7 December the orders were cancelled almost immediately 'when the general was going to beat we were countermanded'.[68] Instead, on the 8th, another council of war was held were it was proposed to march west to Halifax in an attempt to cut off the rebels who were by now retreating north. The possibility of delays, due to the badness of the roads and a lack of provisions,[69] was anticipated and the march did not start till the 10th, the intervening time being spent collecting wood, straw and forage.[70]

On arriving at Wakefield, the route of the march was revised yet again. The retreating rebels were now three or four days' march ahead, so the new plan was now to endeavour to keep the army between the rebels and Newcastle.[71] The men of Pulteney's Regiment were heading north once again, getting ready to march on the 12th, back to Newcastle.

Table 2: The Stages of the March of Pulteney's Regiment from Hexham to Wakefield

Route		Approximate Distance*	Date*	Days March*	Miles per Day*
Hexham	}	21½ miles	20 November	3	7
Newcastle			22 November		
Newcastle	}	34 miles	26 November	3	11½
Piercebridge			28 November		
Piercebridge	}	39 miles	30 November	3	13
Boroughbridge			2 December		
Boroughbridge	}	16 miles	4 December	1	16
Clifford Moor			4 December		
Clifford Moor	}	14½ miles	6 December	1	14½
Ferrybridge			6 December		
Ferrybridge	}	11½ miles	10 December	1	11½
Wakefield			10 December		

*These dates and distances are approximate; the total distance marched was approximately 136.5 miles in which was covered in 12 days of marching over a period of 21 days with an average rate of march of 11½ miles per day when the troops were not halted.

66   James Ray, *A Journey through part of England and Scotland along with the Army 2nd Edn* (London: Printed for T. Osborne, 1747), p.14.
67   TNA, SP 36/76/2/52 Letters & Papers Folios 53-54, copy of Wade to Fawkener, 6 December 1745.
68   *Newcastle Courant*, Saturday 7 December 1745 to Saturday 14 December 1745.
69   TNA, SP 36/76/2/117 Letters & Papers Folios 120-121 copy of Wade to Cumberland, 9 December 1745.
70   TNA, SP 36/76/3/55 Letters & Papers Folios 59-60, copy of proceedings of council of war at Ferrybridge.
71   *The Gentleman's Magazine*, 1745, p.623.

The March North from Wakefield to Newcastle

The army had been marching after the rebels for two months, without any real sense of direction,[72] but it now appeared certain the rebels were retreating north and the necessity of marching to secure Newcastle, either from the retreating rebels or their reinforcements reportedly gathering in Perth, seemed obvious.

While the troops were encamped at Boroughbridge it was decided they should march to Newcastle in separate divisions so that they could be cantoned undercover each night, avoiding the need to camp in such extreme bad weather.[73] The first body of 1,000 English foot then set off, by way of Northallerton, Darlington, and Durham, to be followed by the rest of the army marching in succession. Pulteney's Regiment, accompanied by Barrel's, Blakeney's and Cholmondley's, finally arrived in Newcastle on 24 December, several days after the first contingent of troops had arrived.[74] The return of the troops to Newcastle seems to have aroused mixed feelings as Field Marshal Wade reported the 'inhabitants of Newcastle refuse to billet the English infantry'; conversely 'the town of South Shields was willing to accommodate and supply English soldiers but not the Dutch horse'.[75]

While the army gathered again at Newcastle the time was spent 'securing provisions and forage in Northumberland and southern Scotland; enough bread for 10,000 men for 104 days, oats for 2,000 horses for 111 days, hay at Berwick for nine days'.[76]

Field Marshal Wade's time in command was now coming to an end; he had spent most of the campaign making reference to his ill health when writing to the powers-that-be, and suggesting a more 'active and capable' general should lead the army into Scotland.[77] In this matter, at least, his superiors and subordinates all seemed to agree with him.

The condition of the army however also gave many cause for concern, there was said to be 'Great sickness amongst the men in Marshal Wade's army occasioned by the inclemency of the weather and the hospitals being filled, these fevers ravaged also amongst the towns people and even amongst the surgeons and apothecaries that attended them, many of whom also died'.[78]

On the 28th it was announced 'Lt General Henry Hawley to be commander in chief of his Majesty's forces in Scotland'.[79] The following day plans for the march to Edinburgh began 'eight battalions of English troops are in march for Edinburgh to which place they were ordered to proceed with the utmost expedition'.[80]

72   UNMSC, Ne C 1684, Wentworth to Pelham, Leeds, 12 December 1745.
73   *Caledonian Mercury*, Tuesday 24 December 1745.
74   *Newcastle Courant*, Saturday 21 December 1745 to Saturday 28 December 1745.
75   TNA, SP 36/77/2/143 Letters & Papers Folios 43-151, Wade to Newcastle, 21 December 1745.
76   TNA, SP 36/78/2/58 Letters & Papers Folios 58-60, Wade to Newcastle, 29 December 1745.
77   TNA, SP 36/76/2/14 Letters & Papers Folios 14 & 16, Wade to Newcastle, 5 December 1745.
78   Ray, *A Journey through part of England and Scotland*, p.44.
79   *London Gazette*, 28 December 1745.
80   *Caledonian Mercury*, Tuesday 7 January 1746.

Table 3: The Stages of the March of Pulteney's Regiment from Wakefield to Newcastle

Route		Approximate Distance*	Date*	Days March*	Miles per Day*
Wakefield	} 9½ miles		12 December	1	9½
Leeds			12 December		
Leeds	} 12 miles		13 December	1	12
Clifford Moor			13 December		
Clifford Moor	} 16 miles		14 December	1	16
Boroughbridge			14 December		
Boroughbridge	} 70miles		16 December	5	14
Newcastle			20 December		

*These dates and distances are approximate, the total distance marched was approximately 107½ miles in which was covered in eight days of marching over a period of nine days with an average rate of march of 13½ miles per day when the troops were not halted.

The March from Newcastle to Edinburgh and the Battle of Falkirk

Lieutenant General Hawley continued with preparations for the march from Newcastle. He had sufficient bread for the troops but further rations still needed to be bought in by sea, he was however most urgently in need of money and a map of Scotland![81]

The infantry were to march to Edinburgh in separate divisions; on 1 January 1746 Hawley wrote 'Barrell's and Pulteney's regiments marching tomorrow'.[82] As Pulteney's set off from Newcastle on the 2nd, the first two battalions to have marched would be arriving in Edinburgh that same day, having completed the final stage 'with the help of country horses' when they 'came from Berwick to this place in two Days.'[83]

Their route took them along the coast and it was reported that there was 'plenty of fish which was our chief subsistence such as skate, cod and haddock'.[84] The magistrates at Dunbar 'made a grand entertainment to every Regiment that passed through; the private soldiers had all a certain quantity of bread, meat and drink allowed them'.[85] 'Each soldier got a pound of beef, a pound of bread, a glass of Scots spirits and a bottle of Ale'.[86] By the time they reached Edinburgh the troops were said to be 'in good health and spirits'.[87]

Having been the last division to set off from Newcastle, Pulteney's and Barrel's Regiments finally arrived in Edinburgh on 10 January. 'Some of the troops were billeted in the city suburbs and Leith but the greatest part were quartered in public buildings and empty houses; the inhabitants furnishing them with blankets by the direction of constables'.[88] As each new

---

81   TNA, SP 36/78/2/64 Letters & Papers Folios 64-65, Hawley to Newcastle, 29 December 1745.
82   TNA, SP 36/80/1/21 Letters & Papers Folios 21-22, Hawley to Newcastle, 1 January 1746.
83   *Stamford Mercury*, Thursday 16 January 1746.
84   Ray, *A Journey through part of England and Scotland*, p.53.
85   Ray, *A Journey through part of England*, p.56.
86   *The Scots Magazine*, Friday 3 January 1746.
87   *Stamford Mercury*, Thursday 16 January 1746.
88   *The Scots Magazine*, Friday 3 January 1746.

batch of troops arrived there were 'bonfires, illuminations and all other demonstrations of joy by the well affected of the city who entertained the whole army most heartily'.[89]

Not all the troops marched to Edinburgh though: the hospitals in Newcastle were still full of sick soldiers and £300 was 'remitted for one thousand pairs of Stockings and one thousand caps to the Mayor of Newcastle for the benefit of the sick soldiers in those parts'.[90] Similarly Lieutenant General Hawley estimated 'ten men in every hundred will visit hospital in Scotland'.[91]

Starting Monday 13 January and continuing on the Tuesday and Wednesday, the battalions of foot marched by brigades from Edinburgh 'westward in quest of the rebels'. 'There was a great quantity of bread distributed among the Soldiers and some thousand pairs of blankets generously furnished by the inhabitants of this city to the Troops in this cold season'.[92] It was expected that there would also be a 'supply horses for the men, but none appeared when they marched out'.[93] A few days later they were 'given 12 guineas to each regiment of foot to buy beef',[94] a gift from Lord Hopton. By Thursday 16 January the whole army was assembled and encamped to the west of Falkirk.

The next day reports were received of the rebels marching by the south side of Torwood heading for Dunipace, this supposedly taking the rebels within five or six miles of Falkirk. A series of contemporary accounts summarise the course of the action that ensued:

> [At 1 o'clock in the afternoon the] troops got under arms and formed immediately in front of the camp and marched towards the same rising ground as the rebels. When all was formed our first line was within 100 yards of the rebels. Orders were given for the advance and a body of dragoons attacked them sword in hand but the rebels giving fire they gave ground and a great part of the foot of both lines did the same after making an irregular fire. Brigadier Mordaunt rallied the scattered battalions into their corps. A great storm hindered the men from seeing and a great many of the firelocks were so wet not one in five that attempted to fire went off.[95]
>
> A tempest of wind and rain blowing incessantly at that instant, that nobody could either see or almost keep their feet, and a regiment of foot, said to be Poulteney's finding that the fire came from that quarter, and not perceiving the dragoons were betwixt them and the Highlanders, kept a running fire did more harm to the Dragoons than the enemy.[96]
>
> The whole troops continued on the field till near dark for a full hour after all firing had ceased. But finding that rain had greatly spoiled the arms and ammunition it was judged proper not to pursue the advantage. The army marched that night to Linlithgow and continued its march next day to Edinburgh. Most of our

89   *Stamford Mercury*, Thursday 16 January 1746.
90   *Glasgow Courant*, Tuesday 14 January 1746.
91   TNA, SP 36/78/2/64 Letters & Papers Folios 64-65, Hawley to Newcastle, 29 December 1745.
92   *Caledonian Mercury*, Monday 13 January 1746.
93   TNA, SP 36/80/2/117, Letters & Papers Folios 117-118, Wentworth to Newcastle, 16 January 1746.
94   *The Gentleman's Magazine*, 1746, p.27.
95   *Glasgow Courant*, Monday 27 January 1746.
96   John Veitch, *Border Essays* (Edinburgh & London: William Blackwood & Sons, 1896), pp.206-210.

artillery and ammunition and a considerable number of tents were left behind which was occasioned by the country people flying off with their horses which drew the artillery.[97]

The army was to remain at Linlithgow where it had retreated to on the night of the 17th but it being found that the troops had no powder that would take fire due to excessive rain for 4 hours before a resolution was taken on the morning of the 18th to march to Edinburgh and places adjacent where the whole army arrived that afternoon about four o'clock.[98]

The performance of the army came in for criticism and it was said the 'handsomest looking regiments behaved worst'.[99] A private soldier of Barrel's Regiment wrote 'The R----- ---- being [in] the right of the front ran before they were engaged we [marched up, and] took their ground'.[100] Lieutenant General Hawley reported 'such a scandalous cowardice I never saw before. The whole second line of foot ran away, without firing a shot'.[101] For its part, Pulteney's Regiment, which had been in the centre of the first line, suffered casualties of one killed, three wounded and 10 missing.[102]

The cheering crowds were absent on their return to Edinburgh and 'the mob, and lower orders of people, were very free in their expressions, and some of the higher also spoke very warmly, in favour of Prince Charles'.[103]

Once back in Edinburgh 'a court martial was ordered for the trial of some officers and men who behaved ill' at the Battle of Falkirk.[104] The losses suffered in men by the army were soon made up by replacements and 'the universal cry of the soldiers is to attack the rebels again',[105] 'the men promise their officers to redeem their credit at the first occasion'.[106]

By coincidence, on the 23rd three soldiers were hanged in the Grass Market of Edinburgh not because they had behaved ill at Falkirk but because they had deserted from the British before Fontenoy and then enlisted in the French service. One of these men was David Welch of Pulteney's Regiment.[107]

Provisions were a constant concern and at the end of January, Hawley felt it necessary to issue orders against:

The inconvenience occasioned to the army by a great number of idle people following the troops in their march by wasting and consuming the provisions and forage; therefore all the persons as come within a mile of the army after the march

---

97   *Glasgow Courant*, Tuesday 14 January 1746. The abandoned tents were burnt to render them useless to the rebels; see *Newcastle Courant*, Saturday 18 January 1746 to Saturday 25 January 1746.
98   *Glasgow Courant*, Monday 27 January 1746.
99   Stamford Mercury – Thursday 30 January 1746.
100 *The Gentleman's* Magazine, 1746, p.41.
101 TNA, SP 54/27/29B Letters & Papers, Hawley to Cumberland, 17 January 1746.
102 Jonathan D. Oates, *King George's Hangman* (Warwick: Helion & Company 2019), p.140.
103 Metcalf, *The Life of John Metcalf*, p.94.
104 *Newcastle Courant*, Saturday 25 January 1746 to Saturday 1 February 1746.
105 *Stamford Mercury*, Thursday 30 January 1746.
106 TNA, SP 54/27/32A Letters & Papers, report from Lieutenant General Hawley.
107 *Caledonian Mercury*, Friday 24 January 1746.

from Edinburgh without having a pass from the Lord Chief Justice, his Excellency General Hawley or one of the general officers shall be punished and must blame themselves if they be fired on, except such as bring provisions and forage to the army who are to be paid ready money for what they bring to whom all protection is to be given and excepting those also whose information may be useful to the army.[108]

Despite the best efforts to keep the army supplied, Hawley also wrote 'the foot are as near naked as can be described'.[109]

Lieutenant General Hawley's time in command was however now coming to an end. He would continue in a subordinate role for the rest of the campaign but for now the soldiers awaited the arrival of their next commander. It was reported that,

in order to animate the troops in Scotland his Majesty is pleased to direct the Duke of Cumberland to go to Scotland and his Royal Highness set out on the 24th for Edinburgh. Though his royal highness will have the chief command whilst he is in Scotland His Majesty is so well satisfied with General Hawley his authority is not to be lessened in any other way.[110]

Table 4: The Stages of the March of Pulteney's Regiment from Newcastle to Falkirk & Edinburgh

Route		Approximate Distance*	Date*	Days March*	Miles per Day*
Newcastle	}	15 miles	2 January	1	15
Morpeth			2 January		
Morpeth	}	11 miles	3 January	1	11
Felton Bridge			3 January		
Felton Bridge	}	9½ miles	4 January	1	9½
Alnwick			4 January		
Alnwick	}	15miles	5 January	1	15
Belford			5 January		
Belford	}	14½ miles	6 January	1	14½
Berwick			6 January		
Berwick	}	8½ miles	7 January	1	8½
Eyemouth			7 January		
Eyemouth	}	13½ miles	8 January	1	13½
Dunglass			8 January		
Dunglass	}	8 miles	9 January	1	8
Dunbar			9 January		
Dunbar	}	28½ miles	10 January	1 (mounted)	28½
Edinburgh			10 January		

---

108   *Caledonian Mercury*, Monday 27 January 1746.
109   TNA SP 54/27/48 Letters & Papers, Hawley to Cumberland, 29 January 1746.
110   *Glasgow Courant*, Monday 27 January 1746.

Route		Approximate Distance*	Date*	Days March*	Miles per Day*
Edinburgh	}	18 miles	15 January	1	18
Linlithgow			15 January		
Linlithgow	}	8 miles	16 January	1	8
Falkirk			16 January		
Falkirk	}	8 miles	17 January	1	18
Linlithgow			17 January		
Linlithgow	}	18 miles	18 January	1	8
Edinburgh			18 January		

*These dates and distances are approximate; the total distance marched on foot was approximately 147 miles in which was covered in 12 days of marching over a period of 17 days with an average rate of march of 12¼ miles per day when the troops were not halted. The infantry were mounted for the later portion of the march to Edinburgh, so it is possible that the earlier stages may have included one or more rest days and that further days may have been completed on horseback.

The March from Edinburgh to Perth

On the morning of Thursday 30 January, the Duke of Cumberland arrived in Edinburgh and 'having found the army in readiness to move his Royal Highness proposes to march as far as Linlithgow tomorrow with 14 battalions and Cobham's and Lord Mark Kerr's Dragoons'.[111]

Later that evening before their march westward from Edinburgh a privately produced 'Address to the Army' 'was dispersed among the common soldiers in their respective quarters'.[112]

An Address to the Army
Edinburgh Jan 30, 1746.

Gentlemen
The only apology I can make for troubling you with this short address is the hearty and sincere zeal I have for the noble cause you are now engaged in.

[A short section is faded and illegible in the copy referred to]
To meet an enemy on equal term is common, but it is the distinguishing characteristic of the British alone to despise numbers and even to advance with undaunted steps to the mouth of devouring cannon. After what you have already done, you'll find it an easy matter with a very small share of your wanted resolution to surmount this present difficulty, to crush the insolence of a set of thieves and plunderers, who have learned from their fathers to disturb every Government they have lived under. Some of you indeed have had no opportunity of showing your valour in foreign wars, but then that difference is owing only to chance: Sure Gentlemen, you think yourselves as all the word does just as good Men as them, and had you the same

111 *Newcastle Courant*, Saturday 1 February 1746 to Saturday 8 February 1746.
112 *Newcastle Courant*, Saturday 15 February 1746 to Saturday 22 February 1746.

opportunities, would have been no less distinguished your courage and valour than they were and many of you belong to Corps that never turned their backs before an enemy. Consider Gentlemen what character you bear; remember you are the free soldiers of a free people Recollect how happy the condition of soldiers of the British Army is, when compared with the starved and oppressed military slaves of France, whom you have always looked down upon with disdain and contempt. Encouraged then with the sincerest love of liberty, prompted by the strictest ties of religion, duty and gratitude and animated by the goodness of your cause, go forth shew your-selves like men and your enemies will as snow in the sun melt before you. Almighty God, who has often wrought Deliverance to these nations in so remarkable manner, will not fail powerfully to bless your endeavours against an attempt so destructive and bloody. Despite these cowardly intentions of such of our bosom enemies as craftily endeavour to magnify the courage as well as cruelty of these vagabonds in hopes thereby to impress you with fear. The experience you already have of them is a demonstration of how inconsiderable and contemptible their boasted broad-swords are against the close and regular fire of well-disciplined troops. Tis a maxim of war that those who behave best, suffer least; the more brave the less danger. If you but stand still and look them in the face they'll fly form you; they have not the smallest chance unless you turn your backs and then indeed you wantonly throw away both your lives and your honour. Remember you are fighting under generals who have often with glory distinguished themselves abroad and in consequence of the high trust committed to them will share every danger at home and observe your valour so as to faithfully reward it. Think then Gentlemen upon the noble cause you are contending for, follow your brave Generals, and under God there is not the least fear of the consequence. I expect to see you returning with Glory and Success amidst the applauses and acclamations of all the friends of Liberty crying in the triumphal procession, Victory! Victory! These are the Guardians of Liberty! These the deliverers of their Country! Be of good Courage, and play the Men for our People and the Cities of our God and the Lord do that which seemeth him good.[113]

Next day, early on 'Friday morning the Army began their March to the westward. The whole troops expressed the greatest eagerness to attack the rebels. General Huske led the van and his Royal Highness the Duke of Cumberland set out soon after the artillery passed through the city'.[114] The army marched from Edinburgh in two columns with Pulteney's Regiment heading for Linlithgow in the first column where they cantoned for the night.[115]

For the following days march the camp colour men were assembled at 4 o'clock in the morning and marched with the quartermaster general to Falkirk. The rest of the army assembled on the plain outside Linlithgow at 5 o'clock before they marched in a single

---

113 *Newcastle Courant*, Saturday 8 February 1746 to Saturday 15 February 1746.
114 *Newcastle Courant*, Saturday 1 February 1746 to Saturday 8 February 1746.
115 Stennis Historical Society 'Cantonment Register of the British Army in Scotland, 1746-52', Version 1.2, 13/01/19, <bit.ly/StennisHS>

column to encamp at Falkirk.[116] The Duke wrote 'our troops in general showed all the spirit that I could wish and would have retrieved whatever slips are past'.[117] That night the soldiers endured a hard frost and scarce supplies as they camped in their tents, the rebels having consumed all the provisions thereabouts.[118]

Next day the foot and artillery marched in one column for Stirling where the rebels had been laying siege to the castle, the march was accompanied by the sound of two large explosions from the nearby Church of St Ninian when the retreating rebels blew up their powder magazine.[119]

The army arrived at Stirling at 1 o'clock in the afternoon but they were then forced to halt in order for repairs to be carried out to the arch of the bridge over the river. This had previously been broken down by the garrison of Stirling Castle.[120] On the same day that the troops arrived at Stirling a vessel (the *Elizabeth and Mary*) with a great quantity of timber and house carpenters on board sailed from Leith for Stirling in order to repair the bridge.[121] The repairs however were mostly completed 'using timbers gathered by the Jacobites for the same purpose'.[122]

While halted at Stirling the men of Pulteney's Regiment were cantoned at St Ninians. The army halted at Stirling for two days and some spent the time indulging in macabre forms of entrepreneurship looking for booty and souvenirs within the trenches of the rebel siege works:

> [T]hey were continually digging in the trenches to find dead men, for their cloaths, sand bags etc. and others seeking out where cannon balls had razed the earth then they dig for them and by this means they got much money in selling them. Great numbers of rebels brought in to the Duke some of these our men as soon as taken stripped of their cloaths and dressed themselves up with their targets etc. and strutting about in this manner made a very comical appearance.[123]

Repairs to the bridge where completed by six in the morning of 4 February and at noon the same day the army marched in a single column heading for Dunblane where Pulteney's Regiment were cantoned.[124] Next day the army marched in a single column from Dunblane to Crieff. Pulteney's Regiment was cantoned that night in several villages about one mile

116 Stennis Historical Society 'Cantonment Register of the British Army in Scotland, 1746-52', Version 1.2, 13/01/19, <bit.ly/StennisHS>
117 *Newcastle Courant*, Saturday 8 February 1746 to Saturday 15 February 1746.
118 Ray, *A Journey through part of England and Scotland*, p.103.
119 Stennis Historical Society 'Cantonment Register of the British Army in Scotland, 1746-52', Version 1.2, 13/01/19, <bit.ly/StennisHS>
120 *The Gentleman's Magazine*, 1746, p.92.
121 *Caledonian Mercury*, Tuesday 4 February 1746.
122 *The Gentleman's Magazine*, 1746, p.92.
123 Ray, *A Journey through part of England and Scotland*, p.106.
124 Stennis Historical Society 'Cantonment Register of the British Army in Scotland, 1746-52', Version 1.2, 13/01/19, <bit.ly/StennisHS>

from Crieff.[125] On the same day 'a great quantity of Butcher Meat and Bread went from the City [Edinburgh] to the army by way of Stirling'.[126]

On Thursday 6th February at about 7 o'clock in the morning the army marched for Perth and the whole army arrived there about 5 o'clock in the afternoon 'in good spirits, after a march of 14 miles'.[127] The army marched from Crieff to Perth in two columns with Pulteney's regiment in the first column. Pulteney's Regiment were then cantoned in Perth from the Cross to Cutluggs Vennal, both sides of the street, the Meeting House and the Hammermen's Hall.[128]

While in Perth the soldiers 'made a kind of military auction or public sale of household goods, sheep, hogs etc. with what little silver they have been able to find in the houses of such Gentlemen as are with the rebels'.[129] More orthodox military activities were also taking place; time was spent 'laying in magazines of bread and forage and to rest the Foot regiments after the great fatigue they have undergone'.[130] The commissary of the army set out for Perth and carried 30 bakers with him to provide the troops with bread.[131] Boats were provided at Leith and horses at Kinghorn to carry a quantity of ammunition for the army at Perth.[132] The army could not march from Perth until a supply of coals had been sent to Aberdeen, Montrose, Inverness, and the other places in the north through which the army was to march, so on the 11th a considerable number of ships and vessels laden with coals was sent from the River Forth to the different ports in the north.[133]

Weather conditions were poor and the Duke omitted 'no opportunity to canton the army in such a manner to secure the soldiers from the intolerable cold'.[134] Back in Leith the *Rose in June* landed several packs of flannels, gloves and stockings for the Army, while the *Isabella* arrived with 'all sorts of provisions for the army.[135]

Measures were also undertaken to improve the efficiency of the troops and several orders were given out to the army while it was halted at Perth:

> When pieces cannot be drawn, an Officer to assemble the men, and see them fired together in a safe place.
> When the piquets are ordered out, the men are to have their ammunition, bread, knapsacks, and the pay in the Officers hands.

125 Stennis Historical Society 'Cantonment Register of the British Army in Scotland, 1746-52', Version 1.2, 13/01/19, <bit.ly/StennisHS>
126 *Caledonian Mercury*, Friday 7 February 1746.
127 *Stamford Mercury*, Thursday 20 February 1746.
128 Stennis Historical Society 'Cantonment Register of the British Army in Scotland, 1746-52', Version 1.2, 13/01/19, <bit.ly/StennisHS>
129 *Stamford Mercury*, Thursday 20 February 1746.
130 *The Gentleman's Magazine*, 1746, p.93.
131 *Glasgow Courant*, Monday 10 February 1746.
132 W.B. Blaikie (ed.), 'Origins of the Forty Five', *Scottish Historical Society*, series 2, vol. 2, (1916), p.366.
133 Blaikie (ed.), 'Origins of the Forty Five', p368.
134 *Newcastle Courant*, Saturday 15 February 1746 to Saturday 22 February 1746.
135 *Caledonian Mercury*, Monday 10 February 1746.

Whenever a guard or detachment which is marching by with arms passes by any guard, that guard is to be under arms; and if the guard or detachment which is marching by the beat of their drum, the other is to do the same with rested arms.

When any Officer makes a report in writing, he is always to mention his rank and the regiment he belongs to.

No drum to be beat for orders after the retreat.[136]

Despite the severity of the weather which was delaying the troops at Perth, detachments were sent out to Dunkeld, Creiff and Coupar in order to distress the rebels; piquets were also advanced several miles to keep a good look out and ensure the rebels could not draw supplies from the surrounding area.[137]

Table 5: The Stages of the March of Pulteney's Regiment from Edinburgh to Perth

Route		Approximate Distance*	Date*	Days March*	Miles per Day*
Edinburgh	. }	18 miles	31 January	1	18
Linlithgow			31 January		
Linlithgow	}	8 miles	1 February	1	8
Falkirk			1 February		
Falkirk	}	11½ miles	2 February	1	11½
Stirling			2 February		
Stirling	}	6 miles	4 February	1	6
Dunblane			4 February		
Dunblane	}	16 miles	5 February	1	16
Creif			5 February		
Creif	}	17 miles	6 February	1	17
Perth			6 February		

*These dates and distances are approximate; the total distance marched was approximately 76 miles in which was covered in 6 days of marching over a period of 7 days with an average rate of march of 12¾ miles per day when the troops were not halted.

The March from Perth to Aberdeen

On 14 February His Royal Highness the Duke of Cumberland sent forward a brigade consisting of three battalions of foot and a regiment of dragoons, the former to Coupar Angus the latter to Dundee. The infantry component (The Royal Brigade) of this advance guard comprised 2/Royals, Pulteney's Regiment and Fleming's Regiment, Pulteney's were billeted that night at the south end of the town. On the 15th the advance guard marched to Forfar where Pulteney's were billeted at the west end of the town and next day they marched to Montrose then halted. This halt was required to allow time for the other three infantry

---

136 Thomas Simes, *The Military Guide for Young Officers* (London: J. Milan, 1776), p.349.
137 *Glasgow Courant*, Monday 10 February 1746.

brigades, which had set off from Perth on the 19th, 20th, and 21st, to catch up with the advance guard.[138]

An officer wrote from Inglismaldie (about nine miles from Montrose) on the 22nd:

> We are the advance guard of the Army and shall be at Aberdeen on Tuesday next…
> We are just now in a dismal country, among mountains covered with snow up to
> the clouds, no coals nor any sort of fuel to be seen, yet I am in perfect health and
> notwithstanding all our fatigues will follow the Duke cheerfully… notwithstanding
> the disagreeableness of the place, its poverty and situation, we had yesterday for
> dinner a salmon just caught out of the river by us that weighed 31 lbs, which cost
> 2s our butter was bad but by the help of excellent vinegar and good claret I made a
> good dinner…[139]

On 23 February the advance guard marched to Bervie and Pulteney's were cantoned in the villages around the town. Next day they marched to Stonehaven were Pulteney's were billeted in the south end of the town. Finally, on the 25th, the advance guard arrived in Aberdeen and Pulteney's took up their quarters, part in the Old Town and part in the New Town.[140] The rest of the army stretched back along the route taken by the advance guard and it was 1 March before all the troops were re-united at Aberdeen. The troops were to stay in Aberdeen for the next month, held up again by bad weather.

This enforced delay enabled further measures to be taken to ensure the efficient running of the Aberdeen garrison and a number of orders were issued by the Duke:

> The surgeons of each regiment to visit their sick twice a day, and make a report to
> the Commanding Officers every morning.
> As soon as any centinel challenges Who comes there? The Searjeant is to answer,
> Rounds; and all centinels (except those who have orders to make rounds stand) are
> to reply, Pass rounds, keep clear of my arms, all is well.
> Officers that mount guard to wear their sashes tucked up short.
> It is recommended to the Commanding Officers of regiments, to order their new
> officers to attend the parade every morning.[141]

Supplies and all sorts of provisions arriving at Leith were now sent forward by boat to Aberdeen;[142] there was 'a considerable quantity of biscuits' to be shipped north.[143] In Aberdeen itself the army could buy beef and pork for a penny farthing the pound,[144] although supplies were somewhat limited there were no shortages due to the provisions arriving in the port by

138 Stennis Historical Society 'Cantonment Register of the British Army in Scotland, 1746-52', Version 1.2, 13/01/19, <bit.ly/StennisHS>
139 *Newcastle Courant*, Saturday 8 March 1746 to Saturday 15 March 1746.
140 Stennis Historical Society 'Cantonment Register of the British Army in Scotland, 1746-52', Version 1.2, 13/01/19, <bit.ly/StennisHS>
141 Simes, *The Military Guide for Young Officers*, p.350.
142 *Newcastle Courant*, Saturday 1 March 1746 to Saturday 8 March 1746.
143 Blaikie (ed.), 'Origins of the Forty Five', p369.
144 *Newcastle Courant*, Saturday 8 March 1746 to Saturday 15 March 1746.

sea. Sick soldiers in Edinburgh, once recovered, also made their way to Aberdeen, weather permitting.[145]

The weather though continually prevented the march of the army, there was 'a great snow' in early March,[146] the weather was 'almost every day snow or sleet and at night frost'.[147] In late March preparations to leave Aberdeen were again halted this time because 'it rained so hard'.[148]

Still the troops were 'all in top spirits wishing that the rebels may come face them'.[149] The regiments were said to be 'all in good health and spirits, the Officers remarkably assiduous and diligent'.[150] They were 'commanded by a brave and capable young general who has the hearts of the whole soldiery'.[151]

On 12 March the dragoons moved out of Aberdeen and the opportunity was taken to consolidate the billets of Pulteney's Regiment in Old Aberdeen.[152] Then, on 26 March, Pulteney's marched from Old Aberdeen to Oldmeldrum where the regiment stayed until 7 April. This redeployment was partly carried out in order to ease the provision of supplies within Aberdeen itself. The army had been reinforced and reorganised and they were now part of the 5th Brigade (the Reserve).[153]

It seems to have been around this time that there was a parting of the ways between Pulteney's Regiment and Squire Thornton. It was reported that:

When Pultney's Regiment was ordered from Old Meldrum to Buchan on a command one day, these gentlemen who declined no fatigue, and had usually joined that corps, marched along. But coming the first night to a little village called Ellon, the Quartermaster would not assign Quarters to the volunteers as Officers, and none of the Officers would give orders for it, which and some other things of this kind effectually disgusted them, so that they immediately left the army and returned home.[154]

By early April Squire Thornton had arrived in Edinburgh on his way home from Aberdeen.[155]

At the end of March the troops in Aberdeen received a welcome supply of winter clothing, part of 'The Guildhall Relief Fund'.[156] The soldiers clothing in general was noted to be in a

145 *Glasgow Courant*, Monday 10 March 1746.
146 *Newcastle Courant*, Saturday 15 March 1746 to Saturday 22 March 1746.
147 *Derby Mercury*, Friday 21 March 1746 to 28 March 1746.
148 *Derby Mercury*, Friday 4 April 1746 to Friday 11 April 1746.
149 *Caledonian Mercury*, Monday 10 March 1746.
150 *Newcastle Courant*, Saturday 22 March 1746 to Saturday 29 March 1746.
151 *Derby Mercury*, Friday 28 March 1746 to Friday 4 April 1746.
152 Stennis Historical Society 'Cantonment Register of the British Army in Scotland, 1746-52', Version 1.2, 13/01/19, <bit.ly/StennisHS>
153 Stennis Historical Society 'Cantonment Register of the British Army in Scotland, 1746-52', Version 1.2, 13/01/19, <bit.ly/StennisHS>
154 Blaikie (ed.), 'Origins of the Forty Five', p158.
155 *Caledonian Mercury*, Tuesday 8 April 1746.
156 Alastair Massie & Jonathan Oates (eds.), *The Duke of Cumberland's Campaigns in Britain & the Low Countries 1745-1748: A Selection of His Letters* (Stroud: The History Press for The Army Records Society, 2018), p.174.

bad condition due to the extraordinary fatigues of the campaign and the soldiers were said to be thankful for the for the items provided.[157]

Table 6: The Stages of the March of Pulteney's Regiment from Perth to Aberdeen and Oldmeldrum

Route		Approximate Distance*	Date*	Days March*	Miles per Day*
Perth	}	13 miles	14 February	1	13
Coupar of Angus			14 February		
Coupar of Angus	}	17½ miles	15 February	1	17½
Forfar			15 February		
Forfar	}	18½ miles	16 February	1	18½
Montrose			16 February		
Montrose	}	12 miles	23 February	1	12
Bervie			23 February		
Bervie	}	10 miles	24 February	1	10
Stonehaven			24 February		
Stonehaven	}	14 miles	25 February	1	14
Aberdeen			25 February		
Aberdeen	}	16½ miles	22 March	1	16½
Oldmeldrum			22 March		

*These dates and distances are approximate; the total distance marched was approximately 101 miles in which was covered in 7 days of marching over a period of 37 days with an average rate of march of 14½ miles per day when the troops were not halted.

The March from Aberdeen to Nairn and the Battle of Culloden

In early April dry weather and favourable winds bought more provisions into Aberdeen along with the prospect that the River Spey would become fordable.[158] On Tuesday 8 April the soldiers were reviewed by the Duke and 'they all seemed in good health and high spirits… they all with one consent gave three cheerful Huzzas and declared they would stand by His Royal Highness with the last drop of their blood'.[159] The army finally set off early in the morning in four separate divisions and from three separate locations.[160] The Duke 'endeared himself exceedingly to the soldiers by walking most of the way on foot with them, generally using one of the soldiers Tenttrees [tent poles?] for a staff'.[161]

It was during the march from Aberdeen that His Royal Highness the Duke 'took pains to confer with every battalion on the proper method of using the musket and bayonet to advantage against the sword and target'.[162]

---

157 See appendix to this chapter for details of the items purchased by the fund.
158 *Derby Mercury*, Friday 11 April 1746 to Friday 18 April 1746.
159 *Newcastle Courant*, Saturday 19 April 1746 to Saturday 26 April.
160 *Caledonian Mercury*, Monday 14 April 1746.
161 Blaikie (ed.), 'Origins of the Forty Five', p159.
162 *Newcastle Courant*, Saturday 3 May 1746 to Saturday 10 May.

On arrival at Banff His Royal Highness the Duke 'ordered all the army to be drawn up in a great field… and ordered a gill of brandy to every man to revive him after his long days march'.[163] The troops halted at Banff for a day before resuming their march to the camp at Cullen; as they marched along the coast they were accompanied by 'a fine fleet of transports not far from us at sea attending our army'.[164]

From Cullen the army marched to the River Spey in two columns. Pulteney's, as part of the reserve, followed the route of the right-hand column; before them was an advance guard formed of all the grenadiers, camp colour men, and a piquet of Kingston's Light Horse.[165] The army reached the River Spey about noon and 'the foot waded over as fast as they arrived and though the water came up to their middles they went on with great cheerfulness'.[166] 'The poor women who among the soldiers are called the heavy train were obliged to wade with their cloaths packt upon their heads'.[167] They crossed the Spey 'with no other loss than one dragoon and four women all drowned'.[168]

Once across the Spey the army encamped on the banks of the river, and, being so close to the rebels at this point, the Duke issued 'a strict order throughout the camp making it death for any Soldier to be found out of the limits of the camp that night'.[169]

From the camp at the mouth of the River Spey the army marched in four columns with the Reserve forming part of the first column. The army was encamped at Nairn on the 15th where 'the Army rested and got their arms and ammunition in excellent order, it being the Duke's Birthday the troops were in the highest spirits',[170] and 'everyman had a sufficient quantity of biscuit, cheese and brandy allowed him at the sole expense of the Duke'.[171] 'That night intelligence was received that the clans were exceeding numerous but this in no manner dismayed the meanest soldier in the Army'.[172]

On the 16th, the army was under arms at 3 o'clock in the morning.[173] Thereafter:

[T]he commanders of every regiment received their full instruction in writing in what manner to act and how the men were to be formed.

Before the Army proceeded on their march general orders of the day were read to every company in line.

If any person taking care of the Train horses or any other Horses loaded with Tents or General Baggage should abscond or run from them He or they should be punished with immediate death: And if any Officer or Soldier did not behave

163 Michael Hughes, *A Plain Narrative or Journal of the Late Rebellion Begun in 1745* (London: Henry Whitridge, 1746), p.33.
164 Ray, *A Journey through part of England and Scotland*, p149.
165 Stennis Historical Society 'Cantonment Register of the British Army in Scotland, 1746-52', Version 1.2, 13/01/19, <bit.ly/StennisHS>
166 *Derby Mercury*, Friday 18 April 1746 to Friday 25 April 1746.
167 Hughes, *A Plain Narrative*, p.34.
168 *Derby Mercury*, Friday 18 April 1746 to Friday 25 April 1746.
169 Hughes, *A Plain Narrative*, p.34.
170 *Glasgow Courant*, Monday 21 April 1746.
171 Hughes, *A Plain Narrative*, p35.
172 *Glasgow Courant*, Monday 21 April 1746.
173 *Derby Mercury*, Friday 18 April 1746 to Friday 25 April 1746.

according to his Duty in his rank or station during the time of the engagement should be liable to the same punishment at the discretion of a general Court Martial according to the nature of their default and misbehaviour.[174]

As they set out from their camp at Nairn, the bat horses and women of each regiment followed their respective columns and the camp colour men marched with their respective regiments.[175] The troops 'moved on being allowed no liquor and no provision but a piece of ammunition bread'.[176]

James Grainger, surgeon's mate in Pulteney's Regiment, wrote an account of the battle that followed:

On the morning of the 16th we decamped by break of day from Nairn and were in sight of the enemy by eleven, who were drawn up in one very long line across Culloden Moor. Upon this our advanced guard came back, the army was in an instant marshalled in order of battle. The cavalry was equally divided on the Flanks, the Campbells were posted at a little distance from the left of the front line, and orders were sent to the bat-men, women, &c., forbidding them to come within a mile of the rear. These material points thus settled, we continued our march, and about 12 were come so near them that I could observe their right wing to be composed of the Clans, the left of the French, and their centre of the Lowlanders. Where their cavalry was I could not see. The ground on which they stood was plain, and the field seemed every way adapted to decide the fate of the Rebellion. Here the whole Army fixed bayonets, and renewed their priming, while our nine piece of cannon were planted at regular distances in the front of the first line. The Duke says a battle without cannon is like dancing without music his ears were soon gratified with that martial music. For the Rebels now welcomed us to the plain from a battery on their right, but they fired too high and the balls whizzed over the Corps de Reserve. The compliment was returned forthwith by a complete round from our Artillery, but to better purpose; most of the shots took effect and laid numbers of them sprawling on the ground. The cannon gave our men infinite spirits. The enemy renewed their charge not only from their first battery but from two others to their left. They only made our gunners fire the faster, and really complimented the enemy at least twenty for one. The wind drove the smoke in the teeth of the enemy; their batteries were silenced in the space of eight minutes, and their line partly raked. The thunder of our cannon was perpetual, and if they had stood still much longer where they were, our matrosses would have done the business. This they were sensible of. Their whole line advanced forward to attack our first line in the order they were drawn up.

The Clans rather flew than marched, consequently our left was not only soonest but hottest engaged, for nothing could be more furious than their onset, which no

---

174 Hughes, *A Plain Narrative*, p.37.
175 Stennis Historical Society 'Cantonment Register of the British Army in Scotland, 1746-52', Version 1.2, 13/01/19, <bit.ly/StennisHS>
176 Hughes, *A Plain Narrative*, p.37.

troops but these, headed by our magnanimous hero, could have withstood. Yet not a regiment was broke, not a soul deserted his colours, true, indeed, their small arms did little execution, but they seemed determined to make amends for this by their broadswords, had not the regiments they attacked prevented them by a very brisk and heavy fire we had some hundreds of them breathless on the ground. This ruder reception (perhaps) than they expected did not, however, dispirit the Claris. They rallied, and before our left, (viz., Barrels, Monroes, and the Highlanders), could load, came again like lions to the charge, sword in hand, but the claymores would make no impression against the bayonet charged breast high. Our men stood like a wall, shoulder to shoulder. Here, however, Lord Robert Ker was killed and Lieut.-Colonel Rich lost his left hand. More officers than these must have fallen had not the battalions in the centre of our line, viz., Scots Fusiliers and Cholmondeley's, before whom the Lowlanders began precipitately to fly almost without attacking, turned part of their fire against the Clans, and with such success that but few of them had leisure to return from the attack.

The confusion of the enemy was now pretty universal, only the French as they marched more orderly so they were only come now within musket shot of our right. At the beginning of the action, our regiment, Pultney's, was advanced from the Corps de Reserve and posted on the right of the Royals, an honour for which we were indebted to the Duke of Cumberland, and here it was that we not only regained our character, but were particularly complimented by his Royal Highness. But what could they or any other troops have done? The Royals and our regiment were ready and eager to engage, and not a man of either the 2nd or Corps de Reserve had discharged. They, (the French), however, made a show to charge and flank us, but after a fire (not like the French) they followed the example of their mountainous friends and made with all the swiftness their feet could carry them towards the town. Our regiment did not miss this opportunity, and with one good volley made numbers of them bite the ground. The whole field on their side was one continued scene of slaughter and dismay. They flew scattered in little clusters everywhere, but most made after the Pretender to the mountains. Our cannon again thundered. Our light horse and dragoons who had never been engaged were sent after them and did terrible execution many they took prisoners, but more they killed, for the pursuit lasted four miles beyond Inverness.

In the field were taken ten 6-pounders. Whilst His Royal Highness advanced at the head of the infantry towards Inverness he was met by an officer from the Brigades who surrendered themselves prisoners of war in town. Inverness was immediately taken possession of by a regiment, where they found 6 more field pieces, and our royal conqueror entered the place about 4 o'clock. Immediately upon the flight of the enemy, I rode over the field of battle. You may be sure it gave me infinite joy to see those who threatened ruin to our glorious constitution of Church and State dead in the field, which joy was not a little augmented by observing how very few, not twenty of our men, were killed. As the Campbells were on the left, and therefore in the hottest of the action, they lost two Captains that is the sum of the slain. That of the enemy cannot certainly be known, for we daily find dead bodies, six, eight miles from the place, it is conjectured to amount to 1,800. Our men have got a great deal of booty. The Pretender's coach and Boger's are taken. On the coach was painted the Welsh arms and below 'Prince Charles' in letters of gold. We have between 2,000 and 3,000 prisoners. Amongst several of distinction are Earls Kilmarnock, Cromarty, and their sons; Lord Drummond, Glenbucket, Stewart of Ardchiel, Appin, &c. They mustered 8,350 the day before the battle, as was found in an officer's pocket; it would have been ended fatal to us had we given way, for their Prince gave orders to spare neither man, woman, or child, and so confident was he of success that in the same orders he forbad any man to stir from his rank to plunder till after the pursuit.[177]

Other reports describe Pulteney's role in the battle from their position on the extreme right of the line. Opposite them the rebels 'came down three several times within a hundred yards of our men firing their pistols and brandishing their swords but the Royals and Pulteney's hardly took their firelocks from their Shoulders so that after those feint attempts they made off'.[178] Another account elaborates on the incident alluded to in the letter from Grainger:

> During the action the French Brigade, being drawn from the Right of the Rebel Second Line to the Left of their Front, made a Motion towards our Right, which the Duke observing ordered Pulteney's Regiment to face about and attack them; but though in coming down the Monsieur's presented and shouldered twice, they never fired a Shot; which was regarded as one of the oddest Circumstances happened that day.[179]

At the end of the battle Pulteney's Regiment had fortuitously recorded no losses amongst its officers and men. A return of the numbers of officers and men in each battalion on the day of the Battle of Culloden gave the following figures for Major General Pulteney's Regiment:

Field Officers 2
Captains 6
Subalterns 14
Serjeants 23
Drummers 19
Rank and File 410[180]

177 George Bain, *History of Nairnshire* (Nairn: The Telegraph Office, 1893), p.356.
178 *Derby Mercury*, Friday 25 April 1746 to Friday 2 May 1746. Despatch from the Duke of Cumberland giving particulars of the victory obtained over the rebels.
179 Samuel Boyse M.A., *An Impartial History of the Late Rebellion in 1745* (Dublin: Edward & John Exshaw, 1748), p149.
180 *Caledonian Mercury*, Tuesday 27 May 1746; note, however, that Massie & Oates (eds.), *Cumberland's Campaigns in Britain & the Low Countries*, p.184 gives 310.

Table 7: The Stages of the March of Pulteney's Regiment from Oldmeldrum to Inverness

Route		Approximate Distance*	Date*	Days March*	Miles per Day*
Oldmeldrum	}	15 miles	8 April	1	15
Turiff			8 April		
Turiff	}	11 miles	9 April	1	11
Banff			9 April		
Banff	}	9½ miles	11 April	1	9½
Cullen			11 April		
Cullen	}	15miles	12 April	1	15
Speymouth			12 April		
Speymouth	}	14½ miles	13 April	1	14½
Alves			13 April		
Alves	}	8½ miles	14 April	1	8½
Nairn			14 April		
Nairn	}	8½ miles	16 April	1	8½
Culloden			16 April		

*These dates and distances are approximate; the total distance marched was approximately 82 miles in which was covered in 7 days of marching over a period of 9 days with an average rate of march of 11¾ miles per day when the troops were not halted.

After the Battle: Inverness and the Return to Flanders

Following the defeat of the rebels at Culloden the army moved on to Inverness the same day and encamped on the moors just by the town.[181]

> Soon after this the Duke sent a party to the estate of Simon Frazer Laird of Lovat with orders to burn down his dwelling house and bring of all that was moveable. His fine salmon weirs were destroyed and salmon in abundance was bought into the camp and enjoyed by the soldiers. Inverness became a wonderful exchange for an odd variety of merchandise, all manner of plaids, broadswords, dirks and pistols; plaid waistcoats, officers laced waistcoats, hats, bonnets, blankets and oatmeal bags; (for in the field near Culloden House there was a magazine or granary of oatmeal that lay scattered about). While our highland fair lasted if a soldier was seen in the streets of Inverness the good wives and lasses would certainly run after him to buy a plaid.[182]

Despite this private trade, military discipline was maintained and a number of orders were issued in respect to the running of the camp:

---

181 *Newcastle Courant*, Saturday 19 April 1746.
182 Hughes, *A Plain Narrative*, pp.51-52.

The beating in camp to be taken regularly by signals, beginning from the right of the first line and continued from the left of the second line; the quarter guard to march off, and to be trooped back at the same time, and no regimental punishment to intercept the marching off or relieving of those guards.

When a regiment sends for bread, coals, straw or forage, the men are to regularly paraded and marched by a Subaltern Officer of each Brigade, and a Serjeant of each regiment to the place of delivery, besides the Quarter-master or the quarter-master Serjeant, the Officers to take care that the men receive it regularly and in their turns, and then to march them back to camp.[183]

The First Brigade, now comprised of the Royals, Pulteney's and Sempill's Regiments, marched from the camp at Inverness on 13 May bound for Perth;[184] it was proposed that they would 'visit the Macintoshes, Macphersons, and the Duke of Athol's tenants about Blair and Dunkeld' along the way.[185] At the same time their baggage was loaded onto ships ready to be transported by sea.

They had left Inverness just in time:

[E]very part of town filled with sick soldiers. Their sicknesses at first where chiefly pleurisies and fluxes, the last of which was thought to be chiefly occasioned by drinking the bad water of the ness. A little while later we had a most terrible malignant fever introduced amongst us by the Regiment of Brigadier Houghton coming from the sea in ships that had before carried rebel prisoners amongst which was the Goal Distemper.[186]

By 22 May Pulteney's Regiment were reported to have arrived in Perth having 'met not with the least disturbance on the road thither'.[187] At Blair Athol they had received the submission of two groups of Macphersons who surrendered their arms and were permitted to 'return home and trust in the Kings Mercy'.[188]

£4,000 had been sent to His Royal Highness the Duke to be used as he saw fit for 'such regiments as behave well in action'.[189] Pulteney's share of this money came to £276. The distribution of the fund seems to have been agreed in early June and the money was distributed to the numbers on the spot which appear to be higher than the totals returned of those who served at Culloden:

183 Simes, *The Military Guide for Young Officers* pp.333, 329.
184 Stennis Historical Society 'Cantonment Register of the British Army in Scotland, 1746-52', Version 1.2, 13/01/19, <bit.ly/StennisHS>
185 *Derby Mercury*, Friday 23 May 1746.
186 Ray, *A Journey through part of England and Scotland*, p.169.
187 *Caledonian Mercury*, Thursday 22 May 1746.
188 *Newcastle Courant*, Saturday 24 May 1746.
189 *Newcastle Courant*, Saturday 3 May 1746.

Serjeants 23
Corporals 26
Drummers 18
Rank and File 479[190]

On 12 June Pulteney's and Sempill's Regiments received orders to prepare for foreign service,[191] and on 24 June *Samaritan* transport ship arrived at Dundee (about 20 miles from Perth) where it disembarked 'clothing for Pulteney and St. Clair's regiments and the wounded'.[192]

The rank and file strength of Pulteney's regiment was recorded as 650 men by 24 June. A further 50 men were to be drafted from the two additional companies in order to bring the regiment up to full strength. The regiment was ordered to take their old tents and field equipage with them from Scotland and complete their arms and camp equipage at London.[193]

By the end of July Pulteney's Regiment was ready to march from Perth to Kinghorn and prepare for embarkation.[194] Boarding the transports took place over three days from 31 July to 2 August and Pulteney's, Wolfe's, and Sempill's Regiments finally sailed on 5 August from the Road of Leith bound for Holland.[195] Next day '36 Transports, with the regiments Sempil, Pultney and Wolfe on board passed by the Bar of Shields for Flanders under a proper Convoy'.[196] Finally the Regiments of Wolfe, Pulteney and Sempil passed by Helvoetsluys on their way to Willemstadt where they arrived on the night of 9 August.[197]

Table 9: The Stages of the March of Pulteney's Regiment from Inverness to Kinghorn

Route		Approximate Distance*	Date*	Days March*	Miles per Day*
Inverness	} 80 miles		13 May	5	15
Blair Atholl			17 May		
Blair Atholl	} 34 miles		18 May	5	11
Perth			22 May		
Perth	} 30 miles		27 July	3	9½
Kinghorn			30 July		

*These dates and distances are approximate; the total distance marched was approximately 144 miles in which was covered in 13 days of marching over a period of 79 days with an average rate of march of 11 miles per day when the troops were not halted.

---

190 Blaikie (ed.), 'Origins of the Forty Five', p.432.
191 Atkinson, 'Jenkins' Ear, The Austrian Succession War and the 'Forty-Five', pp.280-299.
192 TNA, ADM 354/133/58, request for orders from Thomas Corbett, the Master of the *Samaritan* transport.
193 TNA, SP 54/32/24D, state of the brigade ordered to Flanders.
194 *Caledonian Mercury*, Thursday 24 July 1746.
195 *Caledonian Mercury*, Tuesday 5 August 1746.
196 *Stamford Mercury*, Thursday 14 August 1746.
197 *Derby Mercury*, Friday 15 August 1746.

The Men of the Regiment

During the 11 months they had spent in Britain the men of Pulteney's Regiment had marched over 1,100 miles and fought in two battles and, although they are rarely mentioned, the wives and children of soldiers would have marched along with them every step of the way. Though their casualties from battle had been barely a dozen they had probably suffered nearly 250 casualties from sickness and the fatigues of a winter campaign, although many of these would have subsequently recovered and re-joined the regiment.

The individuals have become lost over time; indeed, they were barely recorded at the time beyond references to 'the English Foot' or 'the King's Troops'. Some government soldiers however can be tentatively identified as serving during this period and Dr Jonathan Oates has distilled a list of nearly a hundred or so individuals of Pulteney's Regiment from the Chelsea Pensioners Service Records.[198] These can allow some generalisations to be made about the composition of the regiment in terms of age, occupation and nationality. In turn these can be compared with figures for the army as a whole as presented in Andrew Cormack's recent publication *These Meritorious Objects of the Royal Bounty*,[199] which has analysed over 14,000 individual records.

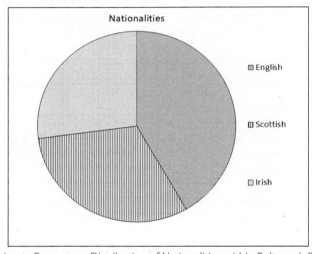

Figure 1: Approximate Percentage Distribution of Nationalities within Pulteney's Regiment in 1746

Estimated figures for Pulteney's Regiment based on selected examples provided by Dr Jonathan Oates		Average figures for the British Army based on *These Meritorious Objects of the Royal Bounty*' Appendix 6-1	
English	42%	English	63%
Scottish	31%	Scottish	20%
Irish	27%	Irish	17%

---

198 Personal communication from Dr Jonathan Oates, drawn from his research into pension records from TNA, WO116/4-7.
199 Andrew Cormack, 'These Meritorious Objects of the Royal Bounty'; The Chelsea Out-pensioners in the Early Eighteenth Century (London: Privately Published, 2017).

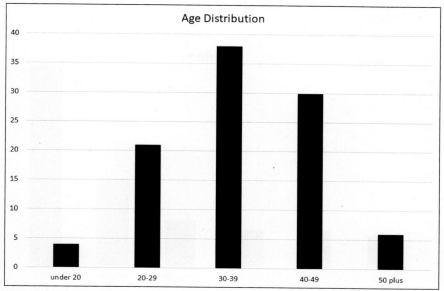

Figure 2: Approximate Percentage Distribution of Ages within Pulteney's Regiment in 1746

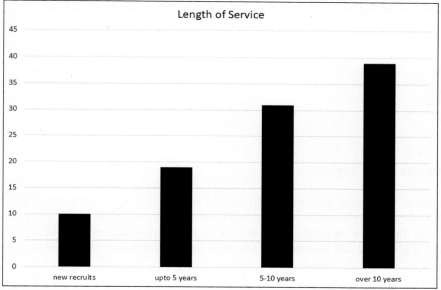

Figure 3: Approximate Percentage Distribution of Length of Service within Pulteney's Regiment in 1746

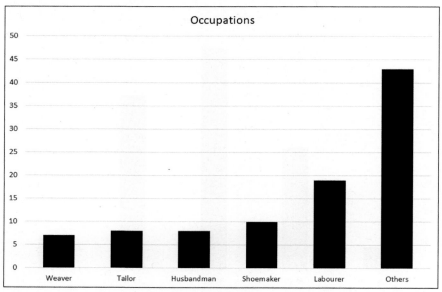

Figure 4: Approximate Percentage Distribution of Occupations within Pulteney's Regiment in 1746

Estimated figures for Pulteney's Regiment based on selected examples provided by Dr Jonathan Oates		Average figures for the British Army based on *These Meritorious Objects of the Royal Bounty* Appendix 9-1	
Weaver	7%	Weaver	10%
Tailor	8%	Tailor	5%
Husbandman	8%	Husbandman	9%
Shoemaker	10%	Shoemaker	7%
Labourer	20%	Labourer	21%
Others	47%	Others	48%

The Officers of the Regiment

A full list of regimental officers for the period can be found in *Cumberland's Army, the British Army at Culloden* by Stuart Reid and it seems unnecessary to repeat it here.[200] Suffice to say that the regiment's colonel, Major General Henry Pulteney, was in charge of the garrison of Hull and not present with his regiment, which was commanded in the field by the Lieutenant Colonel Thomas Cockayne.

---

200 Stuart Reid, *Cumberland's Army, the British Army at Culloden* (Leigh-on-Sea: Partizan Press, 2006), p.46.

Thomas Cockayne was the son of a Mayor of Derby and brother of a Lord Mayor of London; he was baptised at St Peter's in Derby in 1697. He had served with the regiment since 1716 when he was appointed ensign, and was appointed lieutenant colonel in 1744. He had a number of appointments outside of the regiment being made Secretary to the Order of Bath in 1735, appointed Deputy Judge Advocate of the Forces ordered to Flanders in 1742,[201] and Adjutant General to Field Marshal Wade in 1744.[202]

Appendix – The Guildhall Relief Fund[203]

The fund was instituted on 27 November 1745 at the Guildhall, London, in consideration of the particular hardships and inconveniences which may be suffered by such soldiers as now are or shall be employed in his Majesty's service during the winter season.

The monies raised were used to purchase the following items:

STOCKINGS.	
Long hose at 12s per dozen pair	10,000 Pair
Short Hose 11s 10d per dozen pair	6,504 Pair
BREECHES.	
To be made of Kersey half of them red and half blue of three sizes at the rate 3s 3½d each pair, with as good lining and all to be strongly and well sewed; Two thousand pair to be delivered each week till the whole was completed	15,000 Pair
SHIRTS.	
At the price of 3s 6d; each shirt to contain 2 Ells ⅞th of cloth with an allowance of 2d per shirt for 600 to be made somewhat better being intended for Serjeants, 1500 to be delivered weekly until the whole was compleated	12,000
WOOLLEN CAPS.	
To be of blue, red and green at the price of 5d per Cap the whole number to be delivered on the 1st January	10,000
BLANKETS.	
To be nine Quarter wide and not above 13s 6d per pair	1,000
WOOLEN GLOVES.	
Being in different sizes at the rate of 5s to 6s and 2d per dozen pair	12,000 Pair
WOOLLEN ANKLE SPATTERDASHERS.	
To be made in three sizes with flat metal buttons and the straps of Russia Drab of the price of Eighteen Pence Halfpenny a pair	9,100 Pair

---

201 Charles Dalton, *George the First's Army 1714-1727* (London: Eyre & Spottiswoode Ltd, 1912), Vol.II, p.297.
202 *The Gentleman's* Magazine, 1744, p.339.
203 Blaikie (ed.), 'Origins of the Forty Five', pp.429-431.

3

The Noblemen's Regiments

Andrew Cormack

From the birth of the regular British Army it was kept as small as possible. There was much resentment against soldiers in the immediate post-Restoration period because of the way the Commonwealth New Model Army had effectively usurped power, and the governing class was fearful that any military forces would constitute a threat to the liberties of Englishmen. Nevertheless, it was an era in which no country that expected its neighbours to take it seriously could afford to be without an army, though England, as an island was more fortunately guarded by nature, ably assisted by the Royal Navy, than most.

When conflict arose, it was always the case therefore that England's, and after 1707 Great Britain's, armed forces had to be hugely expanded to meet the challenge. However, the persistence of suspicion of land forces, as well as the desire for economy and faith in maritime power, which, even in peacetime, bolstered and protected ship-borne trade, always meant that the Army was much reduced at the end of each war. Expansion, when deemed necessary, was carefully controlled and tended to address the immediate threat rather than providing a generous amount of spare manpower for unforeseen circumstances.

This mind-set was not unknown to Britain's principal enemy on the European mainland, France, and when war broke out, that country always had recourse to the strategic possibility of distracting its enemy from the main theatre of operations by opening a second front within the British Isles in the form of a rebellion of the Jacobite supporters of the monarchy that had been deposed in 1688. William III had been distracted from the defence of his original country, the United Netherlands, by having to conduct a campaign against Franco-Jacobite forces in Ireland during the Nine Years War in Flanders.[1] Queen Anne had been obliged to withdraw troops from the War of the Spanish Succession to counter an expedition of 12 French battalions that sailed from Dunkirk to Scotland in 1708.[2] George I had barely established himself in London, and was not absolutely sure of his popularity with the English people, before an attempt to undermine him was made through Jacobite

---

1   J.G. Simms, *Jacobite Ireland, 1685-91* (London: Routledge & Kegan Paul, 1969) though a little old, provides a good overall account.

2   J.L. Roberts, *The Jacobite Wars – Scotland and the Military Campaigns of 1715 and 1745* (Edinburgh: Polygon, 2002), pp.8-11 contains a brief account of the 1708 expedition.

risings in Lancashire and the Scottish Highlands in 1715.[3] Likewise George II's army was deeply embroiled in Flanders in 1745 when, with French encouragement, later augmented with military support, the Jacobites rose again in Scotland.[4]

The response to these threats was always to withdraw British forces from mainland Europe in order to counter the uprising at home, thereby, as was intended, giving the French an added advantage in Flanders, the main theatre of the war. Once it became clear that Prince Charles Edward Stuart's uprising in Scotland was indeed a serious threat, British troops were withdrawn from the War of the Austrian Succession. Unlike in previous rebellions, however, the Hanoverian dynasty had sufficiently embedded and endeared itself to a significant section of the governing class that an upsurge of loyal sentiment arose that manifested itself in offers by the nobility to raise regiments to assist the regime against its enemies at home. The so-called Noblemen's Regiments – 11 of foot and two of horse – constitute a fascinating story about forces raised for service during a particular war, which disappeared, almost without trace, from the Army after the crisis had passed.[5]

One such regiment of Foot was raised by 'Our Right Trusty and Well Beloved Henry Arthur, Lord Herbert of Chirbury … for Our Service in Our County of Salop' in October 1745. It is referred to in official documents as Lord Herbert's Regiment of Foot, but in internal documents and in the county it was known as 'The Shrophire Fuziliers'. To digress for a moment, although the colonels' commissions of Berkeley's, Herbert's, Edgcumbe's, Cholmondeley's and Harcourt's are written in the form '… to be raised for Our Service in our County of Gloucester/ Salop/Cornwall/Chester/Oxford' respectively, it is clear that this did not mean that they were only to be employed in those counties. The raising commissions for Ancaster's, Bedford's, Halifax's, Granby's, Gower's and Montagu's Regiments of Foot make no mention of their recruiting areas, whilst Falmouth's and Bolton's actually give the regiments' titles as the Cornish and the Hampshire Regiments of Foot. Kingston's Light Horse is qualified as 'to be raised in Nottingham'.[6]

Apart from His Lordship, the first Captain to receive his commission was a certain Forrester Leighton.[7] He was the son of Sir Edward Leighton, 2nd Baronet, who had married in about 1709 and produced his first son in 1713, naming him Forrester, which was his wife, Rachel's, maiden name. Forrester was originally commissioned into Major General Humphrey Gore's Dragoons, the 1st (Royal) Dragoons, in September 1730,[8] though he never rose above the rank of cornet and retired from the service 'on account of the ill state of his health' in April 1739.[9] This was not, however, Forrester's only foray into the military life,

---

3   D. Szechi, *1715 The Great Jacobite Rebellion* (London: Yale University Press, 2006) gives a good survey of the uprising in Lancashire and Scotland.

4   C. Duffy, *The '45 – Bonnie Prince Charlie and the Untold Story of the Jacobite Rising* (London: Cassell, 2003) provides excellent coverage of the 1745 Rebellion.

5   This chapter is an expanded and enhanced amalgam of two articles that appeared in the *Journal of the Society for Army Historical Research* – See: A. Cormack, 'An Officer of Lord Herbert's Foot, 1745-46', *JSAHR*, Vol.81, Spring 2003, pp.1-7, and A. Cormack, 'The Noblemen's Regiments of the Jacobite Rebellion, 1745-'46', *JSAHR*, Vol.82, Winter 2004, pp.279-290.

6   The National Archives (United Kingdom) (TNA), Commission Book, WO 25/21, ff.156-220.

7   TNA, Commission Book, WO 25/21, f.168.

8   TNA, Commission Book, WO 25/18, f.166.

9   TNA, Commission Notification Book, WO 25/133, f.149.

for the disturbances of the Jacobite Rebellion brought him back to the service of his King in 1745.[10] To commemorate that service, Leighton had himself painted by Allan Ramsay, thereby providing what is, almost certainly, the only record of the dress of the officers of Lord Herbert of Cherbury's Regiment of Foot.[11] The portrait features among the illustrations to this volume.

Though slightly unexpected for an officer of the British Army in 1745 to be dressed in blue, it should come as no great surprise that the sitter was thus attired. A few of the other Noblemen's regiments raised were clothed in blue coats rather than red, though it is equally true that some of the new noble colonels chose to make their regiments resemble their fellows in the Regulars, whether of Foot or Horse. The best known of the latter is Kingston's Light Horse, though it has been suggested that Kingston's and Montagu's mounted regiments wore blue clothing.[12] In the case of the latter, reference is made to a notice in the *Ipswich Journal* concerning the proposed raising of an unusually large regiment of 10 troops (the standard number being six), whose clothing was projected as being blue lined red. However, the notice was published in the edition of 17 May 1744, which was 14 months before Charles Edward Stuart landed in Scotland. There is no trace of this regiment ever having come into existence and the likelihood of that clothing being revived 19 months later must be conjectural. It may well be that Morier's painting of a private of the Duke of Cumberland's Dragoons (formerly Kingston's Light Horse) does indeed show a later uniform and not the one that was worn during the '45,[13] but the absence of evidence for or against makes this an unsettled point.

The Earl Gower's Regiment of Foot was certainly clothed in red, though its facings are unknown.[14] Harcourt's was also in red faced with yellow[15] and Berkeley's in red faced in green,[16] while Cholmondeley's appears to have worn red faced in red.[17] The number of blue-clothed regiments amongst the Noblemen's Regiments and other hastily-raised forces was, however, notable: the Duke of Rutland's Foot, known as Granby's Regiment of Foot,

10   Beriah Botfield, *Stemmata Botevilliana: Memorials of the Families of Botteville, Thynne and Botfield* (Westminster: J.B. Nichols, 1858), p.175 (access to this rare work kindly supplied by Sir Michael Leighton, Bt.).

11   A. Smart (ed. J. Ingamells), *Allan Ramsay: A Complete Catalogue of his Paintings* (London: Yale University Press, 1999), Fig. 376, Cat. 315, where the sitter is incorrectly identified. The files at the Heinz Archive of the National Portrait Gallery, London contain portraits of Lt Col Richard Herbert, and of Capt. Sir Francis Charlton. Neither, however, is in uniform.

12   S. Reid, *Cumberland's Culloden Army 1745-46* (Oxford: Osprey Publishing Ltd, 2012), Plate F Fig. 1 and p.46.

13   A.E. Haswell-Miller & N.P.Dawnay, *Military Drawings and Paintings in the Royal Collection* (London: Phaidon Press Ltd, 1969) Vol.1 Fig. 49 and Vol.2, p.15 Cat. 92. See also Royal Collection Trust <www.rct.uk> reference RCIN 400724.

14   TNA, Granville Papers, PRO 30/29/1/13, ff.479-80.

15   Cecil C.P. Lawson, *A History of the Uniforms of the British Army* (London: Norman Military Publications, 1963), Vol.II, pp.25-7.

16   *Felix Farley's Bristol Journal*, No. 91, 4 Jan. 1746.

17   Portrait of George Cholmondeley, Viscount Malpas attributed to Pompeo Batoni at <www.theathenaeum.org/art/full.php?ID=172821#>, viewed 30 October 2019. This portrait does not appear in A.M. Clark (ed. E. Peters Bowron), *Pompeo Batoni – A Complete catalogue of his Works* (London: Phaidon, 1985).

seems to have worn blue,[18] the four Independent Troops of Horse raised by John Ponsonby certainly did so,[19] the Associated Companies of Volunteers of the East Riding of Yorkshire wore blue turned up in red,[20] and, almost certainly, the Associated Companies of the North Riding wore blue turned up in white.[21] It is possible that this preference for blue-faced red clothing reflected a desire on the part of those raising regiments to emphasize their loyalty by wearing the Royal Livery colours – scarlet and blue – but as they could not claim to be Royal regiments, and in addition would probably have wished to make evident their 'special service, volunteer' origins, they contrived to wear them in the form of reversed colours. In the case of Herbert's Regiment, the colours were also the principal tinctures of His Lordship's arms, though his heraldic devices were silver rather than gold.[22]

Although it is clear that several of the new-raised regiments got up to strength very quickly and became sufficiently disciplined to be useful, at least on the lines of communication, it is also clear that some were used as garrison troops for towns in various parts of England and others barely showed their usefulness before the crisis had passed. Kingston's Regiment of Light Horse was reported as being 'with the Duke' as early as January 1746, and four of the foot regiments got as far as Berwick, Carlisle and Newcastle-upon-Tyne, though the other cavalry regiment, Montagu's Carabineers, served exclusively in England. Herbert's, in the first instance, garrisoned the county town of Shrewsbury.[23]

Getting the regiments fit for any type of service was bound to be a struggle and, immediately after the colonels' commissions were signed, the Secretary-at-War suggested that sergeants and corporals be appointed to the corps from the Chelsea Out-pensioners living in the district in which the various regiments were to be raised. He provided lists to assist in routing out these old heroes from the repose they so richly deserved.[24] The use of any such Chelsea Out-pensioners was complicated by the fact that they were specifically forbidden to accept any other employment that would entitle them to pay issued by the Government. However, this problem was overcome by the King issuing a proclamation overturning that regulation during the national emergency. Out-pensioners were therefore engaged – indeed some were pressed – to teach raw recruits the manual exercise and to provide a leavening of experience to these raw formations. They were also directed to act as drill instructors to the various Armed Associations of Gentlemen, which arose in London and elsewhere.[25]

18 Lawson, *History of Uniforms of the British Army*, Vol.II, p.27.
19 Portrait of 'John Long Bateman Esq., Capt. in Col. Ponsonby's Independant [sic] Regiment' by Stephen Slaughter, Sotheby's, 13 Nov. 1991. This picture is often mistaken for an officer of the Royal Regiment of Horse Guards, so similar is the cut of the uniform, though it is clearly not RHG as it bears no gold lace.
20 A. Cormack & A. Jones (eds), *The Journal of Corporal William Todd, 1745-1762* (Stroud: Sutton Publishing for the Army Records Society, London, 2001), p.2.
21 Portrait of Sir Thomas Wentworth of Bretton, 5th Bt by J.T. Heius, Christie's Pictures from Wentworth sale, Lot 31, 8 July 1998.
22 Per pale azure and gules three lions rampant argent. Sir Bernard Burke, *Genealogical and Heraldic Dictionary of the Peerage & Baronetage of the British Empire* (London: Harrison, 1865).
23 TNA, State Papers, Military, SP 41/17, f.18, location of regiments as at 5 January 1746, and Marching Orders WO 5/37, f.174.
24 TNA, Secretary-at-War Out-letters, 3 October 1745, WO 4/40, f.514.
25 TNA, Secretary-at-War Out-letters, WO 4/41, ff.56, 129, 145, &198. Notice of the King's Proclamation appeared in *The London Gazette*, No. 8478, 22-26 October 1745.

Finding arms for the new formations was also perceived as a problem. On behalf of 'Viscount Falmouth's Cornish Regiment of Foot' the Duke of Montagu, who, apart from being colonel of three regiments simultaneously, was Master General of the Ordnance, was requested in late October to instruct the Ordnance officers in the West Country to buy up arms salvaged from a British privateer, which had become stranded in Mount's Bay, near Penzance. The suggestion was also made that arms be purchased originating from the Spanish ship *St Xeriaco*, which had been brought into Bristol by the Privateer *Tryal*. It seems that in neither case were these sources of weapons tapped, as the Ordnance Office clerks wrote in December that they had received no instructions to do so.[26] Montagu evidently had a better grasp of what arms were available in store and did not require the Duke of Newcastle's rather desperate suggestions to assist him to run his department. In fact, warrants for the issue of arms out of the Ordnance stores were regularly signed in the next few months; the warrant for Herbert's being dated 12 October.[27]

Naturally it took some time for the regiments to achieve a state in which they could be taken onto pay and Establishment. This stage was reached formally when they were certified as half-complete, and from that time the Lords Commissioners of the Treasury were obliged to provide them with subsistence. The establishment of each was set at 800 non-commissioned officers, drummers and men, including twenty warrant men.[28] As the Duke of Rutland pointed out, this created difficulties since he was, in the meantime, responsible for quartering the battalion while it gathered strength.[29] The restriction evidently operated as an incentive, however, as only a fortnight later Rutland's was certified as being half-raised.[30] As early as 5 October it was reported that 'the Lord Herbert who is beloved as a Father by his Tenants in Shropshire has enlisted 500 of them',[31] but this could only have been possible if he had greatly anticipated being permitted to raise a regiment, as his commission had only been signed the day before. Forrester Leighton and his fellow company commanders were evidently doing their best to cajole the lads away from their ploughs and into the ranks, and by 9 November his company had 23 attested recruits.[32] The regiment's half-complete stage was officially reached two days

---

26   TNA, Ordnance Letters, SP 41/37. Falmouth's was to receive 'cutlasses with belts' while muskets, bayonets and boxes with belts were to go to George Borlase's Independent Company of Volunteers at Penzance.

27   TNA, State Papers, Military, SP 44/186, f.110.

28   The pay of warrant men was allowed to regiments in order to form a fund from which regimental expenses were paid and which contributed to the personal pay of company commanders – see A.J. Guy, *Oeconomy and Discipline – Officership and Administration in the British Army, 1714-1763* (Manchester: Manchester University Press, 1985), p.10.

29   TNA, Secretary-at-War Out-letters, WO 4/41, f.33.

30   TNA, Secretary-at-War Out-letters, WO 4/41, f.49, dated 7 November 1745. The regiments were certified as half complete in the following order: (day and month in brackets; reports after 7 November shown as later folios) Bedford's 10 October; Kingston's Horse 12 October; Halifax's 18 October; Montagu's Horse and Gower's Foot 22 October; Ancaster's 1 November; Falmouth's 2 November; Rutland's/Granby's 4 November; Harcourt's 13 November, f.83; Bolton's 18 November, f.83; Berkeley's 23 November, f.141; Edgcumbe's – no report seems to have been filed.

31   *Farley's Bristol Advertiser*, No. 84.

32   National Library of Wales (NLW), Powis Castle Papers PC 21718, Capt. Leighton's recruiting account.

later when it was taken onto Establishment.[33] Towards the end of the year the pool of recruits gathered in up to that time appears to have been allocated equally between the companies, as in respect of the 31 days up to 24 December a uniform £47 6 shillings was paid to each company except Captain Whitmore's, which received almost £20 more.[34] There is no explanation for this difference, but perhaps Whitmore was detached from headquarters and his overplus of recruits did not form part of the pool. In the next subsistence period of 32 days each company received varying amounts indicative of its progress beyond the half-complete stage. Leighton's received £68 18 shillings which, if one assumes a full complement of NCOs – three sergeants and three corporals – means that his Company was somewhat over-strength at 76 privates including two drummers. Besides the officers' own efforts, this success in recruiting appears to have been due partly to the assistance received from the very close-knit community of Whig landed gentry in the county, who aided the build-up. Relations of Forrester's on his mother's side, Brook and William Forrester of Old Willey Hall, neither of whom held commissions in the Regiment, appear to have helped, as there are recruiting expense accounts from them in the Powis Castle papers.[35]

Herbert's established its headquarters in 'Shrewsbury and places adjacent' at the end of November 1745.[36] Its only active duty appears to have occurred on 8 December 1745 when the Regiment was ordered to march towards Ashbourne to counter the advance of the Highland host in its progress through Derbyshire. Contemporary records of this incident reveal a wide disparity of view as to the usefulness of this movement, some indicating a degree of fearfulness and disorganisation reminiscent of the scenes scandalously depicted in Hogarth's 'The March of the Guards to Finchley' and others taking a more positive view, applauding the county's willingness to defend itself.[37] The regiment had evidently acquired a number of gentlemen volunteers, though the only one who remained faithfully at his post during this incident was Sir Thomas Whitmore.[38]

The order for this march to Ashbourne must have come as an operational order from the area commander, Brigadier General William Douglas, as it is not reflected in the Secretary-at-War's Marching Orders.[39] When the commotion had died down, Herbert's was ordered to march to Bristol in two divisions in the middle of January,[40] and at the end of the month was dispersed from these quarters on account of a fair to be held in the city. Six companies went to Gloucester and four to Cirencester, though with orders to return to the city three

---

33   TNA, Establishments, WO 24/245, Establishment for two Regiments of Horse and thirteen Regiments of Foot.
34   NLW, PC 21174, General Account of the Rt. Hon. the Earl of Powis's Regiment.
35   NLW, PC 21725 and 21735, Recruiting Accounts.
36   TNA, Marching Orders, WO 5/37, f.174.
37   Montgomeryshire Collections, Vol.8, pp.3-4, and J.B. Owen & H. Blakeway, A History of Shrewsbury (London: Harding, Lepard & Co., 1825), Vol.I, p.507.
38   Bishop William Cartwright's Chronicle, from Transactions of the Shropshire Archaeological Society, 4th Series, Vol.4 (1914), p.67.
39   From 1st Major, 2nd Foot Guards, Douglas was promoted to the colonelcy of the 32nd Foot on 29 May 1745 (having been a colonel by brevet since 29 December 1740) and was appointed Brigadier General on 30 May 1745.
40   TNA, Marching Orders, WO 5/37, f.281.

days after the fair had closed.[41] These orders were rescinded at the beginning of February, notification having been received from the Mayor of an outbreak of smallpox in the city,[42] and the regiment remained split until mid-March when the companies at Cirencester were gather in to Gloucester.[43] During these months its duties and movements were routine in the extreme: clearing out of the towns to surrounding villages when the Gloucester Assizes took place and twice being called upon to provide escorts for deserters.[44] It is pleasing to note that the regiment's major, Charles Collins, was given the task of securing the release of one James Knight, formerly of Richbell's 39th Foot, who had been jailed as a deserter despite having been properly discharged to a Chelsea out-pension, though it seems unlikely in the mood of wounded national pride, suspicion and retribution prevailing at the time that Knight received recompense for his illegal imprisonment.[45]

Indications of a disturbance within the regiment, in the late winter, appear in a letter from Major Collins to an unidentified correspondent including the passage 'on Thursday we had a General Court Martial on the men Mr [illegible] Clive told you of. I fear some of them will be found Guilty of Mutiny.'[46] This was an interesting case illustrative of the naivety and lack of military experience on the part of both the officers and the soldiers in Lord Herbert's Regiment and one for which Lieutenant Richard Larner, the regiment's adjutant, was authorized to act as a Deputy Judge Advocate on 10 March.[47] It also gives indications of the problems encountered as a consequence of having recruited men of different ethnic backgrounds and demonstrates the difficulties that could arise amongst soldiers unaccustomed to, and probably bored by, the drudgery of garrison duties. The court martial took place in Gloucester on 27 March 1746 and concerned five soldiers, Thomas Ward, Thomas Griffith, James Jones and William Palmer who were accused of mutiny and high misdemeanours and John Roberts accused of desertion. The record of the trial is long, but the nub of the incident was that the Welshmen in Herbert's companies stationed in Cirencester were excused duty on 1 March, St David's Day. They also, in accordance with tradition, decorated their hats with leeks in memory of the saint. Their English comrades in response, assembled by beat of drum and scuffles broke out as the sons of St George attempted to remove the vegetables from the headgear of the sons of St David. Commissioned and non-commissioned officers intervened on several occasions to break up groups and generally to quell the disturbance and there was 'bold and impudent' behaviour on the part of the rioters, including some pushing and shoving and the release of a soldier who had been detained in the Guard House by an officer. Lieutenant George Brissac also suffered the indignity of being called a 'French Dogg' and having his life allegedly threatened by Ward and several others. Brissac was presumably an Huguenot, but the subtleties of his theological position *vis à vis* ordinary Frenchmen were not something that

---

41   TNA, Marching Orders, WO 5/37, f.291.
42   TNA, Secretary-at-War Out-letters, WO 4/41, f.238.
43   TNA, Marching Orders, WO 5/37, f.340.
44   TNA, Marching Orders, WO 5/37, ff.313, 314 & 433.
45   TNA, Secretary-at-War Out-letters, WO 4/42, f.35.
46   NLW, PC 21749, dated 25 March 1746.
47   TNA, Courts Martial Records, WO 71/18, f.356.

even his own men cared to take note of in the circumstances.[48] The ring leaders were eventually arrested and on the following day an attempt was made to march them to Gloucester under escort, but a mob of soldiers and civilians stirred up by Griffiths, one of the prisoners, pelted the escort with filth and Roberts, one of the escort, 'deserted' and joined the crowd. The whole incident seems to have been an example of the normal rough and tumble of eighteenth century life, which in a civilian context would have had little in the way of consequences. The fact that the participants were now mostly soldiers, however, put upon it an entirely different complexion and their officers felt they had no choice but to treat the disturbance with the full rigour of military discipline. The court was concerned to throw light on the possibility of a conspiracy – pre-meditation – and to interpret the behaviour in terms of mutiny; the alleged use of the phrase 'One and all ...' by the rioters being particularly indicative of collective guilt in this respect. In all 3,800 lashes were awarded to the participants, but the authorities took a more lenient view than the officers and 'in consideration of the long confinement ... and their appearing to have a just sense of their guilt, His Majesty was graciously pleased to pardon them ...'[49]

The regiment remained in Gloucester until the time approached for its disbandment, and it was ordered back to Shrewsbury on 7 June 1746.[50] The colonels of most new-raised regiments were advised that the King wished to thank them and their officers for their 'Seasonable and Distinguished Marks ... of Fidelity and Attachment to His Majesty', and the officers were enjoined to thank their men 'that there may be no one Person ... unacquainted with the sense His Majesty has of their zeal and Loyal Behaviour'. Herbert's Regiment was finally disbanded on 23 June by Major General Pulteney, but not before the officers had been instructed 'to engage as many, as may be, of your Men who shall be willing and fitt to Enlist themselves in the Old Regiments'.[51] The disbanding generals were given discretion to award four, five or six days' subsistence to each NCO and man,[52] and Leighton's Company received a total of seven guineas to be divided up as disbandment bounty money, which would indicate four days pay each for a full complement of NCOs and drummers, and 61 men.[53] In addition, the men were permitted to carry away their clothes.[54] For some time thereafter, whether at church in their Sunday best or at their ploughs, cobblers' lasts, looms or anvils, many men from Shropshire and the Welsh Marches would have been seen wearing blue and red.

In the course of research on the portrait and career of Captain Forrester Leighton of Lord Herbert of Cherbury's Regiment of Foot, much information was recorded on the other regiments that were raised at the same time. As so little is published on these 15 regiments, most of which existed for less than a year, their locations, movements and various other details

---

48   I am grateful to Mrs Vivien Costello of the Huguenot Officers Research Project for looking into the Brissac family for me. Though George Brissac does not appear in the listings, there are five men of that name in the G.H. Jones card index representing officers of previous generations in the Huguenot Library. It seems highly likely therefore that he was a Huguenot.

49   TNA, Courts Martial Files, WO 71/38, f.46 et seq.

50   TNA, Marching Orders, WO 5/38, f.8.

51   TNA, Secretary-at-War Out-letters, WO 4/42, f.31.

52   TNA, Miscellany and Precedence Books, WO 26/21, ff.6 & 7.

53   NLW, PC 21832.

54   TNA, Miscellany and Precedence Books, WO 26/21, ff.6 & 7.

have been compiled in note form as a contribution towards the history of their service to the campaign and as a record of the particular place that they hold in the history of the British Army of the eighteenth century.[55] All movements were recorded from the appropriate volumes of Marching Orders, though it is clear that not all orders to move were written into those volumes.[56]

Alongside these details is presented information on two surviving grenadier caps worn by Harcourt's Regiment and Granby's (the Duke of Rutland's) Regiment. Although they have been known about for decades, and were recorded by Lawson,[57] their illustration in colour will be of interest to students of uniform.[58]

The Harcourt cap has been displayed for many years on a model head and has suffered at some time in its history from being exposed to sunlight, which has reduced the yellow colour to that of straw. Examining the turnings in the interior, however, reveals that the original yellow was a very astringent, bright shade quite unlike what one would expect from a fairly cheaply produced woollen cloth of the mid-eighteenth century. When new, it must have been dazzling indeed with a visual appearance not very far short of fluorescent modern colours and certainly sharper than the colour of a lemon. The rest of the cap shows the characteristic 'brickish' tone of a good strong red with no pretence towards scarlet. Nothing is known of the particular provenance of this example.

The Granby cap, which is on display in Belvoir Castle, is accompanied by details of its provenance recorded at the time that it entered the collection. They relate that it was presented to Lord John Manners by Mrs Graves, Senior, during Lord John's General Election canvass of Newark on 19 June 1841. It had been originally issued to her great uncle, Jonathan Twelch, 'a Volunteer under the Marquess of Granby during the Scotch Rebellion in the year 1745'. Mrs Graves also handed over her great uncle's sword, but this appears to have become mixed up in the huge collection of infantry hangers, which decorate the walls of the castle's Guard Room and is not presently identifiable. The cap is in astonishingly good condition, its colours bright and the fabric neither worn nor dirty. It has been kept in its folded state and is displayed suspended from a small metal ring sewn into the point.

Both caps are decorated with the beast that features in their respective families' crests, coincidentally in both cases a peacock, which demanded an intricacy of embroidery, with all that that implies in terms of cost and production time, confirming the importance of a showy appearance to the Army of this period. These headdresses stand at the end of an era of independence in matters of dress in the British Regular Army – but not the Militia – and are probably the last manifestations of colonels of marching regiments of foot being able to

---

55   P.A. Luff, 'The Noblemen's Regiments: Politics and the 'Forty-Five', *Bulletin of the Institute of Historical Research*, Vol.LXV (1992), pp.54-73. This article details the political manoeuvrings that took place in order to gain the King's and Ministry's permission to raise the units and the terms of service for officers and men. My thanks to Dr J.A. Houlding for drawing it to my attention.

56   TNA, Marching Orders, WO 5/37 & 38.

57   Lawson, *A History of the Uniforms of the British Army*, Vol.II, p.25.

58   I should like to record my sincere thanks to The Hon. Mrs Gascoigne of The Manor House, Stanton Harcourt, Oxfordshire and to His Grace, the Duke of Rutland and the staff of Belvoir Castle, Grantham, Lincolnshire for their courtesy, help and interest in making these objects available for inspection and photography.

place their personal devices on the appointments of their units, a practice that was specifically forbidden in the Clothing Regulations of 1751.[59]

Alongside these caps, a few other artefacts associated with the Noblemen's Regiments have survived. The portrait of Granby commented upon by Lawson and which he surmised as representing him in the uniform of his Foot Regiment during the Rebellion, now resides in Paris at the *Musée Jacquemart-André*.[60] Though similar in colouring to the uniform of the Royal Regiment of Horse Guards in which Granby is most commonly portrayed – blue coat faced scarlet with gold lace – the style of the cuffs seems to indicate that the picture in Paris does, in fact, show the uniform of his infantry regiment. The grenadier cap noted above would, as Lawson suggests, tend to indicate blue was the background colour of the uniform, and the hesitation which that author expressed in accepting this hypothesis is lessened by the discovery that Herbert of Cherbury's Foot, raised at the same time, wore blue as its coat colour. One might also speculate, though without any evidence to prove it, that Allan Ramsay's attractive but odd portrait, said, unconvincingly, to be Lord John Murray, represents an officer of one of the Noblemen's regiments.[61] An officer he certainly is, wearing sash and gorget, but the dark blue coat with scarlet cuffs and profusions of gold grape vine embroidery are as wide of the mark in terms of 'normal' British military dress as one could hope to find. Although nothing appears to be known of the uniform of Montagu's Ordnance Regiment, nine gilt gorgets bearing the Duke's arms and supporters survive in the Armoury at Boughton House in Northamptonshire. It is most likely that these artefacts derive from his foot regiment.[62] Also present in that armoury is a pair of kettledrums that originated either from the 3rd Regiment of Horse, of which Montagu was colonel from 6 May 1740, and which would have become surplus to requirements when that regiment became the 2nd Dragoon Guards in 1746, or from Montagu's Carabiniers. Although a regiment raised solely for service during the Jacobite Rebellion, the Carabiniers certainly had kettledrums like any other horse regiment. They were played by Richard Warcupp of Derby, who had been a trumpeter in the Royal Regiment of Horse Guards for 11 years before being wounded and taken prisoner at Fontenoy. He returned to his regiment five months later, but his place had been filled and he then became the kettledrummer to the artillery train, from which he was removed by Montagu, the Master General of the Ordnance, to act as kettledrummer in his new cavalry regiment in which Warcupp served 'until it was broke'.[63]

59 Dimensions of both caps as follows: (Harcourt followed by Granby separated by *) Front height 11 3/8in * 11 7/8in. Width of front panel at base 10 1/4in * 9 1/2in. Width base of front flap 8in both. Height of front flap 3 5/8in both. Width top of front flap 4 1/2in * 5 1/2in. Height of rear fold-up 4 1/8in both. Height of rear fold-up at lowest point 3 1/4in * 3 3/8in. Length of plume now existing 1 15/16in Harcourt only. Lettering round the small flap – Harcourt – OXFORDSHIRE; Granby – POUR Y PARVENIR (the motto of the Rutland family).

60 Lawson, *A History of the Uniforms of the British Army*, Vol.II, p.27 and David Mannings, *Sir Joshua Reynolds. A Complete Catalogue of his Paintings* (Newhaven & London: Yale University Press, 2000), Cat. No. 1191, Fig. 211.

61 Alistair Smart (ed. John Ingamells), *Allan Ramsay. A Complete Catalogue of his Paintings* (Newhaven and London: Yale University Press, 1999), Cat. No. 391, Fig. 211.

62 I am most grateful to Mr Stephen Wood, former Keeper of the Scottish United Services Museum, Edinburgh, for bringing these objects to my attention.

63 Boughton House Archives, Ordnance Papers Box 2, Folder 1, Item 162.

Finally, a careful check of the names of the Field Officers of these units in the files of the Heinz Archive at the National Portrait Gallery reveals that none of them chose to have themselves painted in uniform, though there are several portraits of these individuals in civilian garb.

The histories of the Noblemen's Regiments are here presented in note-form. None of the regiments was ever referred to at the time or known by its precedence number, simply being referred to by the colonel's name. Precedence numbers are given here in parentheses.[64]

Ancaster's Regiment of Foot (70th Foot)
Raised by Peregrine Bertie, 3rd Duke of Ancaster (1714–1778)

Movements – six companies to Stamford on 7 November 1745, those six companies to Grantham a week later; the whole regiment to Hull, five companies from Lincoln, three with the headquarters from Stamford and two companies from Grantham 24 November 1745; entire regiment to Newcastle 10 December 1745. However, this order appears to have been countermanded, as Ancaster's was ordered to conduct a deserter from Hull to Boston on 22 February 1746 and two companies were moved from Hull to Lincoln to guard rebel prisoners on 11 March 1746. The remaining eight companies to march from Hull to York to guard prisoners on 20 March 1746. Orders for the Lincoln companies to conduct deserters to the next regiment of Horse or Foot on the road to London on 1 and 16 April, to Boston on 22nd, to Peterborough then on to Wisbech and then to the next regiment on 26 April 1746. It would seem that only two companies moved to York in March, as on 7 June 1746 the two York companies and the six companies at Hull were all ordered to join the companies at Lincoln, thereby bringing the whole regiment together.

Disbanded at Lincoln on 16 June 1746 by Major General George Churchill.

Bedford's Regiment of Foot (68th Foot)
Raised by John Russell, 4th Duke of Bedford (20 October 1710–30 January 1771)

Movements – from regimental headquarters in Westminster, three companies to Bedford 9 October 1745; these companies detached to Oulney, St. Neots and Woburn on 14 October 1745. The company that had been advanced to Coventry to retire to Ampthill 14 October 1745; two companies remaining in Westminster to go to Huntingdon 14 October 1745; the two Huntingdon companies to clear the town for the election 22 October 1745; four companies to concentrate at Bedford 23 October 1745. The 'several' companies to Bedford and places adjacent 12 November 1745 (this concentrated the regiment for the first time since it dispersed from Westminster). The regiment to Birmingham or to the camp at Lichfield if it had been provided with tents etc:, 19 November 1745. All companies to Newcastle and Gateshead 9 January 1746. The company at Durham to escort a deserter to York, collect

---

64   C.T. Atkinson, 'Jenkins' Ear, The Austrian Succession War and the 'Forty-Five', *JSAHR*, Vol.XXII, 1943/44, pp.280-298.

another and take both to the next regiment on the London road 19 March 1746. All companies at Durham to march to Berwick 22 March 1746. The whole regiment to march from Berwick to Bedford when relieved, 27 June 1746. The regiment appears to have left Berwick on 5 August 1746 from where it was said to take about 18 days to get back to its own county.

Disbanded at Bedford in late August by Major General Richard Onslow.

Berkeley's Regiment of Foot (72nd Foot)

Raised by Augustus Berkeley, 4th Earl of Berkeley (18 February 1716–9 January 1755)

Movements – A Drum Major and a Corporal from the 2nd Foot Guards ordered to Berkeley in Gloucestershire, almost certainly to instruct the regiment 30 November 1745; all companies to march to Bristol 10 December 1745; a detachment 'equal to an entire company' to go to Bath to attend Princess Caroline while in the city 27 March 1746; order to conduct a deserter on the road to London 3 May 1746. The nine companies at Bristol and the single company at Bath to march to Gloucester 7 June 1746.

Disbanded at Gloucester on 26 June 1746 by Major General Henry Pulteney.

Bolton's Regiment of Foot (67th Foot)

Raised by Charles Powlett, 5th Duke of Bolton (c.1718–5 July 1765)

Movements – in quarters at Winchester 16 November 1745; entire regiment to Portsmouth 6 December 1745; the Company at Taunton to march to Winchester 19 March 1746; all companies to Salisbury, Fiskerton, Milford and Hainham 17 April 1746. The whole regiment to march from Salisbury to Winchester, 7 June 1746.

Disbanded at Winchester on 13 June 1746 by Brigadier General Charles Armand Paulet.

Cholmondeley's Regiment of Foot (73rd Foot)

Raised by George Cholmondeley, 3rd Earl of Cholmondeley (1702–1770)

Movements – entire regiment ordered to Chester 12 November 1745; ordered to conduct a deserter from Chester to the next regiment on the London road 22 February 1746; a detachment ordered over to Ireland to conduct a deserter to Chester 13 April 1746. Three companies to march from Chester to Liverpool to give Aid to the Civil Power in suppressing rioting against the Catholic inhabitants of the town, 29 May 1746. Order to conduct a deserter from Chester to the next regiment on the London road, 5 June 1746. The companies at Liverpool ordered to return to Chester 7 June 1746.

Disbanded at Chester on 20 June 1746 by Major General Henry Pulteney.

Edgcumbe's Regiment of Foot (79th Foot)

Raised by Richard Edgcumbe, Baron Edgcumbe of Mount Edgcumbe (2 August 1716–10 May 1761)

Movements – raised in Cornwall; the companies quartered in Launceston ordered to vacate the town during the holding of the Assizes 18 February 1746; the officer commanding the company at Exeter ordered to conduct a deserter along the London road 26 April 1746. Order to conduct a deserter from Exeter to the next regiment on the London road, 5 June 1746. At some time the regiment was drawn into the garrison of Plymouth, from which one division of it had been sent back to Cornwall by 18 June 1746; the other probably followed later in the month.

Disbanded in Cornwall on unspecified date, probably late June, by Major General George Reade.

Falmouth's Regiment of Foot (75th Foot)

Raised by Hugh Boscawen, 2nd Viscount Falmouth (20 March 1707–
6 February 1782)

Movements – the regiment's commanding officer at Truro ordered to conduct a deserter along the London road 13 March 1746.

Falmouth's remained within Cornwall for the whole of its existence, and was disbanded in Cornwall on an unspecified date by Major General George Reade.

Gower's Regiment of Foot (77th Foot)

Raised by John Leveson-Gower, 1st Earl Gower (1694–1754)

Movements – 'the 10 companies under your command to be quartered: two at Stafford, two at Newcastle-under-Lyme, two at Wolverhampton, two at Lichfield, one at Uttoxeter, one divided between Stone and Eccleshall' 25 October 1745; five companies to march to Birmingham, the other five to Wolverhampton 12 November 1745; all companies to Chester 'but if the rebels prevent your reaching there you are to go to Shrewsbury' 13 November 1745; order to the officer commanding the five companies at Birmingham to conduct a deserter to the next regiment on the road to London 5 April 1746; order to the officer commanding the five companies at Wolverhampton to conduct a deserter down the road to London 8 April 1746; the five companies at Birmingham to march to Wolverhampton, 7 June 1746.

Disbanded at Wolverhampton on 17 June 1746 by Major General Henry Pulteney.

Lieutenant Colonel Shugborough Whitney and Gardiner's 13th Dragoons at the Battle of Prestonpans.
(Artwork by Peter Dennis © Helion and Company)

Grenadier, Pulteney's 13th Foot, 1745. (Artwork by Christa Hook © Helion and Company)

Captain Forester Leighton, of Lord Herbert of Cherbury's 78th Foot, by Allan Ramsay.
(Reproduced with kind permission of Sir Michael Leighton, Bt.; photograph by courtesy of Sotheby's)

Front and rear views of grenadier cap of Granby's 71st Foot.
(Belvoir Castle Collection; photographs © Andrew Cormack)

Front and rear views of grenadier cap of Harcourt's 76th Foot.
(Private Collection; photographs © Andrew Cormack)

Volunteer of the Derbyshire Blues, 1745. See p.167 for discussion of the sources for this reconstruction.
(Artwork by Christa Hook © Helion and Company)

Granby's Regiment of Foot (71st Foot)

Raised by John Manners, 3rd Duke of Rutland (1697–1779). Known as Granby's and commanded by John Manners, Marquess of Granby (1721–1770)

Movements – the quarters for 10 companies to be as follows: six at Leicester, two at Loughborough, two at Harborough 7 November 1745; entire regiment to Nottingham 12 November 1745; ordered to join the army concentrating in the Midlands at the camp at Lichfield or, if not yet provided with tents, to quarter at Warwick 19 November 1745; the whole regiment to march to Newcastle and Gateshead 9 January 1746; two of the 10 companies at Newcastle to go to Gateshead 10 May 1746. Order to conduct a deserter from Newcastle to the next regiment on the London road, 30 May 1746. On 27 June 1746 the whole regiment to march from Newcastle to Leicester when relieved by Harrison's Foot.

Disbanded at Leicester during the second half of August by Major General Richard Onslow.

Halifax's Regiment of Foot (74th Foot)

Raised by George Montagu Dunk, 2nd Earl of Halifax (1716–1771)

Movements – the 10 companies to be quartered at the following places, four at Northampton, two at Wellingborough, two at Towcester, two at Brackley, 19 October 1745; one of the Towcester companies ordered to Higham and one of the Brackley companies ordered to Naisby 23 October 1745; the company at Towcester to go to Northampton 11 November 1745; entire regiment ordered to camp at Lichfield or, in the absence of tents to quarter at Shrewsbury 19 November 1745; order to requisition wagons to carry the regiment's arms, tents, clothing and ammunition from Smithfield to Shrewsbury 26 November 1745; a similar warrant to requisition wagons from Northampton to Shrewsbury 30 November 1745; whole regiment to Carlisle 9 January 1746; the company in Lancaster to vacate its quarters during the Assizes 18 February 1746; a company-sized detachment drawn from both Halifax's and Montagu's Ordnance Regiments to march to Whitehaven to guard the rebel prisoners 8 March 1746. The company at Lancaster to provide an escort for a King's Messenger conducting rebel prisoners to London, 7 June 1746. The whole regiment to march from Carlisle to Northampton when relieved, 27 June 1746, but it did not leave the town until after 19 July 1746. Lieutenant Dalton with a baggage guard was left behind in Birmingham and relieved so as to re-join his regiment by a detachment of Ligonier's Horse on 9 August 1746.

Disbanded at Northampton during first half of August by Major General Richard Onslow.

Harcourt's Regiment of Foot (76th Foot)

Raised by Simon Harcourt, 1st Earl Harcourt (1714–1777)

Movements – the companies to be quartered as follows: one at Henley, one at Wallington, one at Bicester, two at Thame, one at Banbury, one at Woodstock, one at Burford and two at Whitney 19 November 1745; quarters at Woodstock to be 'enlarged' with Chipping

Norton 3 December 1745; letter to Headquarters at Woodstock – the regiment to move to Berkshire, the first company to arrive at Windsor Castle to relieve the Composite Foot Guards detachment currently employed on that duty. The other companies to be distributed five in Windsor town, two at Colebrook, one at Chertsey, one at Egham and one at Staines 6 December 1745; a detachment of one Subaltern, 3 Sergeants, 3 Corporals, 1 Drummer and 24 Private Men to do duty at Hampton Court 7 December 1745; entire Regiment to Harwich to undertake duty at Landguard Fort by companies in rotation 25 December 1745; escort a prisoner to the Savoy 7 January 1746; the Regiment on its march to Essex to be diverted at Kingston and go to Salisbury with instruction to proceed to Portsmouth if the Governor of that place so orders 21 January 1746; ordered to transfer a deserter from Salisbury to the Savoy prison, London 4 February 1746; companies at Salisbury to vacate their quarters during the Assizes 18 February 1746; order to enlarge quarters to Milford and Harnham 22 February 1746; companies vacating from Salisbury for the Assizes are also to stay out of the town during the Cloth Fair, then return 25 February 1746; order to send a detachment from Salisbury to Taunton to escort deserters 8 April 1746. The whole regiment to march from Portsmouth to Thame, 7 June 1746.

Disbanded at Thame on 17 June 1746 by Brigadier General Charles Armand Paulet.

Herbert of Cherbury's Regiment of Foot (78th Foot)
Raised by Henry Arthur, Lord Herbert of Cherbury, later 1st Earl of Powis (1703–1772)

For movements – see above.

Disbanded at Shrewsbury on 2nd June 1746 by Major General Henry Pulteney.

Kingston's Regiment of Light Horse (10th Horse)
Raised by Evelyn Pierrepont, Duke of Kingston-upon-Hull (1711–19 October 1773)

Movements – the regiment raised in Nottingham and environs and the six troops distributed: three in Nottingham, one in Mansfield, one in Newark & one in Retford 16 October 1745; 25 Men and 50 'recruit horses' ordered from London to Nottingham 24 October 1745; 14 Men and horses to Nottingham 4 November 1745; the regiment to move from Nottingham to Stockport and Altrincham (3 troops) and Warrington (3 troops) 9 November 1745; the preceding order rescinded and the regiment to move to Derby (3 troops) and Burton-upon-Trent (3 troops) 16 November 1745.

Disbanded at Nottingham on 15 September 1746 by Major General Richard Onslow.

Kingston's Light Horse was the only regiment raised by the nobility to see active service rather than performing its duties on the Lines of Communication or elsewhere in England. Though the brief summary above is accurately taken from the War Office Marching Orders, it is clear that the regiment joined Cumberland's army assembling in Staffordshire on 29 November 1745. Thereafter it received operational orders from the army commander and not from the Secretary-at-War. In combination with Bland's 3rd Dragoons and some of the Yorkshire Hunters, it took part in the affair at Clifton on 18 December when Cumberland's advanced guard came up with the Jacobite rear guard. The regiment was ordered back to Nottingham at the end of December but was in Forfar 21 miles north-east of Dundee by early March 1746. With the main army it advanced to Strathbogie and sent a detachment of 30 men with 70 loyal Campbell Highlanders to occupy Keith where it was surprised during the night of 20-21 March by a party of rebels. In Cumberland's report of the incident he said:

> I should have had little Concern about this Accident, if it had not been for the Loss of some of Kingston's People, for, I cannot sufficiently commend the Behaviour of that Regiment upon all Occasions, or the Readiness with which they undergo all the Service & Fatigues they are emploied in.[65]

The regiment forded the Spey on 12 April and a detachment of 50, with some infantry, confronted the Jacobite army outside the town of Nairn before pushing the rebels' rear guard through it onto their main body. His Royal Highness reported that 'Kingston's Horse behaved as well as could be expected from the best old Corps, Lord Robert Suttons having driven them more than once, with his fifty, a squadron of sixty six of Fitzjames's Horse in upon their Foot'.[66] On forming for the Battle of Culloden, Kingston's was positioned in reserve behind the army, but was quickly brought up on the right flank when the infantry line had advanced beyond a marsh, which had protected that wing. When the Jacobite army broke and fled, it took part in the pursuit of the rebels, clashing with the Irish Piquets of the French Army and then cutting down the Highlanders fleeing towards Inverness. In the aftermath the Light Horse, with the other cavalry, were posted along the coasts of Moray and Aberdeenshire in an attempt to prevent those wishing to escape by ship.

In late May Kingston's provided vedettes for the advanced and rear guards of the army as it advanced down the Great Glen to Fort Augustus and also an escort to Cumberland when he visited Fort William. Having found such favour, it remained in this role when Cumberland left Scotland in July.

Though officially disbanded as the Duke of Kingston's Light Horse in September 1746, the regiment was reformed immediately as His Royal Highness, the Duke of Cumberland's Dragoons and performed distinguished service in Flanders for the remainder of the War of the Austrian Succession. It numbered as the 15th Dragoons within the Dragoon branch of service. It was finally disbanded on 3 February 1748/49.[67]

---

65   A. Massie & J. Oates (eds.) *The Duke of Cumberland's Campaigns in Britain and the Low Countries, 1745-1748: A Selection of His Letters* (Stroud: The History Press for the Army Records Society, 2018), p.171.

66   Massie & Oates (eds.), *Duke of Cumberland's Campaigns*, p.182. The nominally Irish regiment of Fitzjames Cavalerie of the French Army had been despatched in February 1746 to Scotland from Dunkirk. Most of its men and all the horses were captured by the Royal Navy, but about 130 officers and men arrived at Aberdeen on 22 February 1746 – see F.J. McLynn, *France and the Jacobite rising of 1745* (Edinburgh: Edinburgh University Press, 1981), pp.190-192 and Duffy, *The '45*, p.438.

67   The service of Kingston's Light Horse is taken from A Massie & Oates (eds.), *Duke of Cumberland's Campaigns*; A. McK. Annand, 'The Hussars of the '45' Journal of the Society for Army Historical Research, Vol.XXXIX, 1961 pp.144-160 and J. Prebble, *Culloden* (London: Penguin Books, 1967), pp.119, 165, 176 & 179 the latter partly quoting from Capt. Hinde, *The Discipline of the Light Horse* (London, 1778).

Montagu's Ordnance Regiment of Foot (69th Foot)
Raised by John Montagu, 2nd Duke of Montagu (1690–1749)

Movements – the 10 companies to be in quarters with two companies at Kettering, one each at Rowell, Thrapstone, Oundle, Bridgstock & Weldon, Peterborough, Desborough & Geddington and two at Stamford 8 November 1745; the detachment in London to march to Stamford 12 November 1745; the regiment to march on Monday 25 November 1745 to the camp near Lichfield or, if no camp necessaries have been issued, to quarters at Bridgnorth; the regiment to march to Carlisle 9 January 1746; those companies based at Lancaster to vacate the town during the Assizes to places adjacent and to return afterwards 18 February 1746; a company-sized detachment to be made from the 18 companies of Halifax's and Montagu's Foot at Carlisle to march to Whitehaven to guard the rebel prisoners 8 March 1746. The company at Lancaster to provide an escort to Mr Carrington, a King's Messenger, to convey prisoners to London, 7 June 1746.[68] The whole regiment to march from Carlisle to Kettering, 27 June 1746, but it did not leave the town until after 19 July 1746.

Disbanded at Kettering in early August by Major General Richard Onslow.

Montagu's Regiment of Carbineers (Horse) (9th Horse)
Raised by John Montagu, 2nd Duke of Montagu (1690–1749)

Movements – the regiment of six Troops to be distributed one in Peterborough, two in Wellingborough, and one each in Market Harborough, Kettering and Rowell 8 November 1745; all Troops from their present quarters to Daventry and from there in two divisions to Frodsham, Cheshire on 13 and 14 November 1745; preceding order cancelled, regiment to remain in quarters 11 November 1745; change of quarters to three Troops in Wellingborough, two in Kettering, one in Rowell 14 November 1745; the regiment to move to Tamworth (three troops) and Ashby-de-la-Zouch (three troops); the regiment was then ordered southwards but the order initiating this move is missing; Squadron at St Albans to march to Canterbury 28 January 1746; Squadron at Southwark to march to Canterbury 4 February 1746; the entire regiment at Canterbury to disperse into quarters in detachments to be assisting to the Revenue Officers against owlers and smugglers 1 May 1746. The whole regiment ordered to march from Canterbury to Kettering and places adjacent, 7 June 1746.

Disbanded at Kettering on 20 June 1746 by Major General George Churchill.

As was to be expected, most of the Noblemen's regiments saw no very active service, but they do provide examples of the sort of duties that all regiments undertook during normal times. While the experienced regulars, brought back from the army in Flanders, operated on a campaign footing, some of the new-raised regiments served in what might be called the rear areas of Cumberland's army on the lines of communication. The two regiments raised in the West Country seem to have done very little.

---

68   This was Nathaniel Carrington – See Priscilla Scott Cady, *The English Royal Messenger service, 1685-1750 – An Institutional Study* (Lampeter: Edwin Mellen Press, 1999), p.93.

Although Montagu's Carbineers were posted at the opposite end of the country from the Jacobites, its routine in Canterbury must have been very similar to that of any other cavalry regiment sent to assist the Customs service.[69] The Quartermaster of Major Mathew Swiney's Troop, John Watts, submitted a return every day of the men and horses fit for duty. The four that have survived indicate that on 5-8 June 1746 the trumpeter, John Frederickharp, and 31 privates were fit and the two corporals of horse, Bacchus Smith and George Harrison, and two other men were sick in quarters. Four of the fit men were on Grass Guard looking after the 16 horses that had been put out to grass, 21 other horses were fit but three were lame in stables. How Privates Thomas Sutton and William Cooper and Farrier Thomas Thorpe, the owners of the lame horses, managed when the regiment had to march back to Kettering a few days later is not known.

Other documents in the collection reveal that cavalry regiments sized their men and their mounts in exactly the same way as infantry regiments with the tallest men in the front and rear ranks and the shorter ones in the centre rank. The division of the regiment into two squadrons is also detailed; the first squadron was made up of the Duke's Troop under Captain-Lieutenant George Robinson along with Major Swiney's Troop and that of Captain William Walton. The second squadron comprised the two troops of John Creed, one of which he held as lieutenant-colonel and the other as captain, and the third troop was that of Captain Thomas Webb.

Perhaps the most interesting document, and surely a very rare one, is a nominal roll of the Major's Troop and the names of the public houses in which each of the men were quartered. One man, the Farrier, was accommodated in Ye Fountain; two each were in Ye Chequer, Prince Charly, Ye Angell and The Blue Anchor. The King's Arms found beds for three men, The Three Compasses and Ye Cock lodged four men each, while a dozen men were divided equally between The Mitre and Horn and The Flower de Luce in the High Street.[70] The remaining eight men had quarters in The King's Head and, of course, there were four men camping in the fields with the horses. Such a distribution of a single troop raises interesting questions. Were these the only beds and stable places that each of these taverns could offer, or were other members of the regiment from different troops also accommodated in these hostelries? If so, why were the men split up between 11 different locations if, possibly, a smaller number of co-located inns could each have sheltered a larger proportion of the troop and all 40 men might have been quartered in, say, five public houses? Such an arrangement would surely have made it easier to distribute orders and gather the men together when necessary. Alternatively, if these public houses could only give room to these small scatterings of men, how many other inns and taverns were there in the town to provide quarters for the other 200 men of the regiment? This quarterings roll sheds most interesting light on the administrative problems that the Army faced in the era when, essentially, there were no barracks.[71]

---

69   All of the details of Montagu's Carbineers are taken from Northamptonshire County Records Office, Gompertz of Glendon Collection, Ref.G(G) 126.

70   The Fleur de Lys Inn was situated at 34 High Street. It was first noted in 1376 and was demolished in 1958. See <www.machadoink.com/fleur de lis hotel.htm> consulted 20 September 2019.

71   Details of almost all of the public houses in the list can be found on www.dover-kent.com/ followed by the name of the pub. As Canterbury had been a resort of pilgrims since the murder of Thomas à

The Noblemen's regiments constituted a fertile seed-bed in which several soldiers, who later appear in the history of the campaigns in Germany and North America, started their careers. Matthew Floyer, a captain in Lord Gower's Regiment, ended his days with Braddock in the disaster on the Monongahela in 1755 in the same rank, having volunteered to go on that expedition from the 40th Foot;[72] William Eyre, Chief Engineer in North America in 1762-'63, was a captain-lieutenant in Montagu's Ordnance Regiment of Foot and Thomas Proby of Bedford's was killed leading the 55th Foot's attempted storming of Montcalm's abatis at Fort Carillon (Ticonderoga) in 1758. The most interesting pair however, who would meet on opposing sides in the American War of Independence, were Major Generals William Phillips and Horatio Gates. The former, one of the few general officers to originate from the Royal Artillery and perhaps the only one in the eighteenth century to command War Office as well as Ordnance Board troops, took his first commission in Montagu's Ordnance Regiment of Foot.[73] Gates, to whom Phillips was obliged to surrender at Saratoga, began his service as a Lieutenant in Bolton's Hampshire Regiment.[74] The regiments employed a total of 475 officers and of these 22 returned to the King's service in 1745 having previously retired, and six were re-employed from the Half-Pay List. Forty-nine transferred or exchanged from existing regiments into the new corps, most of them gaining thereby a step in rank, which they may not have been able to find in their original units, and with the possibility of exchanging back into an old-established regiment at this higher grade. Twenty-two officers managed to do so successfully and were doubtless delighted that their gamble in going into regiments that were bound to be disbanded at the end of the conflict, had paid off. Only two of these, however, managed to do so without spending some period on half-pay in their original lower rank. Of these 22, 13 were officers of the newly-raised Marine Regiments and were probably under-employed, as the maritime war against the Spaniards had subsided by 1745 and they were therefore easily available to transfer into new corps. For the majority however, 398 officers, almost 84 percent of the whole, service in these regiments was their

Beckett in 1170, it was abundantly provided with lodging houses.

72   D. Preston, *Braddock's Defeat – The Battle of the Monongahela and the Road to Revolution* (Oxford: OUP, 2015), pp.184 & 343.

73   Only 11 officers whose first commissions were in the Royal Artillery attained general officer rank prior to 1793. (Personal communication from Dr J.A. Houlding.)

74   Phillips, Major General William, (1731-1781) Ensign, Montagu's 'Ordnance' Regiment of Foot 1745, Gentleman Cadet, Royal Artillery 1746, Lieutenant-Fireworker 1747. Commanded a company of Miners but promoted Captain-Lieutenant when his men were transferred to gun service. Captain 12 May 1756, ADC to Lord Ligonier. Distinguished himself at Minden in 1759 and Warburg in 1760, promoted Lieutenant-Colonel by brevet 15 August 1760. Colonel 1772. Served in America under Burgoyne as Major-General, 1777. Captured at Saratoga, exchanged Autumn 1780 and commanded a force in Virginia until his death. Gates, Major General Horatio (1727-1806) Lieutenant, Bolton's Regiment, 1745. Quartermaster, 20th Foot April – June 1748, Ensign, 20th Foot June to November 1748 then to Half-Pay. Captain-Lieutenant, 45th Foot Nov. 1749, Captain, 45th June 1750. Captain, New York Independent Company 1754, Braddock's expedition, 1755. Major, 45th Foot, 1762, Major 60th Foot 1764. To Half-Pay 1765. Returned to 45th Foot as Major 1768, retired 1769. Appointed a Brigadier and Washington's Adjutant General in the American service, June 1775. Major-General, May 1776, Commander, Northern Department, 1777 and President of the Board of War. Commander Eastern Department, 1778. Commander Southern Department, July 1780. Retired after his defeat at Battle of Camden. Re-joined the Army 1782. Retired from military service, 1783.

first taste of the military life and of the overall total, 145 either continued their careers in the Army without a break or re-entered the Army within a short time of being stood down in June 1746. These corps therefore provided a significant point of entry into the military profession for a generation of officers that would serve in the 'world' wars of the eighteenth century.[75]

The brief passage of these units through the Army was not, however, completely tranquil and they left behind a few records of disciplinary problems, which show signs that they were peculiar to regiments 'raised for rank' and in hurried circumstances. The disturbances in Lord Herbert of Cherbury's Regiment have already been noted. All of the regiments were raised on the basis of 'devolved patronage', their titular colonels having the disposal of all the commissions seemingly without the requirement for the gentlemen concerned to be approved by any higher authority.[76] Bedford's Regiment had the misfortune to attract an officer whose presence within a small community living by the rules of gentlemanly behaviour must have been a sore trial. Lieutenant James Norford was eventually court martialled at Newcastle on three counts of misconduct: firstly, having broken open the trunk of his own captain, Thomas Proby, and taken £15 at Southam in Warwickshire on 25 November; secondly with having robbed his quarters in Mr Vernon's house in Abbots Bromley, Staffordshire, of eight cambric handkerchiefs on 1 December and thirdly with having forced the chamber door and broken open the chest of Ensign John McNeal at the Bear Inn, Woodstock, Oxfordshire on 21 December from which he stole 20 guineas belonging to Captain Scott's company. He was cashiered with ignominy and ordered to be handed to the civil magistrates for prosecution according to the law.[77] The sorry tale does at least provide evidence of the perambulations of the unit around the Midlands after it had been ordered to depart from Bedfordshire and confirms that the Marching Orders do not give a full account of movements. The evidence also indicates, in passing, that the officers of Bedford's Foot carried fusils not spontoons.

A General Court Martial in response to collective action on the part of soldiers, somewhat similar to that which had happened in Lord Herbert's Regiment, was held by Berkeley's Regiment on 28 April 1746. The cause of this disturbance arose out of an earlier case for which some soldiers had been sentenced by a Regimental Court Martial to punishment either on the wooden horse or by flogging for some unspecified crime. On the day when this punishment was to be carried out, 25 March, at the changing of the Old for the New Guard, a crowd of off-duty soldiers assembled to object to the punishment and unwittingly put the gloss of mutiny on their actions by raising the cry 'One and all' and 'gave a Huzza that seem'd to be General'. When the Adjutant, Lieutenant David Ross, ordered the prisoners' escort to quell the mutiny amongst their fellows, William Jones refused to load his firelock and when Ross attempted to arrest him for disobedience, Jones pushed the officer away and

---

75   I acknowledge my indebtedness to Dr J.A. Houlding for the statistical analysis of the officers of these corps. The conclusions drawn from this information are, however, my own. Though less easy to plot, these regiments also gave sufficient military experience to a number of other ranks to qualify them, at least in the opinion of their future colonels, for service as NCOs in Militia units raised during the Seven Years War – See TNA, Militia Appointments, HO 51/1, f.67.

76   Luff, 'The Noblemen's Regiments', p.57.

77   TNA, Courts Martial Files, WO 71/38, f.17 et seq.

joined the mob. Grenadier Thomas Forty of the Old Guard also refused several times 'with Oaths' to load when cartridges 'were offered to those of the Guards that had Flints in their Pieces' and was said to have shown his contempt for the order by opening a cartridge and shaking all of the powder out of it. When told by Lieutenant Charles Capel that 'he should go Prisoner, he swore he would not'. The incident was brought to an end by the arrest of Jones, Forty, Richard Sinderly, Robert Waring, and William Bradley who were confined in the Bristol Bridewell. The disturbance led directly to another pair of military crimes when Walter Meek and Edward Steel went absent without leave, fearing, for unstated reasons, that they would be accused of participation in the mutiny. Both were accused of desertion having been easily picked up, as they were guileless enough to go straight home. William Bradley was convicted of mutiny as the ring-leader of the off-duty soldiers objecting to their comrades' punishment. Discontent in the regiment seems to have arisen from a rumour alleged to have been circulated by Bradley that if his comrades 'receiv'd any pay after wensday they sho'd be soldiers as long as they lived' in contravention of the terms of service under which they had enlisted. A total of 3,000 lashes was ordered for these crimes, but all the men were eventually pardoned.[78]

Lord Gower's Regiment stationed in Chester was also not immune from discontent on the part of the men; 18 privates of Captain Floyer's Company finding themselves accused of mutiny and desertion for their conduct on 30 January 1746.[79] At a General Court Martial presided over by the Governor of Chester, the Earl of Cholmondeley, the men explained that they had all been recruited by one Sergeant Wolf largely on his promise that he would 'continue with them' during their service. One assumes that Wolf was some sort of overseer and that he had persuaded his work-mates to join up. On Wolf and one of their company officers, Lieutenant Lane, being discharged from the regiment, the men conceived that they had been 'forsaken by them' and marched out of town at 2 o'clock to bring the two released men back. The privates were also disturbed by news that their families were 'in great distress from sickness and want of subsistance'. Lieutenant Matthew Floyer was sent after them on a horse, and persuaded them to return to the city, but on nearing it they were met by Captain Chetwynde who had been despatched by the Governor with detachments from Gower's and Cholmondeley's Regiments to disarm them and bring them back in submission.[80] On being ordered to hand over their firelocks some did so, but others cocked theirs and one levelled his at Chetwynde. The detachment surrounded the mutineers and the disarming took place peacefully, though not without Chetwynde having to present his pistol at one recalcitrant. The arms were found to be loaded but not freshly primed, as they had not been unloaded after the men's last guard duty. Chetwynde was unable to point out particular offenders, as presumably, by this time late on a winter's afternoon, it was dark. Various mitigating

---

78   The account of these disturbances is compiled from City of Gloucester Records Office (The Heritage Hub) (GRO/HH), Papers and Accounts relating to Capt. Edmund Bond's raising of Lord Berkeley's Regiment, 1745-46, Ref.D2026 X42, items 30, 31, 32, 33, & 35; TNA, Courts Martial Files, WO 71/38, f.97 et seq.

79   TNA, Courts Martial Files, WO 71/126, un-numbered bundle of documents.

80   There were two officers named Matthew Floyer in Gower's Foot: the captain who re-entered the Army in January 1747 by becoming captain-lieutenant in the 40th Foot, and a lieutenant who left the Army when Gower's was disbanded in 1746. (Personal communication from Dr J.A. Houlding.)

circumstances were presented in favour of the group, several tavern keepers in whose prem-
ises the men were quartered testifying that they had asked for their beds not to be given
away as they intended to return by the following day and had left their kit and food behind
them. One Ambrose Gallimore said he only joined in because he was persuaded by his uncle
to do so. The court decided that he and three others who had immediately surrendered their
arms should be sentenced to 100 lashes, but that the rest should receive 500 lashes each.

At the same sitting of the court in Chester, another miscreant of Gower's, one William
Marsh, was dealt with. He was accused of mutiny on the basis of having invited the Glover
Stone Guard near the castle to meet the two Castle Guards on the sands in the afternoon to
have 'a little discourse of their own and to kick at ffootball'. It was further said that he had
asked that the same message might be passed round all the Guards. Marsh admitted that
he had said the words, but that it was a joke and that he had no ill design. The court did not
believe him and convicted him with a sentence of 500 lashes.

On examination of both of these cases in London, His Majesty was pleased to approve the
sentence on Marsh and ordered that it be carried out before the whole regiment. Only after
they had witnessed that proceeding were the 18 men of the Sergeant Wolf incident to be
advised that 'in consideration of their ignorance of their offence and the several favourable
circumstances in the report of the Court Martial of their intention to return to duty and
their submission to Captain Chetwynde, that if the men will on their knees ask pardon of
His Majesty for their offence' they were to be pardoned. Any who declined to beg forgive-
ness were immediately to receive their punishment.

The fifth court martial concerned one Sergeant John Bobbitt of Bedford's Foot who,
having been demoted by a Regimental Court Martial, probably for irregularities in the
management of his company's pay list, refused to wear a private's coat and was accused of
mutiny. His defence at Newcastle on 4 February 1746 was that he had been promised on
enlisting by His Grace and his agent, a Mr Butcher, that he would serve as a sergeant and
that he understood that he was enlisted on those terms and none other. He was convicted
and sentenced to 500 lashes and to serve as a private, but the punishment was reduced to
100 lashes and demotion.[81]

All of these courts-martial shed interesting light on the problems that could arise from
the hurried raising of units such as the Noblemen's regiments. The disadvantages inherent
in relying solely on the presentation of commissions through patronage brought the hazards
of introducing a 'bad apple' like Lieutenant Norford into a regiment, an occurrence that
the requirement to purchase a commission may have averted. The collective actions of the
men in Herbert's, Gower's and Berkeley's Regiments serve to emphasize the lack of understanding by the rank and file of the absolute nature of the change in their status as free
men on taking the King's shilling. Doubtless the Articles of War had been read to them
several times during their, albeit, brief service, but it is clear that their comprehension of
the military life and its discipline was significantly deficient. It might be imagined that in
a longer-established regiment old soldiers, who knew the form, would at least have pointed
out the dangers of such collective action, but in these regiments there were none to give that
advice. It is clear that the officers however, whether experienced or new, had no hesitation in

81   TNA, Courts Martial Files, WO 71/126, un-numbered bundle of documents.

invoking to the letter the stringency of military discipline. These lapses seem to indicate a perception on the part of the men that theirs were temporary regiments, which had volunteered in response to a national emergency, and that somehow they considered themselves different from and not subject to exactly the same discipline as the marching regiments. The first part of this notion was certainly correct and was explicitly stated by the Duke of Bedford, but the second part was not; the new regiments being 'raised upon the same foot with the other regiments in His Majesty's service ...'.[82] The behaviour of Gower's mutineers appears to illustrate the problems that might arise when men were raised from small communities and allowing them to remain in the same company and under the perceived protection of a character of influence from home. The case of the unfortunate Bobbitt points up his own perception that his terms of service were a matter of private agreement between him and the people who recruited him and his understanding was clearly that the normal rules did not apply to him. Perhaps there is a suggestion here that in order to get good men, particularly non-commissioned officers, misunderstandings of this type would have been allowed to continue rather than be corrected with the risk of losing a useful recruit.

The particular ethos of these regiments is also illustrated by a flurry of correspondence between Lieutenant Colonel Thomas Brudenell of Montagu's Ordnance Regiment and his colonel, the Duke.[83] In May 1746 the commanding officer asked his patron the extraordinary question as to whether His Grace wished deserters to be pursued and brought back to the regiment to face the consequences, or whether Montagu was prepared to let them go, as the regiment would evidently soon be disbanded. His Grace was likewise asked whether the men should be allowed to enlist for General Service, or whether that was to be prevented so that they could return home to work on the estate. Intriguingly, no response to these questions appears to have survived.

The conclusive nature of the Battle of Culloden gave rise to concerns in the Ordnance Regiment as to precisely when it was to be disbanded, as the national emergency was perceived to be over. In June, Brudenell reminded Montagu of the rapid approach of the harvest season and the desire of the men to be at home, representing that 'irregularities' might arise if disbandment were to be delayed. He confirmed that he would prevent, as far as possible, the men engaging with those who were attempting to enlist them for General Service, though he feared that an officer of the 1st Foot Guards might seduce some away with bounty money, as he 'offers pretty largely'. His policy was to encourage the men to return to see their families first and then to re-enlist if they wished. A few days later he reported that the Northamptonshire men were 'begging to be Discharg'd' because if they did not get 'home time enough for the Harvest their Families must inevitably starve all the ensuing Winter'. He had mentioned these concerns to Brigadier Fleming, the officer commanding at Carlisle, and knew that Lieutenant Colonel Joseph Dussaux of Halifax's Regiment – 'whose affairs are in the same situation if not worse' – had done so as well. He realised, however, that the departure of his soldiers would leave the garrison 'greatly distrest' as there were 260 Jacobite prisoners in the castle. Nevertheless, fearing desertions if the men were not released soon, he hoped that a decision could be reached and communicated quickly 'to prevent any

82   Luff, 'The Noblemen's Regiments', p.58.
83   Boughton House Archives, Ordnance Papers, BM1.18.

step that may bring the least imputation upon the Regiment who have hitherto behaved extreamly well ...'

Frustration with their circumstances was shown by Private John Stain of Captain Alexander Cosby's company, which was guarding Jacobite prisoners at Lancaster. Disenchanted with his duty and possibly worried for his family's future, on receiving abuse from the incarcerated rebels he discharged his firelock through the cell door, wounding one of the prisoners and killing the turn-key's son. Stain was probably handed over to the civil magistrates for punishment. As with the disciplinary cases above, Montagu's men clearly thought of themselves as different from other soldiers and their continuing civilian responsibilities, which regulars would not have had, evidently played worryingly upon their minds.

Though they may have considered themselves as different, the men of the Noblemen's regiments, despite the brevity of their service, were as entitled as the regulars to the out-pension of the Royal Hospital, Chelsea if they were appropriately qualified. As we have seen, some men who were already Out-pensioners were summoned to act as instructors and to leaven the new recruits with the experience of 'old hands'. In the West Country the Out-pensioners were called in and examined, and those who were deemed capable of further service were distributed equally between the regiments of Lord Falmouth and Lord Edgcumbe.[84] Some Out-pensioners took advantage of their previous service to offer themselves for commissioned rank. Sergeant Francis Dalton, pensioned out of the 1st Foot Guards in 1740, served as a lieutenant in the Earl of Halifax's regiment; James Varnier, late a Private Gentleman of the 3rd Troop of Horse Guards and pensioned in 1738, got back on his horse as a cornet in Montagu's Carabiniers and Thomas Butler, having last served as a Horse Grenadier Guard in the 2nd Troop and pensioned in 1744, took a commission as a lieutenant in Montagu's Ordnance Regiment of Foot. All of these men continued to receive their Out-pensions while drawing pay for their new regimental service.

Some old soldiers who had been discharged from the Army, but were not Out-pensioners in 1745, showed exemplary loyalty and re-enlisted in the Noblemen's regiments. Thomas Buckley had served in the 19th Foot and James Knight in the 39th Foot but they joined up again in Lord Herbert of Cherbury's Regiment. When it was disbanded, Buckley was put on the Out-pension as 'old and infirm' and Knight because he had had his arm shattered in an accident loading a chest of arms onto a wagon. Two men from Gower's Foot, who had served previously, also entered the Out-pension by way of their service during the rebellion: Thomas Badham because of old age and John Shaw as a result of 32 years cumulative service and having been born in the Army, so he had no other trade to fall back on. Sam Squire and Peter Butler of Bedford's Foot received the pension as being worn out with old age, though Squire had also been injured by a baggage wagon. Robert Harvey, who had been the Drum Major of the 2nd Foot Guards and re-entered the Army in the same role for Halifax's Regiment, received the pension as 'old and infirm', as did Hugh Bingham from the same regiment, who recorded that he had been wounded in the Jacobite Rebellion of 1715.

First-time soldiers also received the benefit of Chelsea as a result of their service. Thomas Haywood of Herbert's, Henry Speller of Bolton's, and James Robinson of Berkeley's suffered disabling injuries due to their own or their comrades' inexperience while performing arms

---

84   TNA, Secretary-at-War Out-letters, WO4/41, f.129.

drill. Haywood had to have his left arm amputated; Speller was disabled in the right hand by a bayonet – presumably the one belonging to the man next to him – and Robinson lost several fingers in a firearms accident. Wounds from combat were rarely the reason for pensioning, but Ascough Horner of Kingston's Light Horse lost his right arm when the rebels made a night attack on the village of Keith on 21 March and accidents claimed other men. Aaron Phillips (Herbert's) suffered contusions from a fall while on guard; Moses Bridgman (Halifax's) lost his right leg at Carlisle and Sam Tysoe (Bedford's) broke his back, presumably in a fall, at Berwick. Illness led to William Clift (Berkeley's) receiving the Out-pension because he lost the use of both arms due to smallpox at Bristol. The men of the Noblemen's Regiments therefore exhibited the full range of causes that could lead to a man receiving 'His Majesty's Bounty of the Royal Hospital at Chelsea'.[85]

Though the majority of the regiments raised by the nobility during the '45 fulfilled routine duties and only one of them participated in the fighting, these regiments do furnish interesting examples of the problems that arose from the hasty raising of men in a national emergency. They perhaps provide pointers as to why in the Seven Years War the expansion of the Army was conducted in the first instance by raising many second battalions for existing regiments, in which the new men could be integrated with old hands whose influence would dilute the tendency towards the continuation of 'civilian' thinking, and why the regiments raised during the latter part of that war were largely used as a pool of available labour from which drafts could be made to fill up the active regiments; a procedure which would have the same diluting effect. Nevertheless, their history provides fascinating material for the military historian and the student of uniform.

Acknowledgements

I am greatly indebted to the staffs of The National Archives, Kew, the Northamptonshire County Archives, the Heritage Hub (County Records Office), Gloucester and to Crispin Powell, archivist of Boughton House, Northamptonshire. Invaluable assistance has been provided by Dr J.A. Houlding from his database of all British Army officers 1724-1794. I am also grateful to Sir Michael Leighton, Bt, Stephen Wood, Esq. and Duncan Sutton, Esq.

---

85   Andrew Cormack, 'These Meritorious Objects of the Royal Bounty'; The Chelsea Out-pensioners in the Early Eighteenth Century (London: published by the author, 2017). Individual details of service are taken from the database upon which this book is based.

4

The Edinburgh Units of 1745-6: The Trained Bands, City Guard, Regiment, and Volunteers

Arran Johnston

Although the political status of Edinburgh had been diminished by the Act of Union and the shift of international trade towards the west, the Scottish capital remained the country's legal and commercial heart. Despite its narrow, crowded closes and high, cramped tenements, the city was also on the cusp of that Enlightenment age which would restore its prestige and see it burst from the constraints of its old town walls. It was also home to Scotland's premier military fortress, Edinburgh Castle, seated at the high western end of the city's spine, whilst the royal palace of Holyroodhouse lay at its eastern terminus. If the former was the symbol of George II's military power, Holyrood emphasised Edinburgh's lost status as a true royal capital. The city was crowded, dirty, and fascinating, little changed since the seismic events of the Civil Wars; the classical facades of the 'capital of the mind' as yet unbuilt.[1] The Jacobite Rising of 1745 therefore occurred at an important moment of transition in the city's history, and the sympathies of the citizens were being pulled in two ways as they sought both future prosperity and their past prestige. This created a tense and uncertain backdrop to the burgh authorities' attempts to raise effective forces for the Government in 1745. This chapter will examine the results of those efforts, following the intertwined narratives of each of the Edinburgh defence units in their turn.

Edinburgh Castle provided the city with the support of a permanent garrison and potential to access Scotland's principal arsenal, but ultimately the castle's main concern was its own defensibility. Its presence was therefore both a reassurance and a threat to the citizens below: then as today, the massive half-moon battery faced straight into the town. In the summer of 1745 the 'Castle-company' consisted of around one hundred Invalids, with the regulars of Lascelles' 58th Foot also currently based there and in the adjacent harbour-town of Leith.[2] The garrison commander was the 86-year-old Lieutenant General George Preston,

---

1   J. Buchan, *Capital of the Mind: How Edinburgh Changed the World* (Edinburgh: Birlinn, 2007).
2   B. Robins (ed.), *Report of the Proceedings and Opinion of the Board of General Officers on their Examination into the Conduct, Behaviour and Proceedings of Lieutenant-General Sir John Cope, Colonel Peregrine Lascelles, and Brigadier-General Thomas Fowke* (London: Faulkner, 1749), p.7.

a Scottish veteran of William of Orange's landing in 1688 who had been in post at the castle since 1715. Born before the Restoration of Charles II, Preston was a bridge to another age, but, according to the senior military commander in Scotland, Lieutenant General Sir John Cope, his infirmities had allowed him to visit Edinburgh Castle only 'two or three times' that year.[3]

When Cope formed his field army in response to the Jacobite prince's landing, all but two 70-man companies of Lascelles' were withdrawn from the capital, along with the castle's experienced master-gunner Major Eaglesfield Griffith.[4] A thousand stand-of-arms were taken north too. Preston was replaced with Lieutenant General Joshua Guest, brought out of retirement despite being only a year younger than Preston. Like his predecessor, Guest was a distinguished veteran. Both generals ended up serving inside the castle simultaneously. Cope left behind him two regiments of dragoons to protect the capital, horses being considered unsuitable for a campaign deep into the Highlands. These regiments had previously been distributed across the Lothians and eastern Borders, but now Gardiner's 13th Dragoons was advanced to Stirling whilst Hamilton's 14th was posted at Leith.

Despite the presence of two generals in the castle, military authority within the city itself was vested by long tradition in its senior civic officer. Elected by the burgh council, as well as heading the urban management of the capital, the Lord Provost of Edinburgh was the interface between the city and the monarch, acting as Lord Lieutenant and Admiral of the Forth. He was therefore given 'authority to command the military force of whatever kind within the City', although the events of 1745 cast into focus whether that authority was directly invested by the crown to the office holder or with the council of which he was simply the senior representative.[5] There was, however, no real doubt that responsibility for policing and defending Edinburgh rested on the Lord Provost's shoulders, and past provosts had faced punishment for failing. Archibald Stewart, a successful wine trader from the Borders who had been serving as the city's MP since 1741, was elected as Lord Provost in 1744. Stewart was therefore tasked with 'preserving the city intrusted to his care from falling under the power of the rebels', leaving Guest responsible only for the castle.[6]

Stewart's task was not an easy one. Although the council formally declared its loyalty to George II, the opinion of the citizens was by no means unanimous. The city defences were old and inadequate, and whispers of Jacobite sympathies named both Stewart and some of those on whom his defensive plans would rest. Later rumour even suggested that Guest was a Jacobite and only kept straight by Preston, although this was surely unfounded.[7] Stewart himself would be openly accused by his political rivals, and for his apparent negligence was imprisoned in the Tower of London and twice tried. Despite being found not guilty, his alleged

3   Robins (ed.), *Report of the Proceedings*, p.6.
4   Anon., *The Trial of Archibald Stewart Esq, Late Lord Provost of Edinburgh* (Edinburgh: Gideon Crawford, 1747, p.279.
5   Anon., *Trial of Archibald Stewart*, p.12.
6   Anon., *Trial of Archibald Stewart*, p.114.
7   Guest is accused of Jacobite sympathy by Robert Chambers, writing almost a century later, based on a tradition of the Preston family. The author has not been able to find the original text, although it is quoted by L. Stephen & S. Lee (eds.), *Dictionary of National Biography* (New York: Macmillan, 1890), Vol.23, p.320.

Jacobitism has still been stated as fact.[8] Stewart had, however, received no special training for this huge responsibility, and was bombarded throughout the crisis with contrary opinions. Gauging the mood of both the capital's grandees and its notoriously temperamental citizens had to be balanced against both political and military consequences.[9] Edinburgh had previously come under direct threat in 1715. On that occasion a plot to betray the castle had been almost farcically bungled, but when a Jacobite force surprised the authorities by crossing the Firth of Forth it successfully seized Leith's old Commonwealth fort. The capital had held its nerve and refused to surrender and the Jacobites had withdrawn of their own accord, but these events of only 30 years before reminded the authorities that they faced threats from both within and without. Their best hope of defence lay in a swift victory for Sir John Cope in the north.

Cope marched north on 19 August, the same day that Prince Charles raised his standard at Glenfinnan. At that time, the Lord Provost's priority was to secure the capital from any internal unrest or disloyalty: he had been instructed from London to use 'such precautions as he should judge necessary for preserving the publick peace within the city of Edinburgh.'[10] Stewart had replied that he would 'keep a watchful eye' to prevent disturbances and apprehend infiltrators. In response to this commitment the council agreed three actions on 23 August: the Constables were to make lists of residents within their districts, recording any suspicious comings-and-goings; the officers of the Trained Bands were to make and report lists of their members; and the city magistrates would 'raise the number of thirty centinels to be added to the City-Guard'. The latter would also collate daily reports of unknown arrivals from the inn-keepers.[11] These resolutions demonstrate that the focus was on internal policing, using the forces at the Lord Provost's disposal. These were soon supplemented by the raising of a temporary regiment of foot and, whether Stewart wanted them or not, by the assembly of a corps of volunteers.

The Trained Bands of Edinburgh

The small company of Constables had been founded by royal authority in 1611, to enforce curfew and arrest trouble-makers. Chosen by the council, half were merchants and half craftsmen, and although from 1700 they were permitted to carry batons, many of their more active duties had been assumed by the City Guard. Civic defence was the role of the Trained Bands, officially formed as eight companies of pike and shot in February 1626.[12] In 1645 the Bands were reorganised into 16 companies corresponding to specific urban districts, again officered by a pre-determined proportion of respectable merchants and craftsmen. In

8   R. Chambers, *Traditions of Edinburgh* (Edinburgh: W&R Chambers, 1869), p.61.
9   The population was considered at the time to be far in excess of 32,000, crammed into a very compact urban space. It was probably considerably higher than that. *The Scots Magazine*, Vol.2 (1745), p.611.
10   The exchange of letters, on 13 and 17 August respectively, was read in council on 23 August and the Provost's response approved. Anon. *Trial of Archibald Stewart*, p.37.
11   Anon., *Trial of Archibald Stewart*, pp.37-38.
12   W. Skinner (ed.), *Minutes of the Society of the Trained Bands of Edinburgh* (Edinburgh: Pillans & Wilson, 1889), p.14.

1663 a formally constituted Society of the Captains of the Trained Bands was established. Over time however, the Trained Bands also yielded much of their responsibility to the City Guard. In July 1709 a Bands officer was suspended for insolence towards a counterpart in the Guard, indicative of a tension between the civilian amateurs and the paid professionals as well as suggesting the Guard was considered to have the higher authority.[13]

By 1745 the role of the Trained Bands was already purely ceremonial, parading annually for the king's birthday without any further military responsibilities. Their weapons were provided from the burgh arsenal, purchased privately through a traditional obligation on city burgesses to contribute arms when they were admitted to that status. As a result the arms were, according to Archibald Stewart himself, 'generally old guns without bayonets, bought at half a crown or three shillings apiece, more for shew than use'.[14] When it became increasingly likely that the city might fall, the owners of these guns proved reluctant to allow them to be sent up to the castle, both so as not to leave the city completely defenceless but also because they were considered as private possessions.

The Lord Provost was *ex officio* colonel of the Trained Bands, but in practice they were led by a captain-commandant. In 1745 this was Robert Tennent, a merchant. The company captains carried a half-pike and hanger, and although most captacincies were reserved for merchants the other officers could include bakers, brewers, painters and wrights.[15] John Dalgleish, a watchmaker, commanded one of the craftsmen's companies. The privates were also representative of the trades of the city: Captain Alexander Hepburn had in his company the tailor Robert Brown and the pharmacist Edward Inglis, for example.[16] Each district was known by the colour scheme of the flag carried by its ensign, which bore the city arms over a coloured saltire.[17] Although Lord Provost Stewart instructed the Trained Bands to assemble 'under their proper colours and officers,' suggesting all 16 flags were paraded out for service in 1745, the Bands were deployed for watching duties three companies at a time.[18]

Whether the soldiers of the Trained Bands were uniformed in 1745 remains unclear. In 1687 white feathers tipped with company colours were ordered for the captains' hats.[19] In the later 18th century we know the captains wore cocked hats, dark blue coats, white waistcoats and nankeen breeches, with rose cockades on their left breast in their company colours.[20] Sadly none of this really advances the case for uniform in 1745, although coloured company hat ribbons seem likely. The Edinburgh historian Robert Chambers refers to the Trained Bands as 'ordinary citizens possessed of uniforms', the latter being but 'simple'. No

13   Skinner (ed.), *Minutes*, p.62.
14   Anon., *Trial of Archibald Stewart*, p.127.
15   Skinner (ed.), *Minutes*, pp.133-134.
16   Anon., *Trial of Archibald Stewart*, p.297.
17   Starting with the senior, the colours were: orange; white; blue; white and orange; green and red; purple; blue and white; orange green; green and white; red and yellow; yellow; red and blue; orange and blue; red and white; red, white and orange; red. At some unknown date, all but the orange colour fell out of service.
18   Anon., *Trial of Archibald Stewart*, p.115.
19   Skinner (ed.), *Minutes*, p.42.
20   Skinner (ed.), *Minutes*, p.106.

other detail is given however, and as he was writing in 1827 there is a chance that Chambers is extrapolating from the experience of his own lifetime.[21]

The military efficiency of the Edinburgh Trained Bands was extremely limited. Alongside the low quality of their aged muskets was that fact that the citizen-soldiers were so ill-used to them. An observer writing in 1748, but recalling observations from before the Rising, noted that despite giving themselves a swagger for the king's birthday parade these soldiers invariably closed their eyes when firing their muskets.[22] Although the Trained Bands had given military service on several occasions in the previous century, they had not been put to use during the Jacobite Rising of 1715.[23] In September 1736, after serious rioting, Captain Alexander Maitland of the City Guard was elected as a drill-master to the Trained Bands. It seems likely, however, that the training focused on 'regulating their marches on all solemn occasions'.[24] After a long-running disagreement between two captains in 1740, the log of the Society of Captains' minutes suggests there was little serious activity in the run up to the Jacobite crisis. Worse still, Stewart suspected the loyalty of the Trained Bands, believing 'many were known to be disaffected'.[25] Patrick Crichton, himself a virulently anti-Jacobite burgess of Edinburgh, agreed: 'of the train band captains 12 of 15 were Jacobite, and the commandant'.[26]

Nevertheless, the Trained Bands had a pre-existing organisational structure of established legality, with the right to make use of the town's arms. They were also large, able to field 1,600 men if brought to full strength.[27] As we shall see, however, the burgh arsenal was insufficient to provide for that number, and most companies were only issued 50-60 firelocks as the Jacobites approached. One company received only 24 weapons.[28] It is unclear whether these numbers were more on account of the lack of available muskets or because the companies were understrength, although it was probably the combination of both. Some members of the Trained Bands also enlisted in the Volunteers, preferring to actually serve in the latter.

In the event, the Edinburgh Trained Bands had but a small part to play in the great events of 1745-6. The companies took turns to mount watches in the weeks running up to the Jacobites' arrival, but when infantry support was required for the dragoons west of the city the Trained Bands were held back. Nevertheless, at 3:00 p.m. on 15 September the captains were ordered to 'draw out their companies' so that weapons could be distributed. Three companies were kept on duty whilst the others stood down, ready to react 'at a minute's

21   R. Chambers, *History of the Rebellion of 1745-6, Seventh Edition* (Edinburgh: W & R Chambers, 1869), p.76.
22   D. Hume, *Account of the Behaviour of Archibald Stewart in a Letter to a Friend* (London: M. Cooper, 1748), p.12.
23   Anon., *Trial of Archibald Stewart*, p.195.
24   Skinner (ed.), *Minutes*, p.74.
25   Anon., *Trial of Archibald Stewart*, p.21.
26   Crichton is the presumed author of an anonymous journal of the events surrounding the city's capture. Although clearly partial, his account provides important and well-informed testimony. P. Crichton, *The Woodhouselee MS* (Edinburgh: W & R Chambers, 1907), p.15.
27   Theoretically each company should have been 100 strong: H. Arnot, *The History of Edinburgh, from the Earliest Accounts to the Year 1780* (Edinburgh: Thomas Turnbull, 1816), p.389.
28   Anon., *Trial of Archibald Stewart*, p.317.

notice' if summoned by the tuck of drums.[29] The officers used a tavern called the Crown as their communication post, with captains in one room and subalterns in another ready to disseminate orders. When the Lord Provost met the Bands officers there on 16 September, they told him the city was not defensible.

The three companies on duty on that night were posted at the Weigh House (at the top of the Lawnmarket) and at the West Port (the gate at the western end of the Grassmarket). At the latter, Captain Alexander Hepburn reported that his men were on the brink of mutiny after hearing that the Volunteers had handed in their arms.[30] There was confusion and miscommunication bordering on panic following the arrival of a message from the Prince, and Captain Tennent later gave evidence that during the evening he heard that the Highlanders had already gained entry into the town.[31] Hearing this, he sought immediate permission to stand the Trained Bands down. This he apparently received, but the messenger, George Wemyss, failed to inform Hepburn at the West Port and he and his men accordingly stayed in arms where they had been since 8:00 a.m., until 3:00 a.m. the following morning.

When Tennent heard Hepburn was still in arms, he sent a caddie (one of the capital's enterprising street messengers) to summon him before a group of anxious and exhausted city officers to explain why he and his company were still at their post contrary to orders. The Lord Provost, Hepburn later related, was himself present but his 'head was lying on his hand on the table'.[32] Thus Archibald Stewart was asleep when the last of the Trained Bands were ordered to disarm by their captain-commandant. Hepburn explicitly reported at Stewart's trial that he was told to stack their arms at the West Port, from which they would be collected later in the morning by the burgh store-keeper. Thus, as the vanguard of the Highland army was lurking in the shadows pondering how best to secure entry to the locked gates, the defenders were actively disarming themselves. How culpable Stewart was in this was the cause of much scrutiny at his trials, but Tennent was clearly eager to stand the Trained Bands down as he did not want his men to be 'found by the rebels with arms in their hands'.[33] The city was seized little over an hour after Hepburn stood down, although his company was at the opposite side of town and could not therefore have saved the Netherbow. After this inglorious defence the Society of Captains did not meet again until October 1747.[34]

The Edinburgh City Guard

Archibald Stewart was also head of the Edinburgh City Guard, a paramilitary force responsible for working with the constables to maintain order and to act when necessary as the

---

29   Evidence of Captain Dalgleish, Anon., *Trial of Archibald Stewart*, p.303.
30   Anon., *Trial of Archibald Stewart*, p.306.
31   Others heard similar rumours, but although false they may in fact have been triggered by witnesses detecting the movements of the covert Jacobite advance on the Netherbow that night. Anon. *Trial of Archibald Stewart*, p.302. For the Jacobites' activities at this time, see A. & H. Taylor, *1745 and After* (Edinburgh: Thomas Nelson & Sons, 1938), pp.71-74.
32   Anon. *Trial of Archibald Stewart*, p.299; after the events of that day, it is hard not to sympathise.
33   Evidence of Robert Tennent, Anon., *Trial of Archibald Stewart*, p.301.
34   Skinner (ed.), *Minutes*, p.84.

capital's first line of defence. Whilst the Trained Bands had been intended for wartime defence, the citizens of Edinburgh had responsibility to undertake a rota of nightly 'watching and warding'. This tedious duty was inevitably unappealing, and as early as 1648 the city opted to pay 60 men as a permanent guard instead. This proved short-lived due to the lack of regular funding, restoring the citizens' burden.[35] Policing was left to the inadequate force of gentleman constables, until a series of disorders so frustrated the Privy Council that it threatened in 1679 to quarter troops on the city. Burgh pride instead led to the creation of a small company of grey-coated musketeers.[36] This proved inadequate for the task, and after a riot on 2 May 1682 the Guard's number was raised to 108 privates.[37]

The appointment of the guard's officers was now made a royal prerogative, with the king also assuming the authority to march the City Guard wherever he felt fit.[38] At a time of increasing anxiety over the prospect of a Catholic succession, this was a serious concern to the independently-minded burgesses. When the storm broke in 1688, the city authorities sided with the Edinburgh mob and deployed both the Guard and the Trained Bands against the royal guards at Holyroodhouse. After William and Mary secured the crowns, the Guard was first reduced to just 50 men and then, in order to be rid of the tax which paid for them, the burgh sought permission from the new regime to disband it. Somewhat embarrassingly, the resulting disorders obliged the council to re-establish the City Guard almost immediately, now creating a company of 87 privates in June 1689 which was paid out of the common good fund.

Again facing a funding crisis, the burgh petitioned Parliament for formal consent to maintain the unit and tax the citizens to pay for it. Accordingly, the Edinburgh City Guard gained formal recognition by Act of Parliament, after several false starts, on 19 July 1690. The Act permitted the recruitment and maintenance of 'a company of trained and experienced soldiers' not exceeding 126 men including officers. The company would 'not be obliged to go above a mile without the city and liberties thereof', and in lieu of their former watching and warding obligations the citizens were required to provide up to £15,000 Scots to cover the pay and expenses of the officers and sentinels.[39] The Guards were now uniformed in red, as had become the established custom for the army.

Policing Edinburgh was rough work and the job attracted rough men. The burgh records contain numerous complaints about rough-handling, abusive language, and misdemeanours, and the council periodically published new rules and punishments for the Guard. The cost of paying the surgeons' bills for patching up Guards grew so high that in 1722 the council opted to pay the surgeon a flat annual rate. This also prevented the Guards from charging treatments given to family members to the city funds, as the magistrates suspected them of doing.[40] A barber was similarly provided, suggesting that appearance

35   Arnot, *History of Edinburgh*, p.390.
36   H. Coutts, 'Resurrecting the Town Guard', *The Scots Magazine*, July 1973, p.329.
37   Coutts 'Resurrecting the Town Guard', p.329.
38   Arnot, *History of Edinburgh*, p.390.
39   K.M. Brown et al (eds.) *The Records of the Parliaments of Scotland to 1707* (St Andrews, 2007-2020), 1690/4/126 at <http://rps.ac.uk/trans/1690/4/126> accessed 29 June 2020.
40   Edinburgh City Archives: Burgh Records, Vol.49, p.384. The author wishes to thank Herbert and Angela Coutts for providing the notes of their extensive search of the burgh records for references to the City Guard.

was considered important. In 1725 specific instructions were given that only able-bodied men who stood over 5 feet 8 inches should be enlisted. In return for the Guard being better regulated, the council agreed not to allow pay to fall into arrears as it had previously.[41]

No illustration of the City Guard's uniform in 1745 has come down to us, although they do exist for the Guard in its later life. The best insights come from the burgh records of the 1730s. On 29 November 1738, Spence, Miller & Company were paid £76 1s 2.5d for 'red and blue cloth,' whilst Patrick Manderston received £15 9s 4.5d for 'lining and coarse cloth'. The tailor David Campbell was then commissioned to make 'the coats and furniture' for the sum of £31 15s 1d. Hats were provided by John Newbiggin and pewter buttons by Thomas Simpson.[42] The previous year's listing had also included both 'gold lace' and 'livery lace', probably intended for the officers and drummers respectively, as well as 'cloth for spatter-dashes', leather stocks and clasps, and shoes.[43] Officers' coats had cost £149 4s 6d to be made up in 1731, and they were made by no less a person than the deacon of the Incorporation of Tailors.[44] Soldiers could earn extra pay by cleaning the unit's leatherwork, and occasionally a hatter was paid to re-crease the soldiers' headgear. Watch-coats were periodically purchased in small enough quantities each time to suggest that they were replacements going into a collective stock.[45] In 1737 the clerks recorded with pride that 'this year the Town Guard is remarkably better cloathed than usual, for their vests and breeches are of the same cloth with their coats, whereas formerly it was of a much inferior quality'.[46]

It seems therefore that in 1745 the coats were of red cloth turned up with blue, with pewter buttons and a coarse cloth lining. Whilst it cannot be confirmed from the records, the coat pattern presumably echoed that of regular soldiers; although it is not known for sure whether or not they featured lapels at this date. The waistcoats and breeches were also red. Gaiters covered the lower legs, possibly black as we know them to have been in the 1790s and which would have been most practical for street duties. Cocked hats crowned the heads, with 'broad buff belts' at the waist which were presumably of the common design used by regular regiments as they held both swords and bayonets.[47] An order for 230 cartridge boxes suggests a stock was kept at the town arsenal. New clothes were costed into each year's budget, and along with payments for washing belts, creasing hats and employing barbers, it seems that the capital's 'company of fusiliers' were turned out smartly.

---

41   Edinburgh City Archives: Burgh Records, Vol.51, p.24.
42   The prices are in Pounds Scots, the currency still used for accounting. Edinburgh City Archives: Burgh Records, Vol.59, p.281.
43   The livery lace is something of a mystery, but might suggest an early origin for the ornamental lace later used on drummers' coats such as the one surviving in the National Museum of Scotland. The lace is white with a complex repeating pattern in blue. Edinburgh City Archives: Burgh Records, Vol.58, p.240.
44   Edinburgh City Archives: Burgh Records, Vol.53, p.278.
45   It is possible that some of the characters wearing heavy watch-coats in tableaux from the Penicuik Sketches are intended to show City Guards, although at least one such character is specifically labelled as a Volunteer and their old-fashioned hair styles again suggests they were not the Guard. See Figs 19-20 and 24 in I. Brown and H. Cheape, Witness to Rebellion: John Maclean's Journal of the 'Forty-Five and the Penicuik Drawings (Edinburgh: John Donald, 1996), pp.61-64.
46   Edinburgh City Archives: Burgh Records, Vol.58, p.241.
47   The quotation for belts is from 1722, when they cost 2s 2d per piece. Edinburgh City Archives: Burgh Records, Vol.50, pp.34-5.

Appearances may have become especially important after the Porteous Riots of 1736, when Captain John Porteous had ordered his men to open fire, killing six. The officer was found guilty of murder, but when the mob suspected Porteous would be reprieved they overpowered the Guard at the tollbooth and lynched him. These events caused a sensation in London, resulting in the council being fined and the Lord Provost barred from future public office. The council declared 'all or most of the soldiers of the City Guard are unfit for service'. The whole unit was dismissed and the officers instructed to levy completely afresh.[48] A committee of improvements was established, and only by late summer 1737 was the restored City Guard ready to receive the new uniforms previously mentioned. This shake-up had provided the opportunity for the City Guard to restore public confidence. The reformation seems to have worked, and by 1745 the Guard was considered 'pretty well disciplined'.[49] Writing in 1779, Hugo Arnot recorded that 'the men are properly disciplined, and fire remarkably well'; the evidence suggests they were no less proficient in 1745, and they certainly appear to have commanded more confidence in 1745 than the other Edinburgh units.[50]

The City Guard operated from headquarters on the High Street, located in front of the Tron Kirk. The arsenal was however kept at the more secure tollbooth, a domineering medieval structure further up the street which was also the meeting place of the council. The store-keeper John Hislop confirmed the arsenal's contents in August 1745: 1,250 serviceable muskets which were 'very old, but could fire'; 200 'altogether useless' muskets; 'not quite 200 bayonets'; 300 cartridge boxes in poor condition; two boxes of ammunition; and 'a bag with some loose ball.' The City Guard's arms were accounted separately as '75 firelocks and bayonets and cartridge boxes'.[51] These included the 'twenty-five stand of arms' purchased from the gunsmith John Wilson in 1733.[52] Some of these muskets are still in the council's possession, all long-land patterns with the royal cypher and some with the Tower stamp. For peace-time street patrols the Guard also possessed Lochaber axes.

The strength of the City Guard fluctuated throughout the century, most commonly resting at 75 men. This figure could be raised as the situation required, as was done in both 1715 and 1719. Council resolutions on 23 August and 2 September 1745 brought the Guard to its maximum legal complement of 126. Before the post-Porteous re-structure, the Guard was organised as a single company with three operational shifts, officered by two captain-lieutenants on rotating duty, plus an ensign (no description of a colour survives). From 26 August 1737, however, the ensign's post was replaced by a third captain-lieutenant to create three equal squads within the company.[53] The three officers, one of whom held

48   Edinburgh City Archives: Burgh Records, Vol.57, p.54.
49   Hume, *Account of the Behaviour of Archibald Stewart*, p.11.
50   Arnot, *History of Edinburgh*, pp.390-391. The City Guard gained an unenviable reputation once again towards the end of the century, although many of its critics were those most likely to be on the receiving end of their rough justice. It seems to have become the later practice to recruit from Army veterans, especially after the American Revolution.
51   Anon., *Trial of Archibald Stewart*, p.317. The extra 39 men of the City Guard raised by order of the council were equipped with the muskets and cartridge boxes usually reserved for the Trained Bands.
52   Edinburgh City Archives: Burgh Records, Vol.54, p.530.
53   'Squads' is the word apparently used by one of the Guard captains in evidence at Stewart's trial. Anon., *Trial of Archibald Stewart*, p.321.

senior authority, were required to swear an oath of allegiance 'with assurance to His Majesty King George II'.[54] In 1745 the three captains were: Alexander Maitland, who was elected to replace John Porteous in 1736 and re-appointed after the re-structuring; Thomas Dalziel, who was promoted in 1738 after apparently serving as the Guard's last ensign; and Walter Hamilton. They were paid 4 shillings per day for 28 days of each month. Below them were their three sergeants, who were paid 1 shilling per day and whose halberds can now be seen in the Museum of Edinburgh. The three corporals were paid 8d per day, and the rank and file 6d.[55] The drummers, whose instruments were painted with the city arms and who beat the nightly curfew, appear to have been paid the same as the privates from 1737, although previously their pay had matched the corporals. These rates of pay are all slightly behind those of regular troops, with the captains' pay 8d short of that of an infantry lieutenant.[56] Payday was the first Friday of each month, subject to the presentation of satisfactory rolls and reports from the officers.

On Sunday 15 September the City Guard was ordered to march out of the city to support Gardiner's 13th Dragoons at Corstorphine. Almost three miles from the city, this exceeded the requirements of their terms of service. The only other time the Guard had marched out of Edinburgh was to vainly threaten the Jacobites in Leith in 1715. Captain Hamilton confirmed that on reaching Corstorphine the Guard was to come under the orders of Colonel Gardiner.[57] As a red-coated unit the City Guard would give an identical appearance to regulars, and after seeing them in position Patrick Crichton considered that 'they looked like men for the purpose'.[58] Once he saw that the infantry were now committed, Lieutenant General Guest ordered Hamilton's 14th Dragoons to follow them west, deliberately riding through the streets to give a show of bravado.[59] At sunset, however, Gardiner pulled back to 'a field between Leith and Edinburgh' and returned the infantry to the city overnight.[60]

After judging some of their muskets deficient, some Guards received permission to swap their weapons for those supplied from the castle for the new Edinburgh Regiment (discussed below).[61] Gardiner was superseded in his command of the dragoons by the arrival of Brigadier General Thomas Fowke, and the attempt to hold the road was resumed the following morning. Captain Dalziel led the City Guard out at 10:00 a.m., leaving behind a sergeant and 16 men to make up more cartridges.[62] They joined the dragoons at Coltbridge

54   Edinburgh City Archives: Burgh Records, Vol.58, p.137. The council was not above dismissing those with who it was unsatisfied, as it did to Robert Telfair in 1730 after 12 years in office. Telfair seems to have got himself into something of a mess and he was not turning up for duties.

55   Although the currencies were officially aligned after the Act of Union in 1707, the burgh accounts continued to record these sums in pounds Scots. The 1737 account, on which these figures are based, is particularly confusing as it uses sterling for some figures and Scots for others.

56   Based on comparison to the 1735 figures in R. Seymor, *A survey of the cities of London and Westminster, borough of Southwark, and parts Adjacent* (London: Read, J., 1735), p.897.

57   *Trial of Archibald Stewart*, p.359.

58   Crichton, *Woodhouselee MS*, p.19.

59   J. Home, *The History of the Rebellion in Scotland in 1745* (Edinburgh: Peter Brown, 1822), p.59.

60   Home, *History of the Rebellion*, p.62.

61   Anon., *Trial of Archibald Stewart*, p.323. The Edinburgh Regiment was not of sufficient strength to need all of them.

62   Evidence of Captain Dalziel, Anon., *Trial of Archibald Stewart*, p.321. These men were later forwarded on to their unit at Coltbridge.

on the Water of Leith, Fowke's little army forming in the open country on the Edinburgh side of the bridge and waiting there until mid-afternoon. Then came the infamous Canter of Coltbridge, in which a few shots from Jacobite outriders sent the dragoons into a needless and disorderly retreat. James Murray, a former soldier, considered that 'the City-Guard retired in good order to the town'.[63] They were back inside the walls by around 4:00 p.m., having acquitted themselves somewhat better than the more numerous regulars at their side.

Dalziel was ordered by the Lord Provost to keep the whole City Guard in arms, posting two of the 'squads' to the Grassmarket whilst the third was held in reserve on the High Street. At 8:00 p.m. Dalziel's men were withdrawn to re-join the rest at the guardhouse, at which point the City Guard was ordered to stand one squad down. The day of 16 September had been an exceptionally taxing one, the most significant in the Guard's history since their *annus horribilis* of 1736, and the whole company had been on duty for almost 12 hours. The men were clearly exhausted and their nerves strained. Nevertheless, Dalziel kept 50 men in arms rather than just 42. As the Volunteers had disbanded, he sent 13 men and a sergeant to watch the Netherbow Port in their absence. Although these men were savvy enough to see off a Jacobite who attempted to gain entry in disguise, Dalziel was later informed that they had 'got themselves drunk'.[64] They were relieved by just six men, 'which was all he could find that were fit for doing duty'.[65] At 4:00 a.m. the weary Captain Dalziel went off duty, at the very moment his Netherbow sentries were stopping a coach at the gate.

This coach, returning to its yards after carrying the burgh's anxious deputation back from the Jacobite camp, was stopped by two Guards at the well-head beside John Knox House. They refused him permission to leave only to be overruled by the civilian underkeeper of the port, James Gillespie. After letting out the coach, Gillespie 'shut one of the leaves of the port, but as he was shutting the other the Highlanders rushed in upon him and beat him back'.[66] One of the sentries confirmed that the coach had not gone 12 yards past before the onrush, during which no less a person than Donald Cameron of Lochiel had seized him by the arm.[67] Thus the Guard could at least claim it had made physical contact with the enemy, unlike most of the city's defenders. Unbeknownst to the City Guards at the gate, 24 well-disciplined Highlanders had been posted in the shadows looking for just such an opportunity.

As soon as the Netherbow was secure, and the Jacobites marched quietly and efficiently into the city and took control of the guardhouse and gates. Had the Trained Bands or Volunteers still been in arms, the risk of bloodshed and collateral damage would have been far higher. As it was, only the City Guard had been standing in the Jacobites' way when the moment finally came. Hearing what had happened, Captain Dalziel went in search of the Lord Provost, finding him in a tavern on Writer's Close receiving the terms of his surrender as dictated by the Jacobite Colonel O'Sullivan. What happened to the City Guards thereafter remains unclear, and the Jacobites may simply have been satisfied to have disarmed them

---

63   Anon., *Trial of Archibald Stewart*, p.313.
64   For the foiled Jacobite ruse, see O'Sullivan's narrative in A. & H. Taylor, *1745 and After*, p.72.
65   Anon., *Trial of Archibald Stewart*, p.321.
66   From Gillespie's own evidence; Anon., *Trial of Archibald Stewart*, p.325.
67   Anon., *Trial of Archibald Stewart*, p.327.

without resistance. Those who were not on duty simply needed to keep their heads down until the Prince's army moved on. It is unlikely that any had sufficient time or warning to reach the safety of the castle. The failure of the Edinburgh City Guard to prevent the city from falling should not detract from their efforts to do so whilst others handed in their arms:

> The rebels made themselves masters of the City Guard, who had been so harassed with the extraordinary duty of the preceding week, and by being put under arms for two days before alongside with the dragoons, that they were hardly fit to do any duty; far less able to oppose an Army of Rebels who were numerous and hardy enough to defeat a regular disciplined body of the King's force a few days after.[68]

The Edinburgh Regiment

On Tuesday 27 August, as Sir John Cope was turning his army aside from the Corrieyairack Pass, Edinburgh's council considered how to 'contribute to defeat the dangerous and wicked designs of the enemies of his sacred majesty.'[69] The next day a committee met with the senior legal officers and proposed 'a regiment of a thousand men should be levied, for the defence of the town and the service of the government, to be subsisted for three months, on the charges of such of the inhabitants as were willing'.[70] The regiment's establishment was delayed by concerns about the legality of raising an armed body without express royal permission, the Lord Provost fearing it might amount to treason. The lawyers appear to have agreed and the Lord Advocate accordingly wrote to London for the required warrant, which duly arrived on 9 September. By then it was clear that Cope had been outmanoeuvred in the north.

As soon as the legalities were settled, Archibald Stewart was appointed as commander of the new regiment by virtue of his office. A management committee, requiring a quorum of five members if the Lord Provost was present or nine if he was necessarily absent, agreed to meet twice daily at the Goldsmiths' Hall on Parliament Square.[71] Some of the city's Presbyterian ministers, mobilised by fears of a Catholic restoration, agreed to subsidise one of the ten 100-strong companies 'out of their moderate stipends'.[72] Allan Burns was appointed adjutant, a veteran who had served in Rothes' 25th Foot (now Sempill's), a regiment with strong Edinburgh connections and anti-Jacobite credentials. However, recruitment proved too slow. On 15 September, 'as many men of the Edinburgh Regiment as were fit for duty' were ordered to join the City Guard's march to Corstorphine, but two witnesses confirm only 50 marched out.[73] Patrick Crichton believed the regiment had 120 men however, so perhaps only 50 had yet been armed and

68   Case for the defence, Anon., *Trial of Archibald Stewart*, p.133.
69   Anon., *Trial of Archibald Stewart*, p.103.
70   Anon., *Trial of Archibald Stewart*, p.103.
71   Anon., *Trial of Archibald Stewart*, p.49.
72   Anon., *Trial of Archibald Stewart*, p.49.
73   Anon., *Trial of Archibald Stewart*, p.148.

trained.[74] Since Stewart signed out 200 stands-of-arms from the castle on 12 September for the regiment, and from these there were enough left on 15 September for the City Guard to upgrade their own arms, the Edinburgh Regiment was barely more than a company at this point.[75]

Recruitment had surely been undermined by the competition. The City Guard had just recruited an additional 39 men, others preferred the lighter risks of volunteering with the Trained Bands or, if they had airs, the Volunteers. As a result, the Edinburgh Regiment was only able to appeal to 'desperate persons, to whom the promised pay was a temptation, and who cared nothing for the cause'.[76] When Sir Robert Dickson of Carberry brought in 130-150 men from around Musselburgh, Provost Stewart invited them to join the Edinburgh Regiment and they refused indignantly.[77] The idea was considered 'an insult and discouragement to their zeal, who being tradesmen and husbandmen, did not mean to leave their occupations and inlist themselves soldiers for hire'. Stewart thought he was doing right by trying to bring them into a formal structure and giving them the chance to draw pay.[78] The scale of the crisis had also yet to hit home, which was not the case in Glasgow where the far smaller town managed to recruit 600 men in just nine days.[79]

The Edinburgh Regiment does not appear to have been uniformed, at least not before the city fell in September and possibly not even afterwards, by which point the burgh records fall silent. Both Christopher Duffy and Stuart Reid suppose the regiment to have followed the English practice of issuing blue coats, although the latter acknowledges the lack of evidence and bases a reconstruction drawing on a sketch of a Volunteer.[80] The regiment probably therefore wore their own clothes, almost certainly with black cockades in their bonnets or hats, with standard infantry leatherwork and the 'guns, swords and bayonets' provided by the castle stores. The Lord Provost intended to have soldiers of the regiment trained, along with some of the City Guard and the Volunteers, in 'the exercise of throwing the hand-granadoes', but the necessary munitions 'never appeared'.[81]

On 16 September Adjutant Burns asked the Lord Provost what the regiment should do with their weapons. Stewart and the council now balked at giving any formal orders, not wanting to be responsible for either losing the castle's muskets to the enemy or for squirreling them away contrary to specific instructions in Prince Charles' letter to the city. The compromise was that 'the soldiers of the new-levied Regiment possest of those arms, should

74   Crichton, *Woodhouselee MS*, p.19.
75   Anon., *Trial of Archibald Stewart*, p.53; Home, *History of the Rebellion*, p.58.
76   Chambers, *History of the Rebellion*, p.77. A plausible if not quite contemporary assessment.
77   *Trial of Archibald Stewart*, p.231.
78   *Trial of Archibald Stewart*, p.23.
79   A Cochrane, *The Cochrane Correspondence relating to the Affairs of Glasgow 1745-6* (Glasgow: Maitland Club, 1836), p.82.
80   C. Duffy, *The '45: Bonnie Prince Charlie and the Untold Story of the Jacobite Rising* (London: Phoenix, 2003), p.148; S. Reid, *Cumberland's Culloden Army 1745-46* (Oxford: Osprey, 2012), p.45. Reid (*ibid.*, p.23) refers to the Edinburgh Regiment as 'the only complete provincial corps to be raised in Scotland', an accolade which would be more appropriately given to that of Glasgow, whose regiment also possessed colours.
81   Anon., *Trial of Archibald Stewart*, pp.50-51.

be privately acquainted to return them to the castle'.[82] It seems strange that the regiment dispersed rather than supplementing the castle garrison. The generals presumably had no wish for inexperienced mouths to feed ahead of a potential blockade.

This was not, however, the end of the road for the Edinburgh Regiment. Following the city's recovery by the long-serving but inexperienced Lieutenant General Roger Handasyd, it was reborn. A new subscription was issued following a meeting on 20 November, 'promising a reasonable gratuity' for the previously enlisted men if they now returned. Again, the ministers were asked to help, and the city apparently had 'good success' in filling the ranks this time. It is not however clear how high the strength actually rose.[83] A meeting in London on 27 November decided 'to name the Earl of Home to command the Edinburgh subscription'.[84] The Earl, a regular officer on leave when the Rising began, had volunteered on Sir John Cope's staff at Prestonpans. In early December he was busy leading the Glasgow Regiment out of the path of the oncoming Jacobites, however, so he had little to do with its Edinburgh counterpart. He arrived in the capital with the Glasgow and Paisley men on Christmas Eve. John Home considered these regiments 'not much better trained' than the volunteer companies which again sprang up in case the Jacobites again swung against the capital.[85]

Lieutenant General Henry Hawley found no use for the Edinburgh Regiment for the Falkirk campaign, even though he took the stronger Glasgow Regiment with him. The subscribers of the Edinburgh Regiment handed the blankets which had been donated to their unit over to the field army before it marched. Then 'the Edinburgh Regiment and the city guard were the only troops left in town,' and thus it escaped the dangers of the Battle of Falkirk.[86] In his turn the Duke of Cumberland also left the Edinburgh Regiment in the capital, although Edinburgh was no longer under serious threat. However, the regiment probably remained understrength, and the government had simply lost all faith in the loyalty and usefulness of Edinburgh.[87] The failed defence of September 1745 and the subsequent warm reception given by some to the Prince, combined with rumours about Stewart's loyalty, all served to poison attitudes towards Edinburgh, something Cumberland never tried to hide.

Nevertheless, the Edinburgh Regiment had one service yet to perform. In the wake of Cumberland's victory at Culloden, its soldiers patrolled the south side of the Firth of Forth in search of fugitives. On 29 April 1746, a detachment successfully captured a Jacobite soldier at South Queensferry. Robert Murray had served in the Prince's Lifeguards; he was a solicitor from Edinburgh.[88]

---

82   Case for the defence, Anon., *Trial of Archibald Stewart*, p.127.
83   *The Scots Magazine*, Vol.7 (1745), p.539.
84   Diary of Hugh, Earl of Marchmont, in G.H. Rose (ed.), *Selection from the Papers of the Earls of Marchmont* (London: J Murray, 1831), Vol.1, p.239.
85   Home, *History of the Rebellion*, p.116.
86   *The Scots Magazine*, Vol.8 (1746), pp.34, 44.
87   Rose (ed.), *Marchmont*, p.162.
88   *The Scots Magazine*, Vol.8 (1746), p.237.

The Edinburgh Volunteers

On Saturday 24 August 1745, a number of 'well-affected citizens' approached Lord Provost Stewart wishing to form a volunteer company.[89] Stewart was accused of sneering at their suggestion, not only because he doubted its wisdom but also because it was brought to him by political rivals. Burgh politics were an important factor with the Edinburgh Volunteers from the outset. The Lord Provost seems to have been annoyed by their leaders' badgering nature and distrusting of their motives in equal degrees. He also felt they were hampering recruitment in the new Edinburgh Regiment. In return, 'a number of very respectable gentlemen and burgesses' made common currency of their view that Stewart's zeal was insufficient. On 2 September 20 such men met in a tavern and essentially agreed to act independently of the Provost's authority in forming a company. Stewart had made clear his anxieties over the legality of raising forces, so he was affronted when he was ambushed on 5 September with a petition, 'signed by ninety or a hundred persons', demanding that he authorise the assembly of gentleman volunteers.[90] Amongst the signatories were three former Lord Provosts and three town baillies. This forced Stewart into the position of either explicitly denying influential men their chance to serve the king, or allowing them to form a body which (although ostensibly under his authority) was unlikely to prove manageable.

Attempting to secure some degree of authority over the new corps, Stewart 'did not leave the nomination of officers to the Volunteers'. Instead he authorised them to choose a list of 30-40 names from which he would appoint officers. In the end he selected six officers from their list before delegating back the choice of subalterns.[91] In reality he had little flexibility of choice as some of these men were too influential to slight. The Volunteer captains were: Stewart's chief rival, the past and future Lord Provost, George Drummond; Sir George Preston of Valleyfield, a kinsman of the octogenarian general inside the castle; another former Lord Provost, Archibald Macauley; Baillie and Auditor of the Excise, James Nimmo; the goldsmith James Kerr, who would be replace Stewart as MP for Edinburgh in 1747; and the solicitor Archibald Stevenson. Patrick Crichton called them 'old crassey officers' who 'acted like priests'.[92]

Stewart tried to ensure some military efficiency (and control) was injected into the unit by seeking an experienced officer to lead it. He wrote to the regular army captains John Dalrymple and James Murray, but 'they both refused to accept of a command of men who had not been accustomed to military discipline'.[93] The identity of these officers is not presently confirmed, although there are possible candidates. Dalrymple may be the young Captain John Dalrymple who was the nephew and favourite of Field Marshal John Dalrymple, 2nd Earl of Stair. This large family had immense local and national influence, and the Lothians were their powerbase. Captain James Murray of Harrison's 15th Foot, future general and Governor of Quebec, was about the same age and also from the Lothians. It is possible that he, having been recently wounded in action and possibly therefore at home

89   Anon., *Trial of Archibald Stewart*, p.39.
90   Anon., *Trial of Archibald Stewart*, p.71.
91   Anon., *Trial of Archibald Stewart*, p.193.
92   Crichton, *Woodhouselee MS*, pp.16-17.
93   Anon., *Trial of Archibald Stewart*, pp.111-112.

to recuperate, may be the second officer that Stewart approached. Whatever their identity, the professionals clearly saw the problems inherent in leading a company composed of men more used to making decisions than obeying orders. Thus thwarted, Stewart was obliged to endure a constant barrage of demands from the Volunteers, followed, after the city's fall, by their bitter accusations.

The Volunteers advertised in the local newspapers, and they soon numbered 400 men. These men enlisted at their own expense, 'to serve for the defence of the city at the hazard of their lives and fortunes'.[94] Lieutenant General Guest released for their use: 'two hundred muskets, bayonets, and cartouch-boxes, and the like number of flints, with one barrel of powder and an equal number proportion of ball.' On 12 September Stewart gave a receipt for half of that number, which may reflect that many brought arms of their own.[95] This is supported by the images in the Penicuik Sketches which show weapons of varied length and often without bayonets, suggesting many to have been private pieces.[96] One young citizen, seeing the Volunteers march, 'ran immediately upstairs to his father's house, and, fetching his fowling-piece and his small sword, joined'.[97]

The relevant Penicuik Sketches depict a mix of the local volunteer forces which gathered in Edinburgh either in September or, perhaps more likely, during November-January. There was probably no distinction in dress however between the Edinburgh Volunteers themselves and the smaller groups that came in from the surrounding communities. Two sketches show men with bags and canteens which suggest they have come in from the country, whilst several wear Geneva bands which identify them as ministers. This accords with the evidence of Stewart's trial, which confirms that the 400 Edinburgh Volunteers were supported at various times by a further 42 men from Dalkeith, 100-150 from Musselburgh, 70 excise-men, and 180 Seceders (raised from the congregations of Presbyterian ministers who had split from the Church of Scotland after a rupture in 1733).[98]

All these men will have worn, as depicted by the anonymous Penicuik artist, standard Lowland dress. Some carry canes as well as muskets, and one portly gentleman appears to be wearing gaiters. The sketches show a mix of bonnets, tricorns, and un-cocked round-hats, and they 'put on a badge or wear a cockade as a mark of distinction of their loyalty'.[99] Some sturdy but unhappy-looking Penicuik figures wear long heavy watch-coats, for which reason they have been occasionally identified as City Guards. However, their old-fashioned wigs suggest this is not the case, especially since one is shown seated in a sedan chair while on duty: the artist was probably more interested in illustrating the unusual, omitting regulars and the City Guard and focusing instead on the Volunteers, Jacobites, and Hessians he observed. Some Volunteers are shown wearing belly-boxes, some appear to have no ammunition pouches, and a small number appear to have cartridge bags on shoulder belts.

George Drummond, aged 57, assumed the role of captain-commandant of the Volunteers. He headed the famous College Company, formed from staff, students, and alumni of

---

94   Anon., *Trial of Archibald Stewart*, p.44.
95   Anon., *Trial of Archibald Stewart*, p.53.
96   The relevant figures are published as Figs 17-29 in Brown and Cheape, *Witness to Rebellion*, pp.59-66.
97   Carlyle, *Autobiography*, p.116.
98   Anon., *Trial of Archibald Stewart*, p.196.
99   Anon., *Trial of Archibald Stewart*, p.193.

Edinburgh University. It its ranks were: the maths professor Colin Maclaurin (47), who also oversaw the urgent improvements to the town walls; professor of moral philosophy William Cleghorn (27); the future university principal and Historiographer Royal, William Robertson (24); son of the minister in Prestonpans, Alexander 'Jupiter' Carlyle (23); future playwright and historian John Home (23); the doctor and poet William McGhie; and the classical scholar Hugh Ballantine.[100] These were young men in their prime, and many would go on to be important personalities in the coming Scottish Enlightenment. They received some training by 'a drill-sergeant', although Carlyle had already learned the 'manual exercise' from his father who had volunteered during the Jacobite threat of 1708. Meanwhile, history professor Charles Mackie penned a proposal for raising four regiments of able-bodied women from the Lothians, going so far as to suggest suitable officers![101]

When the City Guard and Edinburgh Regiment were ordered out on 15 September, the Volunteers were also expected to march. They mustered in the grounds of the university for 'a speech of some length' from Drummond.[102] The College Company then marched onto the Lawnmarket, where it cheered off Hamilton's 14th Dragoons as the regiment rode through. However, it all then began to unravel when Volunteer company officers appeared claiming that 'most of the privates were unwilling to march'.[103] The College Company marched down to the Grassmarket and Patrick Crichton thought they looked as if they were going to an execution.[104] There they were joined only by George Preston's company, while locals brought them 'bread and cheese, and strong ale and brandy.'[105] As the men waited for Drummond to return they were harangued by clergymen who warned they would be marching to their doom. The citizens showed their two faces, some reacting to the Volunteers 'with lamentation, and even with tears, and some with apparent scorn and derision'.[106] The effect on morale can easily be imagined. Drummond returned, marched them back to the university, and stood them down.

It may be that Drummond was, on reflection, reluctant to expose the hope of the city to the Highlanders in a risky operation. In which case, Stewart had essentially called his rival's bluff, and here lay the roots of Stewart's later trials lay as Drummond and his supporters wished both to expose his failings in office and to exculpate themselves from blame. Carlyle remained convinced that Drummond's preparedness to march the Volunteers out to battle was genuine, but burgh politics was clearly affecting how decisions were being taken. The politicised nature of the company commanders and the independent spirit of their men meant that the Volunteers were simply outside the reach of military discipline. The Volunteers did return to help with the night watch that evening, but many were already openly talking of leaving the city (and Stewart) and seeking a better way to serve King George.[107]

---

100 A. Carlyle, *Autobiography of the Rev. Dr Alexander Carlyle* (Edinburgh: Blackwood & Sons, 1860), p.111. Carlyle earned his nickname with his imposing stature.
101 Edinburgh University Library (EUL), Laing Collection: La.II.90/7.
102 Carlyle, *Autobiography*, pp.114-5.
103 Carlyle, *Autobiography*, p.115.
104 Crichton, *Woodhouselee MS*, p.16.
105 Carlyle, *Autobiography*, p.117,
106 Carlyle, *Autobiography*, p.116.
107 Carlyle, *Autobiography*, pp.120-121.

On 16 September Stewart summoned a public meeting by ringing the fire-bell, which was also the signal to assemble the Volunteers. Following the resulting 'clamour and discordance,' Drummond returned to his companies and instructed them to march to the castle and hand in their arms. Carlyle admits he was both 'glad' to deny the muskets to the Jacobites and 'a little ashamed and afflicted at our inglorious campaign'.[108] Thus the Edinburgh Volunteers disbanded without the permission of the Lord Provost, who was rightly incensed. The Trained Bands clamoured to follow their lead.

Over the coming days, the most zealous volunteers trickled eastwards towards Lieutenant General Cope's returning army. John Home remained in Edinburgh just long enough to count the Jacobites before carrying that information to the general. Cope was reluctant to issue arms to these civilians, and they were left to fend for themselves until they were joined at Haddington by Drummond, whose status carried more weight with Cope. Sixteen were deployed in pairs as scouts along the various roads to Edinburgh, out of a total of around 80 available men.[109] Under Drummond's command the rump of the Volunteers were given a place in the reserve of the general's battle order, and Cope agreed to re-arm them. However, when the Battle of Prestonpans began unexpectedly early on 21 September, most of the Volunteers missed the action as they were sleeping in nearby houses. Many, like Carlyle, woke to the sound of gunfire and then lay low in the aftermath.[110] Drummond himself reached the field of battle, reporting what he saw the following year for the inquiry into Cope's conduct.

When volunteers again began to assemble after Handasyd recovered the capital, some of the original members of the Edinburgh Volunteers returned for duty. Professor Maclaurin had fled to England, but he came back through the appalling weather to help raise men once more. The effort broke his health, however, and he died in June 1746. Some of his former companions were no longer available for service – Carlyle had accepted the Prince's amnesty and then left the country – but William McGhie and John Home were elected captain and lieutenant of 'some young men at Edinburgh who formed themselves into a company'.[111]

Lieutenant General Hawley, having replaced Handasyd in January, summoned Home to Holyrood Abbey and asked him to take his Company of Volunteers north to 'bring away the officers who had been taken prisoners at the battle of Preston[pans]'.[112] Home's men, however, retained the spirit of the Volunteers by only performing those duties they themselves wished. Although Home was granted leave to consult his comrades, they returned the obvious answer and refused to go on the risky northern operation. Although Hawley apparently remained obdurate, the Volunteers nevertheless marched west with his attempt to relieve the siege of Stirling Castle, and thus found themselves at the Battle of Falkirk on 17 January. According to tradition, amongst the Jacobites that day was one Robert Stewart, an off-duty City Guard who later returned to work.[113]

---

108   Carlyle, *Autobiography*, p.124.
109   The movements of Carlyle and his friends around this time are discussed by the author in more length in, *On Gladsmuir Shall the Battle Be* (Solihull: Helion & Co, 2017), p.120ff.
110   Carlyle, *Autobiography*, p.144.
111   Home, *History of the Rebellion*, p.112.
112   Home, *History of the Rebellion*, p.118.
113   Coutts 'Resurrecting the Town Guard', pp.330-331.

Denied a place in the battle-line, the Volunteers nevertheless trudged up the sodden hillside behind Fleming's 36th Foot. Lieutenant Home had the command since MacGhie had gone to seek out the general prior to the battle and not yet returned. Already parts of Hawley's army were breaking, streaming back through the storm, when Hawley rode up to the Volunteers and ordered them into 'a fold for cattle which was close by'.[114] This was either to give the little company some protection or else to put them out of the way of the professionals. They were then swept up in the rout; Captain MacGhie, who had ended up fighting alongside Blakeney's 27th Foot, found only Lieutenant Home and a handful of their company still together near the army's campsite.

As the tents were fired, this tiny rump of the Volunteers followed the remnants of Hawley's army as it withdrew from Falkirk towards Edinburgh but the company fell behind on the road to Linlithgow, and the two officers were both captured. Taken with them were: Thomas Barrow (an Englishman) and Robert Douglas, both medical students at Edinburgh; their colleague Neil Macvicar, a law student; and Robert Alexander, whose father would become Lord Provost of Edinburgh in 1752. They were taken under guard by the Earl of Kilmanock to his home at Callendar House, where they were observed by Prince Charles Edward from an open window. Before they were transferred to Doune Castle, Alexander was separated from them in the hope that his father would pay a generous ransom.[115] John Home provides a full and fascinating account of how this energetic band contrived their escape from their prison, in the attempt of which Neil Macvicar was seriously injured.[116] The others got away, returning to the Lothians aboard HMS *Vulture*.

Overall, the Edinburgh Volunteers made little impact on the great events happening around them, beyond providing some limited opportunities for civilian loyalists to feel proactively involved. The East Lothian farmer and local wit Adam Skirving, most famous for his song *Hey Johnnie Cope*, penned the following critique of the Volunteers' performance in September 1745:

> The volunteers prick'd up their ears, and vow gin they were crouse, man!
> But when the bairns saw't turn to earn'st, there werena worth a louse, man.
> Maist feck gade hame, O fie for shame! They'd better staid awa, man,
> Than wi' cockade to make parade, and do nae gude at a', man.[117]

Edinburgh's final contribution to the story of the last Jacobite Rising came on 4 June 1746. On that day, 'the City Guard paraded about eleven, and drew up in the Parliament Close, after which they escorted the 28 constables with their battoons to the cross'.[118] There they stood to attention as the public hangman and the city sweeps processed down from the castle carrying the Jacobite colours captured at Culloden. Then, to fanfares of trumpets, each flag

114 Home, *History of the Rebellion*, p.125.
115 Home, *History of the Rebellion*, p.136.
116 Home, *History of the Rebellion*, pp.136-139.
117 A. Johnston (ed.), *Rebellious Scots to Crush: an Anthology of the Arts Engendered by the Battle of Prestonpans in 1745* (Prestonpans: Prestoungrange University Press, 2008), p.56.
118 W. Fraser, *A History of the Carnegies, Earls of Southesk, and of their Kindred* (Edinburgh: Constable, 1867), Vol.2, pp.456-7.

was burned in its turn. The story of the Volunteers had ended with their escape from Doune; the Edinburgh Regiment had disbanded; and the Trained Bands were never re-armed, nor retained for any other purpose than the king's birthday parade. The City Guard continued in service however, commonly recruiting Highlanders and army veterans. The Gaelic poet Duncan Ban MacIntyre, who had fought at Falkirk with the Argyll Militia, was amongst them. However, after the development of the New Town, championed by none other than Lord Provost Drummond, Edinburgh outgrew the capacity of the Guard. Reduced in both number and reputation, the City Guard disbanded in 1817. Although international events would again require the Scottish capital to raise volunteer regiments, Edinburgh would never again face such a dangerous challenge as it had in 1745.

5

'If the Duke of Argyle would arme his Argyllshire men':[1] The Argyll Militia 1745–1746

Jenn Scott

The idea of raising a Scottish militia, even in times of crisis, was not popular amongst sections of the governing elite in the mid-eighteenth century due to a continuing distrust of the Scots as a whole: in their minds there was no distinction between the loyal and the disloyal. All Scots were seen as potentially rebellious, and therefore there was a concern about the loyalty to the Government of those who might be able to raise a militia. As Lieutenant Colonel John Campbell, Younger of Mamore, wrote, the 'unhappy thing that the misbehaviour of a few should give the Government so bad an opinion of all of Scotland'.[2] In his dealings with the Government, Duncan Forbes of Culloden often found his work as Lord President very difficult because of that fear that 'all Scotsmen were inclined to the Pretender and waiting but an opportunity to declare'.[3] As if to confirm the idea that all Scots were disloyal to the Government the Lord High Chancellor, Philip Yorke, Earl of Hardwicke, wrote that Lieutenant General Sir John Cope 'offered some of the highland lords arms but was told they could not sufficiently depend upon their people'.[4]

Nearly a hundred years before the Rising in 1745, in 1663, Parliament had passed a Militia Act which had remained in force, with a few modifications, until eventually a new act was passed in 1757. The Act stated that the King, acting via the secretaries of state, could authorise the lord lieutenants of the counties to call out the Militia in time of invasion or domestic rebellion. In Scotland, the Militia Act declared that a force of up to 22,000 men could march to wherever in England or Scotland that the monarch required them. There

---

1   John Dalrymple, 2nd Earl of Stair, quoted in G.H. Rose, *A Selection from the Papers of the Earls of Marchmont, in the Possession of the Right Honble. Sir George Henry Rose: Illustrative of Events from 1685 to 1750* (London: John Murray, 1831), Vol.I, p.129.

2   Quoted in I.H. Mackay Scobie, 'The Argyll or Campbell Militia, 1745-6', *Journal of the Society for Army Historical Research*, Vol.24, No.97 (Spring 1946), pp.12–29.

3   Quoted in I.H. Mackay Scobie, 'The Highland Independent Companies of 1745-47', *Journal of the Society for Army Historical Research*, Vol.20, No.77 (Spring 1941), pp.5–37.

4   Quoted in J.D. Oates, *The Jacobite Campaigns: The British State at War* (Abingdon: Routledge, 2016), p.167.

had been no provision for Scottish County Militias in the Act of Union in 1707 and, in 1708, when an attempt to was made to renew the Militia Act it did not receive the consent of Queen Anne, therefore at least theoretically making the Militia obsolete.[5] The power of the lord lieutenants to raise militia in Scotland – or fencible men, as they were more commonly called at the time – was less easy to enforce than in England. The Duke of Argyll was, however, the hereditary Lord Lieutenant of Argyllshire and, when finally granted the Royal Warrant, used this power to sign the deputy-lieutenants' commissions which gave them the power to raise men.[6]

The Lord Advocate of Scotland, Robert Craigie, advised that in his opinion 'it would be illegal for any civilians to resist the Jacobites by force', despite the threat that they posed.[7] The Duke of Argyll himself put his finger on the concerns about raising a militia when he wrote that 'several thousand men armed and used to arms, ready upon a few weeks call is what might disturb any government. The Captain of Clanranald has not £500 but yet has 600 men with him'.[8]

Argyll was understandably cautious in wanting to follow the Militia Act to the letter; previously his ancestors had simply sent out the traditional fiery cross across their clan lands and thousands of Argyllshire men had risen in response to their call. However, since his great-grandfather and his grandfather had been executed in 1661 and 1685 respectively for calling out their men and fighting in support of the Whig and Protestant cause, he was reluctant to begin doing so without official sanction. The Duke pointed out in August 1745 that in fact 'it is not yet lawfull for any person in the Highlands to defend the Government, or his own house, family or goods, though attacked by Robbers or Rebells'.[9] This was not an idle fear: for example, in 1714 Sergeant William Scott had been employed by the Hanoverian Society in Edinburgh, where he had taught approximately 80 recruits how to use a musket, and had been imprisoned in Edinburgh Castle for doing so.[10] Eventually in 1715 there were volunteers but in general they had proved little use: volunteers at Perth in 1715 made no attempt at resistance in September 1715; the Berwickshire Militia left Kelso when the Jacobites advanced.[11] Although Argyll was keen to form a militia, he wanted official sanction before he started raising his tenants. In a letter, dated 17 August 1745 he wrote, clearly somewhat irritated, that 'Sir John Cope will march all his foot in a few days to Forts in the Highlands, which is certainly right if the Rebells are not gott together but if they are it will

---

5   R. Black, *The Campbells of the Ark: The Men of Argyll in 1745: The Outer Circle* (Edinburgh, John Donald, 2017), Vol.II, p.203. Oates, *The Jacobite Campaigns*, p.128.

6   Lord Lewis Gordon was made the Jacobite Lord-Lieutenant of Aberdeenshire by the Prince which enabled him to raise men there for the Jacobites in the same way. W.B. Blaikie, *Origins of the 'Forty-five, and other Papers Relating to that Rising* (Edinburgh: University Press by T& A Constable for the Scottish History Society, 1916), p.128.

7   Oates, *The Jacobite Campaigns*, p.132.

8   Quoted in T.M. Devine, *The Scottish Clearances: A History of the Dispossessed 1600-1900* (London: Penguin, 2019), p.47.

9   Oates, *Jacobite Campaigns*, p.133.

10   C.A. Whatley, 'Reformed Religion, Regime Change, Scottish Whigs and the Struggle for the 'Soul' of Scotland, c.1688-c.1788', *The Scottish Historical Review*, Vol.92, No.233 (2013), pp.66–99.

11   Oates, *Jacobite Campaigns*, p.164.

be very dangerous for want of Highland Militia... it is a great mortification to me to be obliged to run away from 300 French & 3 or 4 of my tennants'.[12]

On 6 August 1745, Lieutenant Colonel John Campbell, of Loudoun's 64th Highlanders, arrived in Inveraray to recruit men into this new regiment; this was at that time the only legal way the Campbells could raise men for the Government. The only soldiers in the area were those from Duncan Campbell of Inverawe's company of Lord John Murray's 43rd Highlanders. Argyll wrote that he had sent his 'cosen, Col. Campbell to Inveraray to look after the raising of the men'.[13] Since it was only two weeks after Charles Edward Stuart's landing in Scotland, the Duke had not yet advanced any plans for raising a militia in Argyllshire. He did so almost immediately after the Younger of Mamore's arrival in Inveraray. However, it took until October 1745 for the King to authorise Argyll's militia. Although the Sheriff of Argyll, Archibald Grant of Stonefield, said that in the 'meantime by the laws now in force the town of Inverara may make use of the 200 stand of arms',[14] and another two hundred for Campbelltown, no one from wider Argyllshire could be armed or permitted to join a militia without contravening the 1725 Disarming Act which forbade the carrying of weapons in the countryside in the Highlands. Andrew Fletcher, Lord Milton, the Lord Justice Clerk, wrote that the Disarming Act:

> ... has been found by experience to work the quite contrary effect from what was intended by it, and in reality proves a measure for more effectively disturbing the peace of the Highlands and of the kingdom...for all the disaffected clans retain their arms and ammunition concealed them at the first disarming, or have provided themselves since at the same time that the dutyfull and well affected clans have tamely submitted to this measure of the government and Act of the Legislature and are still disarmed or have no quantity of arms amongst them.[15]

As Lord Milton wrote to Stonefield on 15 August, 'His Grace is very sensible of the inconveniencys arising to the Government and to the countrey, from the want of proper regulations, instructions and orders on this occasion'.[16] The Campbells had in general obeyed these acts, so until further shipments of arms had taken place there were only those few weapons in some of the castles that were beginning to be garrisoned by or already held by Campbells. 'There were fourty stand of arms his Grace's service lying at Ardkinglass which the Duke desires may be put in order and used for the defence of the castle of Inveraray

---

12   University of Nottingham Manuscripts and Special Collections (UNMSC), NE C 1640: Argyll to Henry Pelham, 17 August 1745.

13   Sir J. Fergusson of Kilkerran, *Argyll in the Forty-five* (London: Faber & Faber, 1951), p.21. The Younger of Mamore was strictly speaking the Duke's first cousin once removed since it was his father, Major General John Campbell, 2nd of Mamore, the future 4th Duke, who was the Duke's cousin.

14   Fergusson, *Argyll*, p.22. Burghs had a different set of laws which was why the Duke approved of Stonefield's suggestion and asked that he was informed of how many armed men there were, presumably to ensure they stayed within the permitted limit.

15   J. Home, *The History of the Rebellion in the year 1745* (Edinburgh: P. Brown, 1822), pp.67-68. As Lord Justice Clerk, Milton was the second most senior judge in Scotland.

16   Fergusson, *Argyll*, p.22.

or to supply the newly raised companys, In short where ever they are most useful'.[17] Many Campbell clan gentlemen, just like those on the Jacobite side, had some military experience due to service abroad, in the British Army, or in the Independent Highland companies. This meant it was relatively easy to form infantry companies from the men who were raised in Argyllshire, although by the mid-eighteenth century the plebeian men themselves often had little direct experience of warfare.

Nonetheless, in the time between the Younger of Mamore's arrival in Inveraray and the Royal Warrant being granted to Argyll in October; the Duke and other loyalist Campbells were not idle.[18] Argyll, despite his initial reluctance to recruit thousands of men in the ways that his ancestors had, did assume that he would be allowed to recruit, albeit in more conventional and perhaps less Highland ways. As the Duke of Newcastle, Secretary of State for the Southern Department, wrote to him from London in mid-August:

> [I]f your Grace's proposal had been pursued, we might now have had a much more considerable number in arms for the Government than, in all probability can be brought against it. However, I should hope it might not be yet too late to make some stand of this kind, and the well affected clans might be provided with arms from the Government, which Sr John Cope has had orders to deliver to them. As to the legality of bearing arms in the defence of the Government, those who are entrusted with the administration should surely find out means to give out lawful authority for that purpose.[19]

Lieutenant Colonel Campbell took these words as encouragement and began, with the tacit approval of Argyll, to recruit officers for the militia by promising them commissions and therefore also recruiting orders since there was little point in having officers without men.[20] However, the Marquis of Tweeddale, Secretary of State for Scotland, was lacking in support for the Duke's raising a militia and consequently this made it much harder for Argyll to convince the King to give him the warrant he needed, as 'the Duke of Argyle stood ill in the King's opinion and Lord Tweeddale very well'.[21]

On 16 October 1745 the Younger of Mamore wrote to his father, Major General Campbell that: 'if arms and ammunition was properly disposed of in this part of the country their [sic] might be a body of men raised in a month's time from this shire and there adjacent able to oppose the whole rebell army'.[22]

The men who were raised in Argyllshire and the Duke's other lands were raised in the same way as many of the men who came out for the Jacobites, and, just like them, quite a few

---

17   Fergusson, *Argyll*, p.25, although the 'companys' talked about in this letter would still be for Loudoun's rather than the militia.

18   National Records of Scotland (NRS), GD14/36 Copy of the royal warrant to [Archibald, 3rd] Duke of Argyll to call out the Argyllshire militia, 22 October 1745.

19   Quoted in Black, *Campbells of the Ark*, Vol.II, p.206.

20   Fergusson, *Argyll*, p22. 'Lord Milton asked Stonefield to list blank commissions and the 'Deputy-Leutenant' [sic] which the Duke would sign as soon as the Royal permission is given'. The deputy-lieutenants' commissions were signed on 20 August; *ibid.*, p.27.

21   Fergusson, *Argyll*, p.33.

22   Fergusson, *Argyll*, p.35.

did not have an enormous commitment one way or the other to the cause, whichever cause that might be. They came out because their friends were out, because they needed the money that they might be paid, or because they felt loyalty to what were still effectively – notwithstanding the 1737 changes to the way the Argyll estate was administered – the tacksmen and gentlemen of the clan. Like others throughout Scotland, many would do the bidding of those that they considered to be their betters.[23] However many of course did feel loyalty to the Government and the Whig cause. The Militia had four 'gentlemen volunteers and twenty private men' who took no pay, so presumably these men were not only reasonably well off but also loyal to the Government.[24] Commitment on the part of plebeian men to the Whig and the Protestant cause should not be under estimated. There were loyal associations formed in most of the big towns, chiefly but not exclusively on the west coast – Glasgow, Stirling, Paisley and Dumfries.[25] Argyll and Ross had been strongly Covenanting areas and were therefore more committed to the Government than some other areas of Scotland, but Argyllshire was not alone in its loyalty to the Government. Nor were the Campbells the only loyal clan.[26]

Christopher Duffy describes the Argyll Militia as 'an expression of the role of main branch of the Clan Campbell in defence of the Protestant interest in Scotland'.[27] However, despite all of this, some areas of land controlled by the Duke of Argyll would not come out for the Government, not matter what their heretors or landlords (as well as their ministers in many cases) said. At the beginning of recruitment for the militia, Archibald Campbell of Barnacarray was under orders from Stonefield to raise men in Tiree. However, the men of Tiree disagreed and sent representatives to argue that no recruitment should take place there:

> I used many arguments to convince them (that he should levy the militia) but all to no purpose. I thought then to try another corner of the country where I mett with a greater number of men ready to oppose me and told me if I would not immediately desist I woud soon repent.[28]

Later Campbell of Mamore wrote to the Duke that people in Tiree 'threatn'd to sacrifice the factor, in such a manner that he had reason to make the best of his way thence'. None of

23   Devine, *The Scottish Clearances*, p.46.
24   Oates, *Jacobite Campaigns*, p 141 Fergusson, *Argyll*, p.127, identifies these four gentlemen as Campbell of Airds, Barcaldine, Carwhin and Skipness respectively.
25   D.Wemyss & E. Charteris, *A short account of the affairs of Scotland: In the years 1744, 1745, 1746* (Edinburgh: James Thin, 1973), p.318.
26   There were six clans who fought against the Jacobites in every major Rising: see Whatley, 'Reformed Religion, Regime Change, Scottish Whigs and the Struggle for the 'Soul' of Scotland', p.70; F. Douglas, *The History of the Rebellion in 1745 and 1746: Extracted from the Scots Magazine: with an Appendix, Containing an Account of the Trials of the Rebels; the Pretender and His Son's Declarations, Etc.* (London: Unknown Publisher, 1755) p.45.
27   C. Duffy, 'The Jacobite Wars, 1708-48' in E. Spiers, J. Crang, M. Strickland (eds.) *A Military History of Scotland* (Edinburgh: Edinburgh University Press, 2014), pp.348-379.
28   Black, *Campbells of the Ark*, Vol II, p309-310 also Scobie, 'The Argyll or Campbell Militia, 1745-6', p.13

them joined the militia. Other areas also were less than enthusiastic about joining. Much of Mull was not Campbell territory but that of the Macleans: there no one except Maclean 4th of Brolas and one private man called McKinnon had joined the militia, whereas men were out for the Prince.[29] In Morvern, on the other side of the Sound of Mull, 'they went early into rebellion with Locheill very few excepted'.[30]

Eventually, on 22 October, the Government gave Argyll the warrant for which he had been campaigning for since the Prince has landed in Scotland in August 1745, and he was able to call out the men of Argyllshire. The King authorised the Duke to 'above all things to have in view the restoring the peace of our kingdom by the immediate reducing the rebells by force of arms'.[31] The Duke wrote to Stonefield that 'His majesty has given me orders for the militia acting, so that everything of that nature can be legally done'.[32]

Major General Campbell, who 16 years later would succeed his cousin as Duke of Argyll, had been in London with the Duke since September when he had volunteered to raise men in Argyllshire for the Government. Finally, the major general received orders to raise eight companies of 100 men with 'regular' officers and then to arm an additional 16 companies with non-regular officers. The distinction was that the 'regular' officers would be paid and others would not be, since their companies would be only be raised for a short period; the company under Alexander Duncanson lasted less than a week, for example.[33] These companies were all to be raised from the lands of the Duke of Argyll, and the Earl of Breadalbane. The latter, though also a Campbell, was a Jacobite sympathiser; however, his son Lord Glenorchy raised a company for the militia. All of this was to be done without any bounty money.[34] The private men were expected to serve for a year or until the end of the rebellion.

Major General Campbell wrote to the Provost of Glasgow:

> I think it proper to acquaint you that his Majesty intends to send me to Scotland to command under the Marshall Wade in the west of Scotland and Highlands, and as I flatter myself that my good f[r]iends in Glasgow will in every shape assist me in the publick service, I take this opportunity of beging you will be so good as to inquire if in your town there are any highland shoe- makers who can make brogues. I shall want about one thousand pairs, to be made immediately; and as soon as any tolerable quantety are gott ready. You will order the contractor to send them by parcels to Dumbarton Castle.[35]

---

29   Fergusson, *Argyll*, p.99. Allan Maclean 4th of Brolas, in 1750 chief of the Macleans, subsequently had a distinguished military career beginning in the Highland Independent Companies after the Rising so his presence in the Argyll Militia as a young man seems quite likely.
30   The Dunstaffage MS. quoted in Fergusson, *Argyll*, p.99.
31   Fergusson, *Argyll*, p.36.
32   NRS, GD14/38 Papers of the Campbell Family of Stonefield: Archibald, 3rd Duke of Argyll to Archibald Campbell of Stonefield, 26 October 1745.
33   NRS, GD14/48 Papers of the Campbell Family of Stonefield: [Archibald, 3rd Duke of Argyll] to [Archibald Campbell of Stonefield], 25 November 1745. 'General Campbell has blank commissions for 8 companies of 100 men each, he has writ to his son about it, and I have directed the General to advise with you about the filling them up'.
34   Fergusson, *Argyll*, p.37.
35   Black, *Campbells of the Ark*: Vol.I p.120; Fergusson, *Argyll*, p.36.

Dumbarton Castle on the Firth of Clyde was one of the castles that Wade had improved with a bastion in the years before the Rising. Dumbarton had a garrison although its governor, Captain Turnbull, complained that it was frequently filled with, 'the scum and dregs of the marching regiments'.[36] During the '45, Major General Campbell paid for barracks to be built at the castle to accommodate three companies from the militia.[37]

On 24 October, Newcastle sent an order for 500 muskets with 'ammunition in propor-tion' and the same number of broadswords were also to be sent to Inveraray.[38] The Younger of Mamore wrote to his father, Major General Campbell on 5 November and told him that he had confirmed an order for 1,000 brogues from Glasgow merchant Robert Finlayson although this order was subsequently reduced to 300 due to the price.[39] The broadswords, when they finally arrived in Inveraray on 29 November on the *Britain's Ferry*, having left from Liverpool on the 12th, were discovered to have been shipped without belts.[40] Due to the problem with the delivery of the shoulder belts, Major General Campbell ordered five or six hundred more from Glasgow almost straight away. Eventually 570 shoulder belts arrived, which cost two shillings each, and '2692 pairs of Brogues or Pumps...sent to the castle of Dumbarton and Inveraray at 2s7d a pair'.[41] Argyll wrote two days later to the Sheriff to his evident relief that 'his Majestie has given me orders for the militia of Argylshire acting so that everything now of that nature can be legally done'.[42] It was envisaged that some of the stands at arms might be available to Inveraray afterward. Additionally, Newcastle wrote to the Board of Ordnance ordering 200 horsemen's tents be supplied to 'the order of Major General Campbell'.[43]

On 9 November a meeting was held of the deputy-lieutenants who had been appointed – Donald Campbell of Airds, James Campbell of Ardkinglass, Colin Campbell of Carwhin, James Campbell of Duntroon, John Campbell of Inverliver, Archibald Campbell of Knockboy and Stonefield. There they agreed that for each one and half merkland paying tax or cess, there should be 'one sufficient able body'd man who in his best array shall be ordered to hold himself ready to march'.[44] However even in Campbell-dominated Argyllshire there were areas from which few men were recruited for the militia and some joined the Jacobites, most notably Tiree, Morvern, and Ardnamurchan.[45]

36   Quoted in Black, *Campbells of the Ark*, Vol II, p.287.
37   There was £52 paid to George Campbell, a carpenter to build barracks at the castle; see Black, *Campbells of the Ark*,Vol II, p.287. The militia were there between February and June 1746.
38   NRS, GD14/42, [Archibald, 3rd] Duke of Argyll to [Archibald Campbell of Stonefield], 2 November 1745. 'This goes by Mr. Niel Campbells son to the principal in a vessel from Liverpool with I think 500 arms and ammunition, which will as soon as possible be followed with Gen. Campbell and a large quantity of everything necessary'.
39   Black, *Campbells of the Ark*, Vol.I, p.121.
40   Fergusson, *Argyll*, p.36.
41   Black, *Campbells of the Ark*, Vol II, p.212.
42   Fergusson, *Argyll*, p.37.
43   Black, *Campbells of the Ark*, Vol.I, p.120.
44   A Merk was worth 13s 4d. The assumption here was that one man could be raised per one and half merkland, although elsewhere in Scotland the Marquis of Tuillibardine expected to raise two for the Jacobites.
45   Whately, C A. 'Reformed Religion, Regime change, Scottish Whigs and the Struggle for the "Soul" of Scotland, c.1688-c.1788', *Scottish Historical Review*, Vol.92 (2013), No.233, pp.66–99.

Since there was a possibility of the Jacobites sending recruiting parties through Perthshire in December, it was decided that, to pre-empt this, the militia should be levied from the areas perceived as likely to supply men to the Stuart cause. Therefore:

> The whole of militia formely appointed to be levy'd in the parishes of Glenaray and Glenshiray. His Grace the Duke of Argyll's property on Lochow and the lands of Barnaline, the lands belonging to Innishconnell and Duncan Fisher of Duran, Inistrynich's lands. Inveraw's whole lands, the Earle of Braedalban's property and superiority in Clachandizart Parish. Ardkinglas's whole lands in the division of Cowal, Strachur's lands in the parish of Strachurr, the officiary of Strathurr and the militia of the parishes of Glasrie and Kilmartine.[46]

By December Major General Campbell could inform the Duke of Newcastele that 'I found 450 men rais'd for his Majesty's service in that corner of the country',[47] for whom he had left 200 stands at arms. However, Stonefield was still having to pay for them from the Argyll estate as no money had been forthcoming from the Government. Recruitment continued apace and very soon men were under arms and able to march to Dumbarton under the command of Captain Noble of the 21st North British Fusiliers – the Younger of Mamore's former regiment. Additionally, a further 600 men were assembled at Inveraray and, over all, 2,000 recruits were expected in four days.[48] By 3 January, there were 1,989 recruits. A fortnight later 12 companies were present at the Battle of Falkirk commanded by Lieutenant Colonel Campbell alongside three companies of Loudoun's 64th Highlanders and one additional company of Murray's 43rd. The 12 companies of the Argyll Militia were: Achnaba's, Ardchattan's Gallanach's Glenorchy's, Knochbuy's, Machrihranish's, Melfort's 1st, Melville's, Raray's, Raschouille's and Tirifour's.[49] Raray's company was subsequently discharged between 2 and 18 February as being under strength.

By February 1746, the Militia had thirteen companies: MacVicars, Lochead's – these two companies were described as the 'most incomplete' – South Hall's, Ballochyle's, Carsaig's, Gallanach's, Melfort's 1st, Achnaba's, Glenorchy's, Knockbuy's, Ardchattan's, Ardminish's and Raschoille's.[50] This is by no means a complete list of every company that was raised since there were some that existed for a short period – only a few weeks in some cases – and others that were raised later in the campaign.

Each company had a captain, a lieutenant, an ensign, three corporals and a piper. Most companies had 50 men; a few had more. This had been a source of contention between Major General Campbell and the deputy lieutenants. He and his cousin Argyll saw the militia as having the potential to be a regular force rather than a clan militia, whereas the

---

46   Quoted in Black, *Campbells of the Ark*, Vol II, p.212.
47   Fergusson, *Argyll*, p.49.
48   See Fergusson, *Argyll*, pp.52-3; *Daily Post*, 16 January 1746; Wemyss & Charteris, *Short Account*, p.361.
49   Black, *Campbells of the Ark*, Vol.II, p.220; J.D. Oates, *King George's Hangman: Henry Hawley and the Battle of Falkirk, 1746* (Warwick: Helion, 2019), p.93; NRS, GD87/1/11 Inveraray, letter to John Campbell of Barcaldine from Colin Campbell [of Carwhin], 10 November 1745.
50   Black, *Campbells of the Ark*, Vol.II, p.130, Oates, *Jacobite Campaigns*, p.134.

deputy lieutenants had used the old clan loyalties to call the men out and wished to organise the militia along those lines:

> irregular troops unaccustomed to military discipline, require many officers and that publick service will be carried on more cheerfully & effectually when men are commanded by their natural leaders & landlords, they (the deputy lieutenants) are unanimously of the opinion that every company ought to consist of 50 private men with 3 serjeants, three corporals & a piper & be commanded by a captain, lieutenant & ensign, gentlemen well affected to the Government and of influence with people.[51]

The biggest problem inherent in raising a force such as this was simply that of feeding such a number of people all gathered together in one place. This was particularly so since the two or three harvests before the '45 had not been good and that the Rising was disrupting trade, therefore making it harder to obtain grain and other supplies. Major General Campbell wrote that he 'found upwards of 600 men brought together, a vast number of gentlemen and their followers, and no thought how they or their men were to live'.[52] A large part of the diet in the West Highlands was oatmeal, and getting enough oatmeal to feed all the men was very difficult: 'We are in the utmost distress for the want of oatmeal, which retards my collecting the men that are now ready to come in'.[53] All the oatmeal was carefully rationed to try and ensure that there were enough supplies. Mamore sourced more oatmeal from Ireland and managed to commandeer 250 bolls from Campbelltown.[54] However, by the end of January, despite earlier assurances that he had enough provisions for all the men and garrisons for three weeks, he was obliged to write to Argyll:

> This country & the whole West of Scotland is threatened with famine. I have done all in my power to prevent it, and last night I was comforted by a letter from Liverpoole informing that two ships were sail'd, at my own risk. I pray to God to bring them safe to port for I find by this day's return I have but fourteen days meal left.[55]

At least some of the expenses for militia were being defrayed by the government in London. Mr Bruce, the agent to the lieutenancy, wrote to Newcastle in February looking for 'payment of several sums of money, as well for purchasing oatmeal, for the use of the militia officers and soldiers raised in that country, for His Majesty's service, as for two months' pay for their maintenance and support'.[56] However, until March 1746 the majority of the money spent on the militia had come out of the personal pocket of Mamore or the Argyll estate. In that

---

51   Quoted in Black, *Campbells of Ark*, Vol.II, p.219.
52   Campbell to John Maule, the Secretary of the Duke of Argyll, quoted in Fergusson, *Argyll*, p.58. The description of the militia here does sound very much like the clan regiment that the Duke was so keen to avoid.
53   Black, *Campbells of the Ark*, Vol.II, p.124.
54   One boll of meal was 140lbs or 63.5kg.
55   Black, *Campbells of the Ark*, p.125.
56   Oates, *Jacobite Campaigns*, p.134.

month Sir Everard Fawkener, secretary to the Duke of Cumberland, wrote to Major General Campbell:

> The difficulties in the way of the pay of the Argyleshire militia arose at the Treasury on account form and several papers containing the demand, have from thence returned to His Grace the Duke of Newcastle, to be transmitted to His Royal Highness… he would authorise you to draw on Mr Sawyer at Edinburgh for the pay of those troops…[57]

Eventually the Government agreed to cover expenditure made by the Argyll estate on behalf of the militia from 6 August 1745.

The Argyll Militia had been supposed to be fully equipped and clothed like the Independent Highland Companies, but this did not happen. Weapons did eventually arrive but the accoutrements seem frequently to have been lacking for some companies. Captain Noble, who had been appointed by the Duke of Cumberland to oversee some of the initial militia recruitment, wrote of his men at Dumbarton Castle 'there are some spare shoulder belts which I intend to give to the militia'.[58] Lord Glenorchy's men were described as the 'best appointed' and the Islay men led by the wealthy Daniel Campbell of Shawfield were 'given belts and other necessaries'.[59]

The planned uniform, following that of the Independent Companies, consisted of a short red coat and the slightly longer waistcoats that were worn with Highland dress, with the *breacan an feilidh* (belted plaid), short red and white checked woollen hose, buckled shoes or highland brogues, and knitted blue bonnets. The bonnets bore black cockades with large red or orange crosses made of cloth or ribbon.[60] Of the latter mark, it was written:

> *Na ur ruardh-chroisean breun…*
> *Nach robh ruadh-chroisean claiginn*
> *Sileadh asta 's iad dearg*[61]

[Than your filthy red crosses/that skulls with dull red crosses were not leaking bright red]

The poet was here making the obvious link between the colour of the cockade and the colour of the blood.

However due to the long delays in supply, and the immediate need for men, the uniforms for the Independent Companies were not forthcoming until the end of the Rising and those for militia were simply never issued. The Argyll Militia, therefore, apart from the red/orange crosses and black government cockades on their blue bonnets, would have been virtually indistinguishable from many of the Jacobites who were dressed very similarly in their belted

---

57   Fergusson, *Argyll*, p.89.
58   Fergusson, *Argyll*, p.55.
59   Fergusson, *Argyll*, p.59.
60   See Scobie, 'The Argyll or Campbell Militia', p14. also J.T. Dunbar, *The History of Highland Dress* (Edinburgh: Oliver & Boyd, 1962), p.170.
61   A. and A. MacDonald (eds.), *The Poems of Alexander MacDonald* (Inverness: Northern Counties Newspaper and Publishing Co. Ltd, 1924), pp.316-317.

plaids, so useful against the highland weather. Because of this distinguishing mark, the militia were also known as *ludh nan croisean* [the cross wearers]. The plaids were in a variety of tartans, the colours and quality of which varied with social class and to some extent locality: there were, of course, no specific clan tartans at this time. Originally there had been a plan to have a specific militia tartan; however, time and the pressures of recruitment had made this impossible.[62] The gentlemen who made up the officer class would, for the most part, have worn either Lowland or English dress or tartan trews. As Defoe said in his contemporary work on Scotland, the people wear 'the Plaid and the Trouse; go naked from below the Knee to the Mid-Thighs; wear a Durk and a Pistol at their Girdle'.[63] Trews were considered to be the mark of the elite since they required considerable skill to construct and were therefore made by tailors. Trews were also worn when riding. With the plaid and the trews they wore clothes very much like their planned uniform, although instead of red the jackets were a variety of colours and tartans from undyed wadmal to brilliant scarlet. Mamore and his son spent much time during the Rising equipping the militia with brogues, guns, cartridge belts, boxes, swords and sword belts. It appears the some of the cost of these may have been recouped at least in part from the men. They do not seem to have had targes. The uniform that Mamore had hoped for was finally sent from Glasgow on 6 August 1746, too late for it to be of any practical use.[64]

Major General Campbell in his letters complained that the 'annition' had been 'imbazelled or fired off without orders' and suggested that the cost of these cartridges and flints – 1½ pence – should be stopped from the men's pay. '6000 cartridges, ball and flint were sent to the militia with the suggestion that 8 cartridges each were sufficient and that their boxes should be turned upside down every second day'.[65] There was very little time to train the men who had been raised with such haste and although they were hardy, the lack of weaponry before the Rising among the loyal clans meant that many of the men had little or no experience in fighting or using weapons – in contrast to at least some of their officers – which perhaps explains their enthusiasm for firing 'off without orders'.

The Younger of Mamore wrote on 27 January that the men were 'ready to mutiny every day for want of shoes...for many of them could not be prevail'd upon to take the shoes from Dumbaton when they knew the price of them & what they were pay for them... Brogues are not to be had here'.[66] They had evidently got hold of some shoes, or at least the promise of them, a week later as he wrote to his father on 2 February, 'I shall write to Carwhin to join us immediately and bring all the brogues for our men with [him]'.[67] The provision of shoes and other supplies remained a problem. In April 1746, Mamore wrote to Argyll:

---

62 It is most likely that this would have been a dark Government tartan, probably similar to the Black Watch: see Scobie, 'The Argyll or Campbell Militia', p.14.
63 D. Defoe, *A tour thro' that part of Great -Britain called Scotland. Giving an account of that nation, its manners, laws and customs, their customs their Castles, Forts...* (Dublin: Unknown Publisher, 1746), p.226.
64 Black, *Campbells of the Ark*, Vol.II, p.257.
65 Fergusson, *Argyll*, pp.64-65. This is same amount as their Jacobite counterparts were given. There do not, however, appear to have been any suggestions that any Jacobites were ever made to pay for extra flints or cartridges wasted.
66 Fergusson, *Argyll*, p80 Black. *Campbells of Ark*, Vol.II, p.216.
67 Fergusson, *Argyll*, p85. Carwhin is Colin Campbell of Carwhin.

> There's no doing without tents, for which reason I have sent forward as many as will cover 500 men together with provisions but there being no such thing as straw in the country, heather must do... I have been hinder'd from accomplishing for three days past by a violent storm of wind and rain and by the same cause depriv'd of receiving some camp kettles I bespoke at Glasgow without which and a number of brogues we cannot do.[68]

In January just before joining the army for the Battle of Falkirk, the Younger of Mamore had ordered forty 'tin camp kettles' and had hoped for 200 knapsacks but rejected the samples he was sent from Glasgow on the grounds that they were not made from calves' skin 'such as soldiers always have'.[69]

The first action that the Argyll Militia was involved in was a small skirmish at Loch Fyne on 10 November 1745, when Lieutenant Colonel Campbell, commanding the three companies of Loudoun's 64th, plus one of the Argyll Militia, saw off a Jacobite raiding force commanded by Gregor MacGregor of Glengyle, a nephew of Rob Roy. A report of this incident made it into the *London Gazette*:

> Edinburgh November 19... The Accounts we had of Colonel Campbell defeating and dispersing a Body of the Rebels of about 130, who came into Cowel in Argylshire, in order to raise Men for the Rebel Army, is confirmed; and that Deputy Lieutenants in that shire in pursuance of his Majesty's Orders, are endeavouring, with the utmost Diligence to raise a considerable Number of Men for the service of the Government.[70]

There had been some resistance to the idea of the militia engaging in fighting, especially with other Highlanders, the concern being that the bonds of loyalty and family would be too strong to break and that they simply would not fight. Lord Glenorchy wrote that, 'this must appear very odd to your Lordship but the connections and dependencies amongst the Highlanders are strong and difficult to break, and indeed may be sometimes dangerous'.[71]

Unfortunately for the militia their first real test was to be the disastrous Battle of Falkirk. On the morning of 17 January, '1000 Argyleshire Highlanders, commanded by Lieutenant Colonel Campbell... joined the King's Army'.[72]

> Our generals were ... far from expecting a battle, and consequently were caught unprepared in manie circumstances, among which none of the smallest was their

---

68 Black, *Campbells of the Ark*, Vol II, pp.165, 207. Mamore was waiting for the shoes – 1,500 pairs – to arrive at Lochgilphead from Glasgow. In the militia accounts John Anderson of Greenock was paid £3 18s 9d for expenses in Edinburgh, and a boat to carry them in. They finally arrived on 1 May. It is not clear if he is talking about the same tents that Newcastle ordered in November 1745 or if these are additional ones.
69 J. Dennistoun (ed.), *The Cochrane correspondence regarding the affairs of Glasgow, MDCC. XLV-VI*, (Glasgow: Unknown Publisher, 1836), p.71.
70 *London Gazette* 23-26 November 1745.
71 Quoted in Oates, *Jacobite Campaigns*, p.168.
72 Hume, *History of the Rebellion*, p.118; Wemyss & Charteris, *Short Account*, p.371.

quartering the Argyllshire corps in places both at such a distance from the camp and from one another, that it was impossible to assemble them in time, especially as no post in army had been assign'd them, nor no particular place of rendezvous appointed I am pretty sure too that nobody had reconnoitred the ground.[73]

The Argyll men were not actively involved in the battle, which was fought towards the end of the day, in semi-darkness, with the Government troops struggling up hill in the snow and sleet. Some troops fled the field in the confusion which led to men being trampled by their own dragoons, as well as to spectators from the town being killed since the lack of uniforms on both sides for many of participants made it hard to distinguish who was who. One account said that the volunteers 'fired upon the Argyleshiremen taking them by their Dress for the rebels'.[74] Another account stated:

> I see'd the dragoons ride through & many drummers & soldiers after throwing away their arms & then comes an Argyllshire man. He had his arms. I ask's if he fir'd. He said not, nor none of them, for the foot of the King's army fell so close upon them that unless they poured their shot in the face of the Redcoates they could not fire.[75]

The poet Duncan Ban Macintyre was present at Falkirk as part of Glenorchy's Company, which had been raised at the end of December by Colin Campbell of Carwhin. It was commanded by Duncan Campbell.[76] The poet was paid to join the militia in the stead of the elderly Archibald Fletcher. He ran away from the battle, jettisoning Fletcher's sword – 'His grandsire's ancestral broadsword' – as the night fell.[77] He described the panic and disorder that Argyll Militia suffered in confusion of the battle in verse:

> Dh'éirich fuathas anns an ruaig dhuinn
> 'N uair a ghluais an sluagh le leathad;
> Bha Prionns' Tearlach le 'chuid Frangach
> 'S iad an geall air teachd 'nar rathad;
> Cha d'fhuair sinn focal comannd
> A dh'iarraidh ar naimhdean a sgathadh,
> Ach comas sgaoilidh feadh an t-saoghail,
> 'S cuid againn gun fhaotainn fhathast.

[Panic seized us in the mayhem/when the army moved downhill:/Prince Charles with his Frenchmen/Were about to come our way/We received no word of orders/To try and fight our enemies/But to leave to scatter round the world/With some of us still undiscovered].[78]

---

73 Fergusson, *Argyll*, p.70.
74 UNMSC, Ne C 1720: George Johnstone to Henry Pelham, Musselburgh 21 January 1746.
75 Black, *Campbells of the Ark*, Vol.II, p.221.
76 Black, *Campbell of the Ark*, Vol.II, p.424.
77 A. Macleod (ed.), *The Songs of Duncan Ban Macintyre* (Edinburgh: Oliver & Boyd, 1952), p.4.
78 Macleod (ed.), *Songs of Duncan Ban Macintyre*, p.4; Scobie, 'Argyll or Campbell Militia', p.14.

Macintyre seems to have been able to desert with few consequences except for the bad feeling caused by throwing away the Fletcher's family heirloom and the loss of the 300 merks he was to have been paid.

Lieutenant Colonel Campbell wrote to his father, 'Our militia were not engag'd but half of them are dispers'd & deserted we have been terribly fatigued'.[79]

On 5 March 1746, when it appeared most likely that Inveraray might be attacked by the Jacobites, Major General Campbell told the Duke of Cumberland that he would give 'Captain Noble, Lieut Bellenden and my aid de camp Lieut Anderson' his plan for making a stand at Inveraray and a subsequent withdrawal to Glasgow.[80] 'I gave His Royal Highness a return of the Argyleshire militia before I left Perth… Ther's upwards of one thousand men employ'd in garrisons and posts, seven hundred and sixty-five left with Colonel Campbell including officers and volunteers, and about four hundred more which I think absolutely necessary to prevent the clanns from falling upon Inverary'.[81] During the whole period there were approximately 200 militiamen stationed in Inveraray: however, in this period of panic an appeal was sent out to the gentlemen of Argyllshire for more volunteers. In March 1746, Major General Campbell had earthworks built around the town and volunteers were employed for this. The militia accounts have a payment of £1 4s 11d for these defensive works.[82]

A further 700 men were raised, and 10 more companies were formed: Barnacarry's 2nd, Bruce's, Duncanson's, Dunoon's Fisher's, Forbes', Gillespie's, Jura, Kilchrist's and Melfort's 2nd.[83] Three more companies were formed in the weeks after that, so by 3 April there were an additional 13 companies. The last three were the New Kintyre Volunteers, Rudill's, and Glenfeochan's.[84] On 12 March there were 2,276 men on the strength of the various companies, but almost immediately this number dropped due the number of men captured during the Atholl raids. The panic about the likely invasion of Inverary and Argyllshire was largely removed when the Jacobite siege of Fort William was abandoned, and subsequently 10 of the 13 newly raised of the companies were discharged. By the time of Culloden, only Glenfeochan's, Kilchrist's, and the New Kintyre Volunteers were still in existence.[85] By the beginning of June 1746, 13 companies had been discharged and Major General Campbell was now in charge of approximately 1,500 men.

Cumberland had wished to use some of the militia to garrison a chain of small posts across the Braes of Atholl to stop the Jacobites from trying to raid Perthshire towns:

> Blairfetty, near Blair Atholl – sixty men; Kynachan near Tummel Bridge – one hundred men; Glengoulin and Cushavile at the end of Loch Rannoch – one hundred men; fifty men at the Clachan of Balquidder and the west end of Lochearn, another

79   Black, *Campbells of the Ark*, Vol I. p.160.
80   Lieutenant Anderson was the major general's aide de camp and had been so since 1740; Lieutenant James Bellenden was his nephew.
81   Fergusson, *Argyll*, p.98.
82   Black, *Campbells of the Ark*, Vol.II, p.309.
83   Lieutenant Colonel Campbell said in his letter to Cumberland that he had raised 500 men but Stonehouse reckoned 700; see Fergusson, *Argyll*, p.102.
84   Black, *Campbells of the Ark*, Vol.II, p.231.
85   Black, *Campbells of the Ark*, Vol.II, p.374.

fifty men. This is in addition to the garrisons or out commands already manned: – Fort William with one hundred and six men, Kilchurn Castle and Tyndrum – two hundred and twelve men including four captains, four lieutenants, four ensigns and twelve sergeants; Dunstaffage Castle, near Oban at the entrance to Loch Etive with a garrison of fifty six men; Mingary Castle which overlooks the Sound of Mull had fifty men with one captain, one lieutenant, one ensign and one sergeant, there were the same number of men at Glenfalloch, at the head of Loch Lomond; the garrison at the head of Loch Fyne had fifty-five men; Portincapel by Loch Long was garrisoned by a sergeant and fifteen men as was the ferry at St Catherine's at Loch Fyne and Dumbarton Castle had a garrison of a one hundred fifty nine men with five captains, five lieutenants, five ensigns and nine sergeants.[86]

The Atholl raids by Lord George Murray on the 17 March resulted in the capture of many of these small garrisons principally 'Bun-Rannoch, the house of Kinnachin [Kynachan], the house of Blairfettie, the house of Lude, the house of Faschillie and the public house at Blair'.[87] Ewen Macpherson of Cluny wrote to Lochiel, 'You will soon receive a visit from 400 Campbells, private men & 16 officers'.[88] Quite a few of the men escaped before they were taken to Inverness, where many of them deserted to the Jacobites.[89] The raids should not have come as a surprise; on 10 March revenue officer Gideon Shaw wrote from Perth:

> Menzies of Shion Sr Robert Menzies' factor, has left Inverness and joined the Mcphersons in order as was whispered amongst them to attract the partys of the Campbells at the Fpt of Rannoch, Kennyachan and Blairfetty which covers Blair and Castle Menzies, for by these posts they find they can't raise the Rannoch men, the Menzies and the disaffected of the Braes of Atholl until these partys are dislodged. Capt. Campbell of the Perth company had this intelligence… on Friday night. Capt, Campbell the moment he received this intelligence acquainted Sr Andrew Agnew at Blair with it, and sent for the one of the Captains of the Campbells. So they are warned.[90]

However, as Cluny wrote to Locheil it appeared that, 'Not one of the commands smelt the design till they were fallen upon' although actually it appears the information did get through to some degree. Certainly, this in part was given as the reason why Archibald Campbell of Knockbuy was not at his command since he was anticipating a siege.[91] It appears that Campbell of Glenure and Knockbuy were both absent from their commands. Home says that the men at Bun-Rannoch had been busily drinking themselves insensible at a wake and

86 Fergusson, *Argyll*, p.254 Appendix II; Black, *Campbells of Ark*, Vol. II, pp.396-8; Douglas, *History of the Rebellion*, pp.148, 160.
87 Home, *History of the Rebellion*, p.147.
88 Black, *Campbells of the Ark*, Vol.II, p.232, says that 400 men is probably an exaggeration. Home, *History of the Rebellion*, p.136 says the number was around 150.
89 Glenorchy wrote to Mamore that 20 men had deserted from Castle Menzies: see Black, *Campbells of the Ark*, Vol.II, p.232.
90 Quoted in Black, *Campbells of the Ark*, Vol.II, p.232.
91 Fergusson, *Argyll*, p.152, Black, *Campbells of the Ark*, Vol.I, p.448.

so 'the party entered the house without a shot being fired and made them all being fired and made them all prisoners'.[92] Glenure (he of the Appin murder) wrote to Glenorchy to explain that he had left his command that night in search of oatmeal for the men and only received the news the next morning: 'I came down for meal for the party which I can easily instruct, I crowd not obtain by the letters which I frequently writ'.[93] Surprisingly, despite this rather feeble excuse, Glenure was let off with only a verbal warning. Knockbuy likewise received a verbal warning for his absence from his command at Kenechan.[94] Knockbuy had left his post to look for meal and ammunition, since he had heard rumours of a pending attack. Home says of the men at Kenechan that their 'centinel was surprised and the whole party made prisoners'.[95] Knockbuy retreated to the safety of Castle Menzies with some of his officers and men. He had also sent some of his officers after some of the men who had deserted. Major General Campbell was not impressed by this.

The Atholl raids did not do much to raise Cumberland's opinion of the militia as fighters: 'I think it much more for the honour of his Majesty's forces and of the nation, to finish this affair, without any further any further use of the Highlanders, than plundering, and sending out parties'.[96] This opinion was further compounded by the raid on Keith towards the end of the month where, as Home rather succinctly puts it:

> seventy Argyleshire men and thirty of Kingston's horse occupied the village of Keith...The Highlanders [led by French officer Nicholas Glascoe] informed of the number of this detachment, marched a much greater number of men from Fochabers to Keith; and arriving their [sic] at midnight on 20 March surprised the party so completely, that almost all of them, both horse and foot were killed or made prisoners.[97]

The militia this time defended themselves and fired on the Jacobites. However, the attack on Keith represented the second of two unsuccessful encounters with the rebels in less than a week. Cumberland wrote again to Newcastle on 26 March that 'his Majesty must have observed how negligently these Highlanders who are with us do their duty'.[98]

Following these two disasters the number of desertions rose. The garrison at Castle Menzies lost 20 men on 29 March, causing the Younger of Mamore to write on 5 April:

> [T]here has been great numbers of the Argyll militia deserted and general discon- tent, nay even a mutiny thro' the whole. They complain that they are always sent upon the most dangerous expeditions, that they have much more duty and fatigue

---

92   Home, *History of the Rebellion*, p.209; Douglas, *History of the Rebellion*, pp.167-168.
93   Quoted in Black, *Campbells of the Ark*, Vol.I, p.379.
94   Black, *Campbells of the Ark*, Vol I, pp.448-449. Knockbuy's men were posted along the military road from Crieff to Dalnacardoch at Blairfetty, Kenachan, Glendullen and Coshieville.
95   Home, *History of the Rebellion*, p.146.
96   Cumberland to Newcastle, 19 March 1746, quoted in Fergusson, *Argyll*, p.155.
97   Home, *History of the Rebellion*, p.151. The account written by Campbell of Airds says 60 foot and 20 horse; see Fergusson, *Argyll*, p.156.
98   Fergusson, *Argyll*, p.158.

than the rest of the troops, that their wives and familys have sent them word that there is great scarcity at home and that they are starving.[99]

It was arranged for one boll of oatmeal to be given to each family in Argyll that had a militiaman serving, and this seemed to remove the immediate threat of further mutiny. South Hall's Company's, while not involved in the raids directly, had meanwhile removed to safety of Finlarig Castle fearing attack and feeling that they were in enemy territory.

The prisoners taken in Atholl raids were not released from Inverness in time to join the rest of the Argyll Militia at Culloden; indeed, when they were paroled in April they reached Fort Augustus on the day of the battle, unaware that there had in fact been a battle.

On the day of Culloden, an advance guard of the Argyll Militia along with some of Kingston's 10th Light Horse scouted ahead of the main force: this was perhaps the militia's most effective use. In the battle itself, Captain Colin Campbell of Ballimore of Loudoun's 64th Highlanders led his own company and three companies of the Argyll Militia – Achnaba's, Glenorchy's and Melfort's – into the right flank of the Jacobite infantry.[100] Home related that 'General Bland who commanded the Duke's cavalry on the left ordered two companies of the Argyllshire men, and one company of Lord Loudoun's regiment, to break down the east wall of the inclosure whose north wall covered the rebel army'.[101] This was done, but Ballimore was killed in the fire from the Royal Ecossois and Achnaba was fatally wounded. The Marquis of Tullibardine was reported to have said 'your Argyleshire men flanked their right and did great execution by their fire from a dyke'.[102]

Cumberland's returns from the army show that one captain was killed, Ballimore, and one captain injured, Achnaba. It appears very surprisingly that none of the men from the Argyll Militia were killed or injured after their attack on Culwhiniac enclosure. Traditionally there are supposed to be some militiamen buried on the field, but this seems unlikely in the light of more recent archaeology. Any militia dead are likely to be carefully buried in the Field of the English rather than anywhere else.[103]

Back in February, Hawley had written to Mamore:

As the measures of the rebels seem now to be entirely disconcerted, there remains for us to pursue & punish them in the manner they deserve, for which purpose it will be proper that you come this way with all the force you can get together; & as you must be the best judge what route to take.[104]

---

99   Quoted in Fergusson, *Argyll*, p.140.
100 Scobie, 'The Argyll or Campbell Militia, 1745-6', p.24; Stuart Reid, 'The British Army at Culloden', in Tony Pollard (ed.), *Culloden: The History and Archaeology of the Last Clan Battle* (Barnsley: Pen & Sword, 2009), p.71 substitutes Auchrossan's company of Murray's 43rd Highlanders for Melfort's Argyll company.
101 Home, *History of the Rebellion*, p.168.
102 Quoted in Black, *Campbells of the Ark*, Vol.II, p.343.
103 Black, *Campbells of the Ark*, Vol.II, p242; Pollard (ed.), *Culloden*, pp.124, 159.
104 Quoted in Black, *Campbells of the Ark*, Vol.II, p.224.

The aim after Culloden was to so 'effectually subdue this country… that the rebellion will not in haste raise up its head again.[105] Cumberland had come to Scotland to 'crush the thieves, plunders and robbers who lived there'.[106] However, Stonefield wrote critically about Cumberland's orders to 'burn and distroy' the rebel lands. He felt that 'The inevitable consequences of the execution of this order, is that the tender innocent babes must suffer with the guilty and that it will most probably introduce a horrible scene of murder, blood and rapin'.[107] Argyll agreed that the militia should not be involved and wrote on the 17 March that he was:

> mightily concerned at the order relating to burning houses and committing devastation of that nature, If anything of that kind must be done, it should be done by the garrison at Fort William and the regular troops, but for the militia to burn houses and possibly in the scuffle murder women and children is what I should be very tender of…the nearest rebels to Argyleshire are mine own tenants, the Camerons of Morvens and their houses are mine.[108]

However, this concern was unfortunately too late since by the time this letter had been written the burnings at Morvern had been carried out.

Captain Duff, RN, of HMS *Terror* wrote to Major General Campbell:

> If the intelligence I have this evening received is true, the rebells must have left their country, and in that case I am of the opinion all ought to be burn'd and distroy'd but be that as it will, I have His R H's possetive orders for so doing. In the Isles the ships ought to land some of their men and doe the like, for which purpose I dirsire you will acquaint the several captns with His Royal Highness's commands. The plunder, they will have a right to excepting arms.[109]

Those 'possetive' orders had been carried out. The ship had troops from the militia garrison at Mingary Castle, which overlooked the sound of Mull, and some men of the 21st Royal North British Fusiliers:

> Most of the Morvern men being gone again to join the young Pretender, and having seduced many of the people of Mull & the other Islands to goe with them, by boasting that they had enriched themselves with plunder, and they were no worse treated by his Maj's forces than those who had stayed at home, it was our oppinion that to let them feel how much a very small part of his Maj's forces could distress and annoy them in one day would not only deter such as are not already gone from going, but make many that are now out return to take care of their families

---

105 UNMSC, NE C1725: Letter from Major General Humphrey Bland, to Henry Pelham, Fort Augustus, 9 June 1746.
106 J. Hunter, *Last of the Free* (Edinburgh: Mainstream, 2003), p.198.
107 Fergusson, *Argyll*, p.99.
108 Ferguson, *Argyll*, p.100.
109 Black, *Campbells of the Ark*, Vol.II, p.127.

and effects. On the tenth instant at four in the morning…Captain Campbell with twenty men from Mingary Castle, a lieutenant and fifty-five men from my ship with orders to burn the houses and destroy all the effects of all such as were out in the rebellion. They begun with Drummin McClean's town, and by six o'clock at night had destroyed the Morven coast as far as Ardtornish.[110]

The noise of the naval bombardment could be heard at Castle Stalker on 10 March. Black identifies 'Captain Campbell' as Dugald Campbell of Craignish. Craignish had been a tacksman in Morvern. It had not gone well and after a campaign of intimidation he had been forced to give up his tack in 1732. He was subsequently one of the founding officers of the Black Watch, but he seems to have retired from the Army by the time of the '45.[111] It could be argued that Campbell of Craignish was taking out a personal grievance against the people of Morvern because of his experiences there 10 years before, and so carried out his orders with some relish. This treatment, however, was definitely at the behest of Cumberland who saw the harsh treatment as necessary if there was not to be another rebellion.

Knockbuy on 4 April went to Mount Alexander, near Kinloch Rannoch:

We assur'd them [the people they met] we had no orders against any we found att their labour quietly at home, but if after this anyone join'd the rebels, their houses be burn'd to the ground, their cattle carry'd off & their country depopulated.[112]

Mamore, however, helped Lady Ardsheil reclaim some of the goods that had been seized from her when she was thrown out from Ardsheal House by Captain Caroline Scott, the controversial Scots-born officer noted for his role in the post-Culloden reprisals.

After Culloden, Mamore and the Argyll Militia were given the tasks of looking for Charles Edward Stuart, helping police the Highlands, and disarming the Highlanders. 'From Inverary we are informed that on the 27th of last month General Campbell sailed with 1000 choice Argyllshiremen… Mr Cameron of Dungallon brought in his men and arms to Major General Campbell and with them surrendered to the King's mercy'.[113] In May some of the militia assisted Captain Fergussone, RN, with the burning the island of Raasay, including the laird's house, and others were marched out of Fort William by Captain Scott to assist him in disarming the rebels. Men from two militia companies were with Scott in Lochaber at the end of May where three men 'found in arms were hanged'. As ordered, they burned MacDonald of Keppoch's house. They also burned other houses which were not included in the orders: Lochiels's, Glengarry's, Cluny's and Glengyle's houses were also burnt, as were many common peoples' homes and their livestock carried off regardless of whether they had been out.[114] Fergussone did eventually face some resistance on the 19 May when he

---

110 Quoted in Fergusson, *Argyll*, p.119.
111 Black, *Campbells of the Ark*, Vol.II, pp.384-385; D. Stewart, *Sketches of the Character, Manners, and Present State of the Highlanders of Scotland: With Details of the Military Service of the Highland Regiments.* (Edinburgh: Constable & Co, 1822), p.145.
112 Black, *Campbells of the Ark*, Vol II, p.452.
113 *London Gazette*, June 10-14 1746.
114 Douglas, *History of the Rebellion*, p.232.

landed off Arisaig with 120 men and 'burnt the house the young Pretender had lodg'd att, with two or three villages'. He found that the 'hills being crowded with Men in Armes. They had buried some barrals of gunpowder with trains which they sett faire too'. They burned Kinlochmoidart House where the Prince had stayed at the start of the Rising, and set loose the cattle. Captain John MacLeod and 40 of the Clanranalds were persuaded to give themselves up which condemned them to transportation. Fergussone's greatest triumph was to capture the old fox himself, Simon Fraser, at the Catholic Seminary at Eilean Ban.[115]

On 6 July 1746 Lieutenant Colonel Campbell reported:

> I have ventur'd to send thirty men with Bernacarry to Tirie. You cannot imagin what pains are taken to lessen the service done by our people & to put bad constructions upon one all our endevours, for which reason I have caution'd Bar. To be as active as possible in disarming those concerned'd in this rebellion & to endeavour to apprehend some of the leading men &drive their cattle. Nay I should be glad if he would even burn some of their houses for these measures (tho in my opinion of no service to the cause) suit the taste of the times more the you can imagine. I shall give Bar. my directions in writings & if you send him any instructions.[116]

The 'bad constructions' here was not the burning of Jacobites' houses or the cattle driven away, but the effect that Cumberland's orders to the militia would inevitably have on the Duke's income due to the loss of rents. Indeed, looked at from that point of view, these burnings were also punishing him notwithstanding that he had been a loyal supporter of the Crown.

The destruction along the west coast lasted ten weeks until on the 18 August when Mamore delivered all the important prisoners, including Flora MacDonald and James of the Glen, who were taken to London by sea on HMS *Bridgewater* by Commodore Smith.[117] The majority of the militiamen were recalled to Inverary except for those who were guarding those the few remaining prisoners.[118] By the end of August 1746, the newspapers were reporting that Major General Campbell had returned to Inveraray with 2,000 stands of arms confiscated from the rebels, and that the last companies of the militia were being disbanded and sent home.[119]

115 F. Douglas, *The History of the Rebellion in 1745 and 1746: Extracted from the Scots Magazine: with an Appendix, Containing an Account of the Trials of the Rebels; the Pretender and His Son's Declarations, Etc.* (London: Unknown Publisher, 1755) p.231; Black, *Campbells of the Ark*, Vol.II, p.456.
116 Black, *Campbells of the Ark*, Vol.II, p.311.
117 C. Duffy, *Fight for a Throne: The Jacobite '45 Reconsidered* (Solihull: Helion & Co, 2015), p.487.
118 Douglas, *History of the Rebellion*, p.229.
119 *General Advertiser*, 2 September 1746.

6

The Yorkshire Blues

Jonathan D. Oates

There were a number of regiments of volunteers formed in England during the Jacobite campaign of 1745-1746. These should not be confused with the militia, which was also summoned in some counties. The largest forces were raised in the large county of Yorkshire. There were a number of forces which came into being in Yorkshire; the county forces organised and led by the lord lieutenants and a myriad of smaller ones raised in the towns and cities of the counties; some by the corporations and some by private individuals. This chapter looks at these units; their organisation, financing, leadership, recruitment, arms and uniforms, their actions and their disbandment. It is not a subject that has never been tackled before; a number of articles since the 1950s having been published in county and city history journals,[1] and in postgraduate dissertations,[2] but there has never been much about these units published in book form. Nevertheless, there is a great deal of information about them; at the National Archives in the State Papers Domestic, in the county record offices of Yorkshire and in contemporary newspapers and histories.

We shall begin with the biggest and best resourced of these Yorkshire units; the county forces. Yorkshire, as with Lincolnshire, was, because of its size, divided into three Ridings; West (the largest and most populous), East and North. For 'civil defence' purposes, each was headed by a lord lieutenant, usually a nobleman of political and territorial power; below him were deputy lieutenants, also noblemen and gentry.

By the end of August 1745 Charles Edward Stuart, aiming to overthrow George II and restore his father to the throne, had formed a small army of Highlanders and was marching towards the Lowlands of Scotland. That part of the British army in Scotland had been

---

1   Cedric Collyer, 'Yorkshire and the Forty Five', *Yorkshire Archaeological Journal*, 38, (1955), pp.71-95; N.J. Arch, 'To Stop this Dangerous Mischief', *York Historian*, 3 (1980), pp.27-30; Barbara Whitehead, 'York and the Jacobite Rebels: Some event and people in the York of 1745-1747', *York Historian*, 6 (1985), pp.59-71; Jonathan Oates, 'Independent Volunteer Forces in Yorkshire during 1745-1746', *Yorkshire Archaeological Journal*, 73, (2001), pp.123-131; Jonathan Oates, 'York and the Jacobite Rebellion of 1745', *Borthwick Papers*, 107, (2006).

2   D.B. Bagnall, *York and Yorkshire's military response to the Forty Five*, (unpublished MA thesis, University of York, 1998); J.D. Oates, *Responses in North East England to the Jacobite Rebellions of 1715 and 1745* (unpublished PhD thesis, University of Reading, 2001.)

unable to bring them to battle. The northern English counties were thus facing a potential major military threat. It was on 6 September 1745 that Henry Ingram, seventh Viscount Irwin (1691-1761) of Temple Newsam, the Lord Lieutenant of the East Riding, first made an enquiry to Thomas Pelham-Holles, Duke of Newcastle (1693-1768), Secretary of State with responsibility for co-ordinating civil and military measures to deal with the Jacobite menace. Irwin had met a number of gentry at the Wakefield races and they 'entered into an engagement to form an Association to find arms and to raise men if we are allowed to do it and to supply ye militia'.[3]

Irwin's reference to the militia immediately begs the question as to why the county force was not raised. The prime reason was because the Militia Acts, encoded in legislation following the Restoration of 1660, had fallen into abeyance in 1735. Parliament was not sitting in September 1745 and would not to do for some weeks; until it amended the Militia legislation, the Militia could not be legally raised.[4] Furthermore, Irwin was unimpressed with the Militia's activity in a similar situation three decades ago. He told Newcastle of 'ye little effect ye militia would be of, unless we could imagine that they would behave better than in ye year fifteen'.[5] Newcastle approved of the proposed Associations, telling Thomas Watson-Wentworth, Earl of Malton (1693-1750), Lord Lieutenant of the West Riding, 'This is the only method the King's servants could suggest for the purpose'.[6]

It was on 11 September that a number of Yorkshire nobility and gentry met at Birom, Sir John Ramsden's seat. These included Malton, Irwin, their host, Thomas Herring (1693-1757), Archbishop of York, Sir Rowland Winn of Nostell Priory and three others. They decided that a morale boosting activity was essential. They also decided to hold a more general meeting, to be held in the county's social and ecclesiastical centre, York, on 24 September. It was envisaged that it would be there that the county association would be created.[7]

Malton had been given authorisation to offer officers' commissions to those willing to raise and lead companies. He drew up a blue print by 19 September and informed Newcastle of it. A subscription rate of sixpence in the pound would be levied on all with property in the county to raise funds; those refusing would be obliged to provide men and arms instead. The Archbishop would chair a council at York to superintend the work in each riding. Cavalry and infantry would be raised. Yet the scheme was dropped; perhaps because of the element of compulsory finance was illegal and smacked of tyranny.[8]

On the day before the great public meeting, there was a smaller gathering. As had been envisaged by Herring, although run by the county's premier Whigs, it also included opposition Tory MPs, too, as a county consensus was desired. Among the four main points which were unanimously agreed on were, firstly, that an association should be formed and secondly that subscriptions would have to be raised to fund this amateur military effort,

---

3   The National Archives (TNA), State Papers Domestic, 36/67, f141r, Irwin to Newcastle, 6 September 1745. Note that the title is generally given as Viscount Irvine; however, the Irwin spelling reflects that employed by the man himself in his letters and has therefore been retained here.
4   British Library (BL) Additional Manuscripts, 35598, ff.54v-55r, Hardwicke to Herring, 17 September 1745.
5   TNA, SP36/68, f.54r, Irwin to Newcastle, 14 September 1745.
6   TNA, SP36/67, f254r, Newcastle to Malton, 12 September 1745.
7   BL. Add. Mss, 35598, ff.47r-48r, Herring to Hardwicke, 13 September 1745.
8   Leeds Local and Family History Library, Plan for the defence of Yorkshire in 1745.

forming volunteer companies of infantry. They also resolved that there was a danger to the King and government and that a loyal address be formulated to the King and government.[9]

Money was to be raised by voluntary subscription. This was a commonplace system of raising money for projects. What it entailed is that those who wished to contribute would contact the county, or in this case, riding, receivers, two being appointed per riding. They would state how much they wished to contribute and would then pay the first instalment, which would be a quarter of the amount promised. Their promises would be made public. The wealthiest inevitably promised most; Irwin put himself down for £200, as did Sir Conyers D'Arcy (c.1685-1758), acting Lord Lieutenant of the North Riding. Winn and Ramsden promised £100 each. Many lesser people did so, too, and in some cases there were contributions by villages and hamlets. The total promised was £32,402 1s 6d.[10]

Similar methods were used to raise money in the City of York and the town of Hull. Money was to pay to uniform and pay the men, but not to arm them; that was the government's responsibility. Other forces were raised by private individuals. In Leeds, Sir Henry Ibbetson, a wealthy young man with political ambitions, did so. In Halifax companies were formed, and there was also another force raised in York.

The county forces were divided into three regiments, totalling 41 companies, with one regiment for each county. That of the North Riding was of seven companies, that of the East Riding was nine companies and that of the West Riding 25 companies. The latter was further sub-divided into three battalions. Each regiment was naturally headed by its lord lieutenant as colonel, except in the West Riding, where there were three colonels; Winn, Ramsden, and Lord Higham, Malton's 15-year-old son. Each had a lieutenant colonel and a major beneath them, and in Higham's case, also a brevet major. It should be noted that none of these men had any military experience whatsoever.[11] Below the senior officers there were the captains, who were given commissions to appoint their junior officers (lieutenant and ensign, as per the regular army) and to raise the men to make up the rank and file. At least six of the West Riding captains were knights, as was one of the majors.

All the men were infantry, though, as noted, Malton had envisaged raising cavalry forces as well. He was not the only man to suggest this. Irwin thought so, too. Initially, Malton had been ambitious in his hope that six troops of 80 dragoons in each could be raised. However, a few days later, he realised 'we find our finances would not make any show in buying horses &c. proper for a dragoon service, therefore we propose to raise companys of Foot only'.[12] Irwin thought that 'some light horse would have done better but it is indeed the difficulty of getting horses to mount the men was not to be got over'.[13] However, out of his own pocket

9   BL. Add. Mss. 35598, f.67r, Herring to Hardwicke, 23 September 1745.
10 Anon., *AN EXACT LIST OF THE Voluntary Subscribers WITH THE sums subscrib'd and paid for the SECURITY of His MAJESTY'S Person and Government, And for the Defence of the County of YORK, Begun at Bishopsthorp, the 23rd of Sept. 1745* (York: John Gilfillan, 1747).
11 TNA, SP36/69, f.275, Malton to Newcastle, 30 September 1745; TNA, SP36/72, f363r, Malton to Newcastle, 30 October 1745.
12 TNA, SP36/68, f.167r, Malton to Newcastle, 19 September 1745; TNA, SP36/69, f274r, Malton to Newcastle, 30 September 1745.
13 TNA, SP36/69, f.197r, Irwin to Newcastle, 28 September 1745.

Malton did employ a dozen armed horsemen as a bodyguard; they had apparently intended to sail to the American colonies just prior to the emergency.[14]

The volunteers were also paid. They received a bounty of five shillings on enlistment and a regular daily wage of a shilling. NCOs received more. This would have been a powerful incentive to join. Pay was better than in the regulars whilst the service would be far less dangerous, with no danger of being sent overseas. Furthermore, the commitment was only for the duration of the emergency.

Officers, being gentlemen or merchants, were not paid. As Captain Danby remarked, his two subordinate officers were both 'possessed of a considerable landed estate'.[15] Irwin remarked that his officers 'embarked on this affair without thought of pay'.[16] Yet in late November, Malton suggested that the junior officers receive pay. D'Arcy agreed with him, too. Eventually Irwin conceded the point that this be universal through all the Ridings' troops.[17]

Recruiting was easy. Malton wrote of 'the whole mob of the county [are] with us'.[18] According to Gertrude Saville, her brother, who was a captain, 'raised his company of fifty men in three or four days, which was looked upon as uncommonly quick'.[19] In part this was due to economic reasons. Herring wrote that the crisis 'has put an absolute stop to trade and business... the want of business in the W. Riding has made it much easier to raise soldiers there, for the manufacturer has no other way to get bread'.[20] The experience of William Todd (1724-1791), born in Preston, Holderness, who was employed on the roads in 1745, gives an insight into the recruitment process. Initially he was reluctant to enlist but his misgivings were overcome and join he did, as he explained. On 8 October he noted:

> Captain Grimston of Kilnwick who is raising a Company of Blues at Beverley came past me as I was sitting at Sutton Salts and he seeing that I was young & likely for the Service Ask'd me if I would Inlist to which I told him I had no Inclination. He told me as the Rebellion was broke out so strong he greatly question'd but every one must as able to bear arms & he desired me to consider of it & enter with him.[21]

He refused, but that was not the end of the story as more pressure was brought to bear on Todd, when one Mr Featherstone, probably his employer, told him that he had been in conversation with Grimston, who had asked him to try and convince him to enlist. Todd continued the story:

---

14   Northampton Record Office (NRO), Malton to Fitzwilliam, 16 November 1745.
15   Borthwick Institute of Historical Research (BIHR), Bp, C & P, XX1/1 Danby to Unknown 15 October 1745.
16   North Yorkshire Record Office (NYRO), ZPB, 1446/1253, Irwin to Malton, 17 November 1745.
17   TNA, SP36/75, f255r, Malton to Newcastle, 29 November 1745.
18   NRO, Malton to Fitzwilliam, 14 October 1745.
19   E. Milner, *Records of the Lumleys* (London: George Bell and Sons, 1904), p.213.
20   BL. Add. Mss. 35598, f.102v, Herring to Hardwicke, 26 October 1745.
21   A. Cormack and A. Jones (eds.), *The Journal of Corporal William Todd* (Stroud: Sutton Publishing for the Army Records Society, 2001), p.1.

he said that the Turnpike must be given Over, & that all Businesses would be at a stand until the Rebellion was ceas'd. As he told me, I should only Inlist for two Months, & have a shilling a day, & he would give Either me or my father a Bond of what sum we pleas'd, that I should be at liberty at two Months End if I chused it. As he said, that both he & everyone that could carry Arms should be obliged to go if the Rebels was not stop't very soon.[22]

Featherstone also promised Todd that he would tell Grimston of Todd's good character, that he would have good quarters and would receive no ill usage. Todd was convinced. He went to Beverley on 9 October and enlisted in Grimston's company.[23] His example would seem to bear out Herring's comment that economic motives were a major motivation in men joining these companies.

John Metcalf (1717–1810, better known as the blind roadbuilder) recorded how he was recruited by William Thornton, who had a commission to raise a company. Metcalf was a fiddler and had performed at Thornton's house at Christmas previously so there was already a connection between the two. Metcalf wrote that on this occasion, Thornton 'treated him liberally with punch and informing him that the French were coming to join the Scots rebels, the consequence of which would be, that if not vigorously opposed, they would violate all our wives, daughters and sisters'. Metcalf agreed to enlist 'instantly' and was then asked if 'he knew any spirited fellows who were likely to make good soldiers'. Metcalf then assisted with recruiting and 'promised great military advancement, or in default of that, places of vast profit under the government... thus following the example of other decoy ducks, by promising unlikely things'.[24]

Yet there was another concern which served to hold back recruitment in some places. News of the Jacobite victory at the Battle of Prestonpans, fought on 21 September near Edinburgh, was in wide circulation, and the fearful casualties inflicted by the Jacobite Highlanders' weaponry caused understandable worry. One Mr Draper of Bridlington wrote 'ye men [were] under such a terror of ye highland swords that they were backward in associating with Captain Boynton'. Draper solved the problem by enlisting himself as a private in Boynton's company, sharing the men's quarters with them and performing the same duties as they did. His example had the desired effect and within two days the company was complete.[25]

Certainly, recruitment was helped by the men knowing their officers beforehand. Irwin wrote that men many had volunteered for service 'out of love and regard for ye gentlemen who command each company'.[26] What is more, the class of recruit was generally good. Irwin wrote that 'by far the greatest part of the seven East Riding companies are farmers' sons or servants'.[27] Captain Hall of the North Riding companies claimed that he had been

22   Cormack and Jones (eds.), *Corporal Todd*, p.1
23   Cormack and Jones (eds.), *Corporal Todd*, p.1
24   John Metcalf, *Life of John Metcalf* (York: E. and R. Peck, 1795), pp.77-78.
25   TNA, SP36/71, f.33r, Irwin to Newcastle, 10 October 1745.
26   TNA, SP36/71, f.33r, Irwin to Newcastle, 10 October 1745.
27   TNA, SP36/78, 189r, Irwin to Newcastle, 27 December 1745.

inundated with volunteers that he could afford to be selective, those he chose were 'pick'd men, young, tall and strong'.[28]

In some Yorkshire volunteer units, the rank and file soldiers were made up of gentry and merchants. This was the case with the 'Gentlemen Volunteers of Leeds' who were all either 'Heirs apparent to Great Estates or considerable Merchants'. Likewise, the independent York Volunteers were mainly taken from the middling and upper middling classes.[29] However, elsewhere the rank and file had a distinctly lower social status. At Halifax, '450 working clothiers came and voluntarily entered themselves into an Association to bear arms and conform to military discipline'.[30] In the city of York itself, the Corporation companies were manned chiefly by shopkeepers and craftsmen of the city; including seven tailors, five labourers, four joiners and four bricklayers to name the most common professions among the ranks.[31] Metcalf recalled that the men who joined were carpenters, smiths and artificers; 140 volunteered, but only 64 were chosen.[32]

The total number of men serving in the county forces was over 2,555.[33] D'Arcy stated he had almost 500.[34] Irwin's companies, by December, were composed of 17 officers and 359 men.[35] Malton's forces therefore presumably amounted to a little over 1,600.

A more difficult task, because it was out of the immediate control of the men raising the companies, was arming the men. There were very few arms in the county. A survey of the West Riding Militia armoury revealed that there were merely 45 pikes, 30 halberds, 30 drums and 45 drum sticks.[36] Initially Irwin had been advised to place an order with Birmingham gunsmiths, but it seems he did not do so.[37]

On 19 September, Malton wrote to Newcastle to tell him, 'Winn is now with us and it is his opinion as well as that of other gentlemen, to desire of your Ma[jes]tie to promise us a sufficient quantity of arms and ammunition to be sent immediately into this county'.[38] Several days later, Irwin and D'Arcy made similar requests.[39] Newcastle promptly passed on this request to the Board of Ordnance on 21 September: 'give immediate directions for sending to Hull 1200 stand of arms with a proportionate quantity if ammunition… [to]…be delivered…as shall be necessary for the Troops that may be raised by virtue of the commissions'.[40]

On 25 September Newcastle wrote to Malton to tell him that he would 'send immediate Directions to the Master General of the Ordnance to send by land carriage to Hull the arms

28   BIHR, C & P, XXI/1 Hall to Unknown, 12 October 1745.
29   West Yorkshire Archive Service (WYAS): Leeds, NH2875/12, Bowes to Robinson, 9 December 1745.
30   *The General Advertiser*, 3414, 17 October 1745.
31   York City Archives (YCA), E41B, pp.11-14, York Poll Book, 1741.
32   Metcalf, *Life*, p.78.
33   TNA, SP36/69, 275v, Malton to Newcastle, 30 September 1745.
34   TNA, SP36/74, f82r, D'Arcy to Newcastle, 23 November 1745.
35   WYAS: Leeds, TN/PO3/3D/1-7, Returns of men recruited.
36   NYRO, MIC 1446, 1228, Returns of arms.
37   WYAS: Leeds, TN/PC3/3C/11, Williamson to Irwin, 8 September 1745.
38   TNA, SP36/68, f167r, Malton to Newcastle, 19 September 1745.
39   TNA, SP36/69, ff.23r-24v, Irwin to Newcastle, 24 September 1745; TNA, SP36/69, 68r-69v, D'Arcy to Newcastle, 25 September 1745.
40   TNA, SP44/132, p.413, Newcastle to Montagu, 21 September 1745.

and ammunition desired...and directions will be given to the officer at Hull to deliver them when required to your lordship, my Lord Irwin, Sir Conyers D'Arcy'.[41] On the same day he gave the order that 1,500 muskets be sent by the Board to Hull.[42]

However, Malton thought that 1,500 muskets would be inadequate. He told Newcastle that the Yorkshire forces' strength would be 2,555 men, so far more would be needed.[43] With the issue unresolved as the weeks went by there was anger in the county. Herring wrote to the Earl of Hardwicke, the Lord Chancellor, in strong tones, 'What no news of ye arms yet? Do they tend to despise all we do to defend ourselves, and tell the world so?... Will they put us...at the mercy of these ruffians?...Have we deserved this neglect?...Are the ministers asleep?'[44] Malton even considered resignation, 'I am in a violent passion and am very desirous to beg all my commissions may be superseded and put into worthier hands nothing restrains me from taking that step but the confusion it must put the affaires of the publick into in this county'.[45]

Meanwhile, on 22 October, the Board could not understand the difficulty that the Lieutenancies were experiencing. There was a routine to be followed:

> [T]he constant practice and custom of the Office of Ordnance, which is not for the Office of Ordnance to send arms to those that want them, but only to pack them and deliver them to the agents of the persons by whom the arms were ordered, who always receive them from the Tower and send them to the respective places.[46]

What had been done was that on both 2 and 8 October 1,200 muskets and bayonets had been sent to Hull, along with 360 swords and the like number of carbines and pistols. The storekeeper at Hull would be told that he must contact the lord lieutenants to inform them that their arms had arrived. Newcastle forwarded a copy of this letter to all three Yorkshire lord lieutenants on the following day.[47] Irwin probably spoke for his fellows when he stated 'The Custom and practice of the Office of Ordnance I am a perfect stranger to'.[48]

The parishes of York had a rather better supply of arms, taken from their own resources: 260 guns, 208 bayonets and 83 swords with which to supply the city volunteers. They were distributed and whitesmiths employed to clean then and make any necessary repairs. However, most were found to be not in working order and 160 muskets had to be found from other sources. Robert Watkin of Birmingham agreed to supply muskets and bayonets at 23 shillings per pair and the corporation placed an order with him for 100. Fortunately, Malton had 60 surplus muskets and he exchanged these for a dozen blunderbusses, which the corporation also ordered from Watkin.[49] Meanwhile Thomas Alanson and Martin Croft

---

41   TNA, SP36/69, f.53r, Newcastle to Malton, 25 September 1745.
42   TNA, SP44/132, p.416, Newcastle to Montagu, 25 September 1745.
43   TNA, SP36/69, f275r, Malton to Newcastle, 30 September 1745.
44   BL. Add. Mss, 35598, f.98r, Herring to Hardwicke, 19 October 1745.
45   NRO, Malton to Fitzwilliam, 14 October 1745.
46   TNA, SP36/72, f132r-133v, Montagu to Newcastle, 22 October 1745.
47   TNA, SP36/72, ff.163v, Newcastle to D'Arcy, 23 October 1745; TNA, SP36/72, 167v, Newcastle to Irwin, 23 October 174; TNA, SP36/72, 170v, Newcastle to Malton, 23 October 1745.
48   TNA, SP36/72, f275r, Irwin to Newcastle, 26 October 1745.
49   York Corporation Association Accounts (YCA), E30, f9; E41, pp.7, 122-123.

were instructed to make bullets from lead and Thomas Taylor made 240 cartouche boxes.[50] On 25 October four casks of gunpowder were ordered.[51]

The men were given blue coats as their uniforms, hence the term 'Yorkshire Blues'. Richard Milnes, a Wakefield clothier and known government supporter, was given the contract to supply these. In detail, the uniforms were blue coats lined with red and these were supplied to all men by the end of October. They were also supplied with hats, breeches, knapsacks and cockades, though it took longer for them to have these. In part this was because the knapsacks had to come from London. Their uniforms were noted as being similar to those worn by the Dutch troops serving in the British Isles.[52] The West Riding regiments also carried two colours each, presumably the union flag and a regimental standard, as the regular battalions did.[53]

The York City companies had their uniforms supplied by city drapers, though it is not known what colour they were. They were of different money values, with captains to be clothed in uniforms costing eight guineas each, lieutenants six and ensigns four. Costumes for privates were a mere 18 shillings. Each company had a standard. It seems that all the men were uniformed on 7 October.[54] When Thornton went to Leeds to acquire uniforms for the men, he arrived on a Sunday and the clothiers initially refused to work on the Lord's day and so Thornton said 'You rascals! If your houses were on fire, would you not be glad to extinguish the flames on a Sunday?' and they got to work.[55]

Training also took place. The lieutenancies were urged to find old soldiers and employ them as NCOs and officers in order to turn the recruits into soldiers. Irwin was approached by Major Charles Wedell, who had once served in the regiment of foot of Irwin's late elder brother the fifth viscount, who offered his services. Irwin believed that the training would take about a month, beginning on 10 October.[56] Retired Lieutenant Colonel Charles Greenwood, a veteran of Dettingen, and Captain Rowland, a former dragoon, came forward to assist Malton.[57] Irwin was also fortunate that three of his seven company captains had also seen military service.[58] D'Arcy seems not to have had the service of any former officers, but one of his officers could report that there were 'sergeants and corporals, two of whom

---

50   YCA, E41b, 16a.

51   YCA, E41b, 20.

52   Historic Manuscripts Commission, *Manuscripts in Various Collections*, VIII, (London: HMSO, 1913) p.154; WYAS: Leeds, TN/PO3/3C/52, Milnes to Irwin, 19 October 1745; WYAS: Leeds, TN/PO3/3C/99, Milnes to Irwin, 21 November 1745.

53   Anon., *West Riding Account, The Account of Money Paid for Raising, Subsisting, and Cloathing Twenty-four Companies of Foot, and Also Trophy-money, and One Month's Subsistence of the Company Commanded by William Thornton, Esq; Raised in the West Riding of the County of York, for the Support of His Majesty's Person and Government, in Consequence of the Association Entered Into, and of the Subscription Begun, at the Castle of York, on the 24th Day of September, 1745* (Unknown Publisher, 1746).

54   YCA, E41B, 8, 10, 16a-b, 18.

55   Metcalf, *Life*, p.78.

56   TNA, SP36/71, f.33r, Irwin to Newcastle, 10 October 1745.

57   TNA, SP36/72, 220r, Malton to Newcastle, 25 October 1745; TNA, SP36/73, f.363r, Malton to Newcastle, 25 October 1745.

58   TNA, SP36/69, f23r, Irwin to Newcastle, 24 September 1745.

seem to know their duty'.[59] The government also despatched eight Pensioners from the Royal Hospital, Chelsea to assist Irwin, though they did not arrive until late October.[60]

There are various references to training. Malton recorded that with the aid of Greenwood as 'General' and an 'excellent sergeant', he had his own company make 'severall movements in the slope and down to the Parterre', presumably at Watson-Wentworth near Sheffield.[61] Herring referred to the men undergoing drill, presumably before the arrival of the muskets, by exercising with broomsticks.[62] Captain Chomley, though, does not seem to have begun training the men until late October, writing towards the end of that month: 'I shall endeavour to have them learn their exercises as soon as I can'.[63] How proficient the men were must remain open to question, but some certainly looked impressive, for in December when Major General Pulteney saw the East Riding companies go through drill and musketry practice, he 'expressed himself highly satisfy'd with their behaviour and complimented their officers'.[64]

The next question is to ask what the purpose of the Blues was. According to Herring, 'though they cannot oppose a regular force, they will employ indigent and idle people, awe the papists and are more than a match for any home commotions'.[65] Malton wrote that whilst 'we cannot repel a great force, we may protect the quiet of the county'.[66] He expanded on this theme on 11 November, 'perhaps we of ourselves may be unable to make a real stand I daresay we shall be able to prevent their being joined by any in this county had they an inclination for it'.[67] There was a concern that without a loyal force under arms, local Jacobites might rise and join the main Jacobite army.

The Jacobite army entered England on 8 November. The following day Carlisle was placed under siege, the garrison surrendering on 15 November. The northern counties were exposed, with Field Marshal Wade's army at Newcastle and the second army only beginning to assemble in the Midlands. The question was what the associated companies could do. D'Arcy was far from being confident, informing Newcastle on 19 November, that his men were 'just cloathed and armed, consequently...very ignorant in military discipline and exercise'.[68]

Newcastle had few instructions to give, but he did write to both D'Arcy and Irwin that they could usefully employ their men by hindering the progress of the Jacobite army should it march through Yorkshire. This could be done, he suggested, by wrecking bridges or roads in their path, denying them foodstuffs and by sniping at them. Lieutenant General Wentworth, whose advice Malton sought, gave similar suggestions, 'manning passes and by harassing the rebels in small bodies from behind hedges and in the night which may easily

59   BIHR, Bp C & P, XX1/1, Danby to Unknown, 15 October 1745.
60   BIHR, Bp C & P, XX1/4, Moody to Irwin, 10 October 1745.
61   NRO, Malton to Fitzwilliam, 12 October 1745.
62   BL. Add.Mss. 35598, f.97v, Herring to Hardwicke, 19 October 1745.
63   BIHR, Bp C & P, XX1/1, Chomley to Unknown, 25 October 1745.
64   *The London Evening Post*, 2826, 15-17 December 1745.
65   BL.Add.Mss. 35598, f.171v-172r, Herring to Hardwicke, 1745, 23 January 1746.
66   TNA, SP36/68, f292r, Malton to Newcastle, 23 September 1745.
67   NRO, Malton to Fitzwilliam 11 November 1745.
68   TNA, SP36/74, f82v, D'Arcy to Newcastle, 22 November 1745.

be done should they enter Yorkshire'. Neither of the lord lieutenants thought that any of these proposals were realistic, given time constraints.[69]

There were other difficulties in accepting these proposals. Irwin explained that there were too many routes which the Jacobites might take. The East Riding was too open to allow effective harassment of the rebel forces, and to stop them taking provisions would be difficult given the recent bumper harvest. D'Arcy echoed these concerns, though he did have his men undertake a survey of the roads to locate those which were sufficiently narrow to make obstruction a possibility. He also had men prepare material to throw up as earthworks to block a Jacobite march. Captain Robinson, one of his officers, paid four masons and 23 labourers to prepare blockades near Greta Bridge if there was a Jacobite march there.[70] Greta Bridge was astride the main road from Westmorland into the North Riding and was near Barnard Castle, and so was a route that the Jacobites might have taken.

The volunteers would be unable to stop any major Jacobite advance, however. Should this happen, D'Arcy wrote 'any opposition we can give them must be ineffectual and end in nothing but the loss of our men with their arms'. If this did happen, he would station five of his companies in Richmond where, if 'parties of them might come into this part of the county', his men could deal with them.[71]

Yet some men were not so hesitant. William Thornton, one of D'Arcy's captains, was eager for action and wanted to attach himself and his company to the regulars. He addressed them thus, 'I have the pleasing confidence that all of you are willing to join them' and they replied, 'We will follow you to the world's end'. Thornton was a liberal commander; providing them with a fat ox for a feast and liberal quantities of beer. They marched off, to the sound of tunes played by Metcalf, such as 'Britons strike home' 'and other loyal and popular airs' in October to join Wade's forces at Newcastle. They subsequently marched into Scotland with and were present at the Battle of Falkirk on 17 January, before going home at the end of January 1746.[72] However, D'Arcy was alarmed and wrote to Malton, 'Should the rest of the troops be so impatient for action, what shall become of us?'[73] As it turned out, he not have worried; a Mr Sowray was given a commission to raise another company of volunteers to replace Thornton's.[74]

A defence of York, despite its walls, was not considered to be a realistic proposal. Malton and D'Arcy, though, had thought about this. This is despite the fact that they knew the walls were weak and that there was a lack of artillery. However, they believed that if Wade could offer speedy relief it was feasible.[75] Captain Francis Pierson opposed such a step, probably

69   TNA, SP36/74, ff.82r, D'Arcy to Newcastle, 9 November 1745, TNA, SP36/74, f.198r, D'Arcy to Newcastle, 22 November 1745; Sheffield Archives (SA), WWM2/311, Wentworth to Malton, 23 November 1745.
70   TNA, SP36/74, f.111r, Irwin to Newcastle, 20 November 1745; TNA, SP36/74, f.198r, D'Arcy to Newcastle, 22 November 1745; BIHR, Bp C & P, XX1/2, Accounts.
71   TNA, SP36/74, f82r, D'Arcy to Newcastle, 9 November 1745; WYAS: Leeds, TN/PO3/3C/78, Hutton to Irwin, 12 November 1745.
72   Metcalf, Life, pp.79, 91.
73   SA, WWM1/342, D'Arcy to Malton, 1 November 1745
74   NYRO, ZPB, 1446/1253, Resolutions, 1 November 1745.
75   BL.Add.Mss. 35598, f.102v, Herring to Hardwicke, 26 October 1745, SA, WWM1/380, Malton to Wentworth, 22 November 1745.

because there were insufficient men to hold three miles of wall against 800 attackers for long.[76] Wade's failed attempt to relieve Carlisle a few days prior to this would not have given anyone confidence that the aged soldier would have been successful in coming to the aid of a besieged York.

Internal security was a task envisaged as being feasible. There were concerns that the Jacobites had sympathisers throughout Britain, especially among the Catholic minorities of which there were numbers in Yorkshire. These men might well try and join the Jacobite army as it marched through England. There might even by localised risings by the gentry as had occurred in Northumberland, Durham, and Lancashire in 1715. Winn stated that 'we think ourselves capable to prevent and curb any riots or insurrections that so near an approach of the Rebels might encourage, for your Grace can but be sensible of how fatal it might be should any tumults cause a diversion of any of the Regular forces necessary'. Finally, the volunteers could guard bridges in the county, presumably to stop and question travellers and arrest any who were deemed suspicious. Likewise, small foraging parties from the Jacobite army might be dealt with. Winn thought that they could 'prevent their detaching any small partys cross the border for plunder of provisions from this side'.[77]

Others thought so, too. A group of Leeds gentlemen known as 'The Leeds Parliament' applied to D'Arcy for his companies to march to the town for they were worried that groups of Jacobites might visit them.[78] Retreating Jacobites were also feared and a Yorkshireman thought that 'a company or two of the Blues might now be of service here… it may not be amiss to address Lord Malton to this purpose'.[79]

In order to accomplish these goals, it was decided in November to spread the 25 West Riding companies throughout the Riding. Higham's would be stationed in Pontefract, Winn's in Leeds and Ramsden's in Wakefield. Therefore, they could unite at Leeds in one day, or in two days if needed in either Wakefield or Pontefract. Malton thought that Winn might be able to block Blackstone Pass if the Jacobites marched into Yorkshire that way. At the beginning of December, Malton ordered Winn's force to Sheffield for 9 December. A few days later the men marched to Halifax. Presumably all this was to protect the western border of Yorkshire from any parties that the Jacobites might detach on their march through Lancashire. They would also have been thereby in a position to assist the regular troops, as Wade was then marching to Halifax and planned to cut off the Jacobite retreat in Lancashire, a feat he never achieved. It was all very exhausting, as Malton wrote on 14 December, 'I have been some days on the march had a very long one yesterday so rest here for some time'.[80] Soon afterwards, there was a suggestion that there might be a French landing on the East Riding coastline and there was a plan for the West Riding companies to march thither, but there is no evidence that they actually did so.[81]

76   SA, WWM1/376, Pierson to Malton, 22 November 1745.
77   WYAS: Leeds, NP1602/11, Winn to Herring, 3 November 1745.
78   TNA, SP36/74, ff.231r-232v, Malton to Newcastle, 23 November 1745
79   WYAS: Leeds, Birkbeck Papers. 12, Unknown to Birkbeck, 10 December 1745
80   WYAS: Leeds, Birkbeck Papers, 12, Anon to Birkbeck, 10 December 1745, WYAS: Leeds, NP1514/3,
     Malton to Winn, 5 December 1745; NH2875/12, Malton to Winn, 11 December 1745; WYAS: Leeds,
     NP1595/9, Bowes to Robinson, 9 December 1745; NRO, Malton to Fitzwilliam, 14 December 1745.
81   SA, WWM2/339, Malton to Herring, 5 December 1745.

Volunteer troops could undertake some routine tasks that otherwise would have been the lot of the regulars. Major General James Oglethorpe thought so, 'which will save the diminishing of the army by leaving troops behind when they march northwards'. These included guarding Jacobite prisoners. On 26 Dorothy Johnson noted the arrival of the prisoners in York and that they were bring guarded by men of the north riding companies. She hoped they would remain in the city to continue their guard duties.[82] Likewise Winn took into custody prisoners from the army and presumably he used some of his men to guard them.[83] One Mr Scot of Woodsome's House had his house searched by the volunteers in case he had any concealed arms there.[84]

The East Riding companies were also active. The Dean of York, in December, told Irwin that the Scots in the Dutch troops which formed part of Wade's command, were deserting. They would attempt to leave by taking ships between Bridlington and Hull. Irwin's men were posted on the coast, with a company at Beverley, and some men at Brough and Hasle. There was liaison with the county constables and beacons were erected on the coastline. There is no further evidence that any action took place.[85]

Yet for most of their existence their activity may have been minimal. Todd only recorded that in October and November that they were billeted in inns in and around Beverley and that he had six pence per day deducted from his daily pay of a shilling for food and lodgings. He was quartered at the Cross Keys in Lairgate.[86]

The Jacobite retreat from Derby on 6 December saw them retrace their route through Staffordshire, Cheshire, Lancashire, Westmorland and Cumberland in the next fortnight. This was a relief to those in Yorkshire. Malton wrote on 7 December, 'I hope they'll return the way they came' and D'Arcy echoed these sentiments. Given that Field Marshal Wade's army was marching through Yorkshire it seemed improbable that a Jacobite retreat would aim for Yorkshire.[87]

Rather than their military benefits, Newcastle looked to the political value of the volunteer forces. As early as 4 September he had informed Malton that 'in this conjuncture it must be very proper for all counties and especially so considerable a one as the county of York to express their zeal and affection for His Majesty and Government by addresses and all other proofs they can'.[88] An example of the forces being used for ceremonial occasions in public occurred in York, after the East Riding companies marched to Pocklington and Market Weighton, in two columns. After staying at these two villages overnight, they arrived at York on the next day. Here they were billeted in inns, Todd staying at the Pack Horse in Micklegate. On 21 they undertook drill at Campus Ing Parterre. Todd wrote that

---

82   Nottingham University Library, NeC 1661, Oglethorpe to Pelham, 20 Octocopter 1745; NRO, ZAL, Box 40/4, Johnson to Thomas Mayer, 25 December 1745.
83   WYAS: Leeds, NP1547/39, Fawkener to Winn, 21 January 1746.
84   C.E. Whiting (ed.), 'Two Yorkshire Diaries', *Yorkshire Archaeological Society Record Series*, 117, (1952), p.113.
85   TNA, SP36/78, f189r, Irwin to Newcastle, 27 December 1745.
86   Cormack and Jones (eds.), *Corporal Todd*, p.2.
87   NRO, Malton to Fitzwilliam, 7 December 1745.
88   TNA, SP36/67, f124v, Newcastle to Malton, 4 September 1745.

the numerous spectators 'seem'd well pleas'd with the Appearance we made & gave us 7 guineas to drink His Majesty's health etc.'[89]

The role of the city forces was more localised. The preamble to the association ran as follows, 'For the securing of the ill effects of the Rebellion and the Houses of and within the city and Ainsty from being plundered by those who are now in open rebellion or by any other wicked persons, whether Strangers or living within this City or Ainsty'.[90] A guard house for the men was established at Robert Sowerby's school room above Thursday Market Cross, where beds were also provided.[91] It seems that their main role was to keep guard at the city's main gates. Herring wrote 'none permitted to come in and go out of the city without examination'.[92] There was concern that the men might abuse their responsibility, for on 25 October and order was made that any man who relieved any citizen of money or drink would be severely punished.[93]

It seems that men from the Leeds volunteers and the independent city volunteers of York took part in a search of Catholic properties in York on 7 December. The corporation refused to undertake this, so Malton gave these other men a warrant to do so. Guards were placed at house doors during the searches. In all 26 horses were found and were transferred to the army.[94] Herring was shocked at such a proceeding, despite his anti-Catholicism, writing 'Tho' I applaud the measure, I am extreamly mortified at ye manner of putting it in execution – it looks like an insult on the magistracy and such a cruel representation of them to the world'.[95]

The Blues also had a ceremonial role to play, too. On 30 October, to celebrate the King's birthday, the four city companies marched down Micklegate, through Coney Street and then to the Pavement before finishing at All Hallows Church. There they drank the King's health. The purpose of this was to show that they were able to march in a soldierly fashion. Two later parades also involved bonfires, as well as ale being drunk; on 5 November and in January.[96]

As time went on and the Jacobites returned to Scotland, enthusiasm began to wane. Duncombe unilaterally disbanded his North Riding company by 15 December. He did this because he was concerned that his men might be obliged to march outside the county boundaries. This ran against the oath that they had taken on enlistment.[97] D'Arcy was concerned that this might spread to the rest of his companies. In fact, there was discussion that the companies should be disbanded now the danger was over. Malton suggested to Newcastle on 13 December that because the regular army needed more men, that the men form the volunteer companies be called upon to enlist therein.[98] Malton met his fellow lord

89   Cormack and Jones (eds.), *Corporal Todd*, p.2.
90   YCA, E41B, pp.1-2.
91   YCA, E41B, p.16b.
92   BL. Add.Mss. 35598, f.140r, Herring to Hardwicke, 13 December 1745.
93   YCA, E41B, p.20.
94   WYAS: Leeds, NH2875/12, Bowes to Robinson, 9 December 1745; BL. Add. Mss. 35889, f.64v, Herring to Hardwicke, 8 December 1745.
95   BL. Add.Mss., 35889, f.64r, Herring to Hardwicke, 8 December 1745.
96   YCA, E41B, pp.20, 57.
97   TNA, SP36/77, f.125r, Irwin to Newcastle, 15 December 1745.
98   TNA, SP36/77, ff.20r-21r, Malton to Newcastle, 13 December 1745.

lieutenants on 30 December, but they disagreed with his proposals. Thus, the volunteer companies were kept in being.[99] D'Arcy thought that they should be kept in being 'we think ourselves far from being in a state of security in this part of the country'.[100]

In January 1746, Malton left the county for London, leaving Winn and Ramsden to 'act in concert with the other two', though convinced that his scheme for recruitment was right.[101] It was not until 8 February that the decision to disband the Yorkshire forces was taken. Some of the remaining money from the subscription funds was to be used as bounty money of four guineas per man, for any of the volunteers who wished to join the regulars. Alternatively, anyone wanting to be discharged could be given two shillings discharge money to return home.[102]

Not many chose the first option; 17 out of the 350 men from the East Riding companies chose to enlist; 90 men out of a gathering of 750 men of the West Riding companies did so.[103] The reason was because, as D'Arcy wrote, in doing so, it was asking men 'to quit an easie comfortable life with 12d per day, for severe discipline, fatigue and but 6d'.[104] Captain Hall, who disbanded men in Whitby on 16 February, found that none would join the army because 'the wages given there for sailors are so extravagant that makes labour here so dear, that even a farmer in the county, cannot get a servant to live with him, for scarce double the wages'.[105] One of Irwin's officers sought a military career and Irwin wrote to the Duke of Cumberland in March to recommend Robert Hampton, his former adjutant, as an ensign in Wolfe's 8th Regiment of Foot, 'where no man could possibly behave better than he did or more to ye satisfaction of all ye officers'. His wish was granted.[106]

The city volunteers' existence was put in question at a meeting on 23 January 1746. It was deemed that 'the Rebells are far distant from this City the Town quiet, no appearance of Tumults or Disorders & therefore no occasion to keep Guards in Thursday market at the Barrs'. Furthermore, the money raised was running out. In any case the 200 men of the independent city volunteers were still in being and so the decision was taken to keep the men in being for only one day a week. The officers and men unanimously rejected the proposal and so the city recorder, Thomas Place, drew them together in the Guild Hall, thanked them for their services and dismissed them.[107] The last of the Yorkshire forces to disband were the York independent volunteers, who were recorded as being in existence since July 1746. This was in order that they could form part of the York display on the Duke of Cumberland's return from Scotland after his victory at Culloden.[108]

The action of the Yorkshire Blues had not affected the military campaign of 1745 one whit and to that extent those historians writing about the campaign are correct to dismiss them.

---

99 SA, WWM2/354, Malton to Newcastle, 1 January 1746; SA, WWM2/359, Irwin to Malton, 10 January 1746.
100 TNA, SP36/77, f.278r, D'Arcy to Newcastle, 17 December 1745.
101 WYAS: Leeds, NP1614/6, Newcastle to Winn, 9 January 1746.
102 SA, WWM1/376; BIHR, Bp C & P XX1/3, Resolutions, 19 February 1746.
103 TNA, SP36/78, f.189r, Irwin to Newcastle, 27 December 1745; Anon., West Riding Account.
104 SA, WWM/2, 334, D'Arcy to Malton, 20 December 1745.
105 BIHR, Bp, C & P, XXI/1, Hall to Unknown, 16 February 1746.
106 Royal Archives, Cumberland Papers, 12/80, Irwin to Fawkener, 12 March 1746.
107 YCA, E41B, pp.26-27.
108 The General Advertiser, 3657, 19 July 1746.

Had there been a Jacobite advance through Yorkshire it is probable that all these local forces would have acted in a similar manner to their like in Lancashire or Derbyshire; disbanding themselves as the Jacobite army advanced towards them or fleeing to a place of safety. This can hardly be construed as cowardice for they would have been badly outnumbered and were never meant to fight a battle, despite their military trappings of uniforms, weapons, and ranks.

However, this assessment is not entirely fair. Their actual significance was twofold. Firstly, they were to deal with any local Jacobite sympathisers. As seen little action was needed, apart from a search and seizure of Catholic property in York. It may have been the case that there were very few in Yorkshire whose sympathy to the Jacobite cause was such that they wished to physically assist it; or perhaps the dominance of such local forces deterred them. Secondly, they helped give the impression that there was strong support in the counties for the King and Government and thus help raise morale both locally and nationally and this they did by simply being in existence and carrying out various ceremonial duties. These modest tasks were achieved and to this extent the Yorkshire Blues were effective, not as a military force, but as an armed police force with political significance.

Appendix: The Yorkshire Hunters

There was another pan-Yorkshire force raised during the emergency. On 24 September a number of Yorkshire gentlemen desired to raise their own corps independent of the county association. Major General James Oglethorpe interceded on their behalf with the Duke of Newcastle. Oglethorpe suggested that they might number 300 men, including servants. As this would be a cavalry unit, the men desired to be called the Royal Hunters.[109] Newcastle agreed readily enough and stated 'They shall be distinguished by the name they desire, of His Majesty's Regiment of Hunters' and suggested Oglethorpe be their colonel.[110]

The unit mustered on 30 September on the Knavesmire, a piece of open ground beyond York's city walls. They were described thus:

> The Gentlemen who composed the first Rank, were all dress'd in Blue; trimm'd with scarlet, and Gold Buttons, Gold Lac'd Hats, light boots and saddles, etc., their Arms were short Bullet Guns slung, Pistols of a moderate size and string plain swords. The second and third ranks which were made up of their servants, were dress'd in Blue, with Brass buttons, their Accoutrements all light and serviceable, with short Guns and pistols, and each with a Pole-Axe in his hand.[111]

Estimates of their numbers varied from between 20-40 gentlemen: if each brought two servants, then the number would be about 90.[112] Stephen Thompson, who was probably a

---

109 TNA, SP36/69, f.8v, Oglethorpe to Newcastle, 24 September 1745.
110 TNA, SP36/69, f.166r, Newcastle to Oglethorpe, 30 September 1745.
111 *The London Evening Post*, 2795, 3-5 October 1745.
112 Anon., *Report on the Manuscripts of Lady du Cane* (London: HMSO, 1905), p.77; BL.Add.Mss., 35598, f.70r, Herring to Hardwicke, 27 September 1745.

lawyer, named some of their members, 'The bucks such as Zach Moore, Hall, G. Thompson, Boynton, Wood, Lascelles'.[113] William Lister, nephew of the Rev. John Lister, was another,[114] as was George Clerk of Penicuik, a lowland Scot.[115] Nathaniel Hodgson 'an honest young clergyman' was their chaplain.[116]

On 25 October they rode into Newcastle to join the army assembling there under Field Marshal George Wade. They were to form part of that force's vanguard and did so when the army marched to Morpeth.[117] In the next month they rode westwards to bring information about the Jacobite march south. Oglethorpe wrote that along with his green-clad Georgia Rangers 'the Royal Hunters…bring me the best intelligence and I have made them send the last to Sir John Ligonier by express'.[118] Yet there were criticisms. Stephen Thompson wrote 'They make more noise than they deserve; their numbers being much magnified'.[119] Ralph Reed noted similarly that they 'might have done good service by watching the rear of the rebel army'.[120]

In December they formed part of a flying column of cavalry led by Oglethorpe to harass the retreating Jacobite army. John Daniel, an English Jacobite, was unimpressed, 'the Yorkshire Hunters endeavoured to shew themselves against us, but little to their honour'.[121] However, according to another observer they 'have done well, for being informed that abt 2 or 300 of ye rebels were at Lowther Hall, they went there and attacked them, kill'd 10 and dispersed ye rest'.[122]

They seem to have been disbanded at the end of December, once the Jacobite army had retired to Scotland. Around this time, they were thanked for their services by the Duke of Cumberland, possibly at Carlisle prior to his return to London.[123] It is worth noting that unlike the Yorkshire Association companies, but in keeping with the Liverpool Blues, they were willing and able to operate outside their county boundaries and in unison with the regular troops.

113 Anon. *Lady du Cane*, p.77.
114 WYAS: Halifax, SH7/HL/36.
115 W.A.J. Prevost, 'Mr George Clerk and the Royal Hunters', *Cumberland and Westmorland Architectural and Archaeological Society Transactions*, 63, (1963), p.232.
116 BL. Add. Mss, 35598, f.244r, Herring to Hardwicke, 20 May 1747.
117 *Manchester Magazine*, 461, 12 November 1745.
118 TNA, SP36/74, f.266r, Oglethorpe to Newcastle, 24 November 1745.
119 Anon. *Lady du Cane*, p.77.
120 Anon. *Report on the Manuscripts in Various Collections*, VIII (London: HMSO, 1913), pp.133-134.
121 W.B. Blaikie (ed.), 'Origins of the Forty Five', *Scottish History Society*, 2nd series, II (1916), pp.183-184.
122 University of Hull Library, Special Collections, DDSY (3)1, 48, Readshaw to Sykes, 20 December 1745.
123 *York Journal*, 7 January 1746.

7

'Your Provincial Guard': The Derbyshire Blues and the Chatsworth Contingent

Andrew and Lucy Bamford

The pivotal role of Derby in the events of the '45 is well known, for it was there that the fateful decision was made to abandon the Jacobite advance on London and to return to Scotland. What is perhaps less well-known, since the Jacobites were able to enter Derby without a fight, is that a sizeable force of locally-raised troops had been assembled in the town, only to leave it in something of a hurry once it became apparent that to remain would have been to stand unsupported against some 5,000 heavily-armed Scotsmen. The blue-coated soldiers who were assembled for review on Derby Market Place on 3 December 1745 came from two sources. The majority were raised by a local association similar to those that existed in Yorkshire, Liverpool, Durham, and elsewhere, but a portion – 146 out of the total of around 750 – were the product of an abortive scheme by William Cavendish, 3rd Duke of Devonshire, to raise a regiment of his own from his estate at Chatsworth. Since Devonshire was also Lord Lieutenant of Derbyshire, he had been identified from the outset by the leaders of the county association as the obvious figurehead for their endeavours and thus the two forces to all intents and purposes merged, once it became apparent that the Jacobites posed a genuine threat to the county.

Regrettably for the subsequent reputation of the corps, one of the main sources for the activities of the Derbyshire Blues, once embodied, is a scurrilous eight-page pamphlet, written in mock-biblical style and attributed to 'Nathan Ben Shadai A Priest of the Jews', entitled *The Chronicle of the Derbyshire Regiment with the Mighty Acts of D---sh-re their Colonel and L-w- their Captain*. This, however, was published 15 years after the events that it relates, and is primarily concerned with mocking those involved in the endeavour for the purpose of political point-scoring. Although its satirical tone has greatly coloured perceptions of the Blues and their activities during the '45, when taken alongside other accounts it does, in fact, contain a surprising amount of useful information.[1] Other source material

---

1   'Nathan Ben Shadai', *The Chronicle of the Derbyshire Regiment with the Mighty Acts of D---sh-re their Colonel and L-w- their Captain* (London: Unknown Publisher, 1760).

has been brought out in studies of Derby and Derbyshire in the '45 by L. Eardley-Simpson and Brian Stone, but the primary focus of both these works is the Jacobite forces and their activities in the county, coupled, in the case of Eardley-Simpson, with an apparent desire to demonstrate that as many representatives of the county families as he could possibly implicate were, in fact, closet Jacobites.[2] Further useful primary material is contained in Robert Simpson's 1826 collection of documents relating to the history of the county.[3]

All these sources have been drawn upon to assemble the following account, but the greater part of what follows is based on papers held in the archives at Chatsworth House. Much of the correspondence there has also clearly been used by Eardley-Simpson and Stone, as well as in an essay by John Beresford, which serves as a useful summary of the whole.[4] However, one source which all of these authors seem to have missed is the list of 'Money Paid by Alexr. Barker on Account of raising men &c. in the Rebellion, the 19th George Second 1745'. The fact that it is hidden away at the back of the Chatsworth kitchen weekly accounts for 1743-1745, would seem, reasonably enough, to be the cause of its having previously been overlooked. The list provides details of all the men raised by Devonshire for his own abortive regiment – their bounties, wages, and lengths of service, but also the costs of their uniforms and equipment – as well as detailing all the expenses entailed by the Duke and his son, the Marquis of Hartington, during the sojourn of the Derbyshire Blues around the East Midlands in December 1745.[5] As such, it enables an accurate picture to be obtained of the sheer expense of raising provincial, volunteer manpower at this time, and, when taken in conjunction with other correspondence, of the administrative and organisational problems such activities involved. A separate list, totalling 37 names, specifies ages, occupations, and places of abode for some of those who were amongst the first to enlist.[6] Whilst it is true, therefore, that the Derbyshire Blues did little of great import in the suppression of the Rising, the fact that it is possible to obtain so detailed an understanding of their internal economy means that they can stand as an exemplar for other locally-raised units for which such details are lacking.

It is clear that to some extent, the efforts of Derbyshire's loyal associators took their cue and inspiration from those of counties further to the north. Certainly, events in Yorkshire were already being followed with interest at Chatsworth by the time that Devonshire, as Lord Lieutenant, received a warrant to seize arms from those thought to be disaffected,

---

2   L. Eardley-Simpson, *Derby in the 'Forty-Five* (London: Philip Allan, 1933); Brain Stone, *Bonnie Prince Charlie and the Highland Army in Derby* (Cromford: Scarthin Books, 2015). The authors are obliged to V.R. James of the Charles Edward Stuart Society of Derby for the loan of his copy of the former work.

3   Robert Simpson, *A Collection of Fragments Illustrative of the History and Antiquities of Derby* (Derby: G. Wilkins and Sons, 1826).

4   John Beresford, 'The Crisis of 1745', in his *Storm and Peace* (London: Cobden-Sanderson, 1936), pp.11-64.

5   Devonshire Collection Archives, Chatsworth (DCA), C/5/A/2, Chatsworth kitchen weekly accounts 1743-1745. The authors are obliged to Fran Baker, Archivist and Librarian, for alerting them to the existence of this source.

6   DCA, C6, Chatsworth Cash Book 1739-1756.

and a second authorising the raising of troops.[7] The 3rd Duke seems not to have been the most active member of the family to have held that title during the course of its history. He had written to his son and heir – also William Cavendish, known by his courtesy title as Marquis of Hartington and then in London where he had a seat in the Commons – expressing the view that the Lord Lieutenants were unlikely to be able to do anything 'but in the ordinary way of the militia… except they get authority from the King to raise companies Troops or Regiments … such authorities have been given formerly. I shall have one but shall not mention it unless I find occasion to make use of it'. At this early stage in the Rising, his belief was that the main threat was a French invasion on the south coast, and that little more would be required of him and his fellow lord lieutenants than to 'keep things quiet in the northern counties where there will be scarce any regular Troops'.[8]

The Royal Warrant, when it arrived, required a more active response, noting that:

> Whereas several of our Loyal Subjects in Our County of Derby, and divers other Counties, have testified unto Us their earnest Desire, at this time of common Danger, when a rebellion is actually begun within This Our Kingdom, in Favour of a Popish Pretender, to enter into Associations for Taking up Arms for the Common Defence, and have desired Our Royal Approbation, and Authority for Their so Doing.[9]

The warrant gave Devonshire authority to 'form into Troops, or Companies, such Persons as shall be willing to associate Themselves for the Purposes aforesaid' and to grant commissions. Along with this presumption of loyal support from above, the Duke was also receiving a certain amount of pressure from beneath, with Thomas Gisborne, a magistrate and former mayor of Derby, twice writing to him with news of meetings that had been held at the George Inn in the town to discuss the threat posed by the Rising and the means that might be taken to resist it, up to and including the acquisition of arms.[10] Whilst Early-Simpson's history endeavours, not entirely successfully, to paint a picture of a county gentry with Tory or even Jacobite sympathies, Derby itself had done very well out of the era of prosperity that had followed the Hanoverian succession, and could be counted on as suitably loyal and Whiggish: 'Upon ye whole never soe good a dispatch to serve theire Country or to Appear in Arms', as Gisborne assessed the prevailing mood.[11] Gisborne himself, 'a spirited magistrate, who governed the men, granted his favours to the women, and excited dread in all',[12] was one of the driving forces behind the formation of the association and its fundraising

---

7   DCA, CS1/163.98, Warrant for the seizure of arms in the County of Derby, addressed to the Duke of Devonshire, 5 September 1745; CS1/163.99, Royal Warrant addressed to the Duke of Devonshire, authorising the raising of troops to resist the rebels, 6 September 1745.
8   DCA, CS1/163.7, Devonshire to Hartington, 5 September 1745.
9   DCA, CS1/163.99, Royal Warrant addressed to the Duke of Devonshire, authorising the raising of troops to resist the rebels, 6 September 1745.
10   DCA, CS1/319, Gisborne to Devonshire, 12 September 1745; CS1/319.1, Gisborne to Devonshire, 14 September 1745.
11   DCA, CS1/319.1, Gisborne to Devonshire, 14 September 1745.
12   William Hutton, *The History of Derby; from the Ages of Antiquity to the Year MDCCXCI* (London: J. Nichols, 1791), p.274.

activities; however, he was not alone in calling upon the Lord Lieutenant to act, and similar appeals came in from all quarters of the county. From Willesley Hall – so far south that shifting boundaries have now placed it in Leicestershire – Sir Thomas d'Abney twice called for the Justices of the Peace to meet in Derby,[13] while from the other extremity of the county, Joseph Offley begged to 'ask your Grace if a meeting at Chesterfield might not be useful at this juncture with your Graces presence, or Ld. Charles, or Ld. Hartingtons'.[14]

Thus prompted, Devonshire gave his blessing and support to a third meeting at the George Inn, on Irongate in Derby, to take place at noon on 28 September. The cost of the event was 'generously defrayed by his Grace', and the subscription towards raising troops was not opened until the attendees had dined and drunk: thus lubricated, the subscribers were persuaded to put up a total sum of £6,169.[15] With this not-inconsiderable total, it was proposed to raise 10 companies of 50 men apiece (inclusive of officers). Two companies were to be raised in Derby and two in Chesterfield; the remainder were to be respectively furnished by the hundreds of Ashbourne, Alfreton, Bakewell and Tideswell, Sudbury and Hilton, Duffield and Belper, and Repton and Gresley. It was proposed that these companies were to be regimented to form either one unit 500-strong, or else two of 250 men each, and it was felt that if the Marquis of Hartington was to agree to be one of the colonels 'it would give Grt. life & incouragm't' to the endeavour. Sir Nathaniel Curzon of Kedleston Hall was also identified as a likely candidate for a senior commission or command. Moving to appointments of lesser stature, something of a surfeit of officers was proposed for the two Derby companies – four captains (the list headed by Gisborne's son John), three lieutenants, and two ensigns – but it was hoped that the Duke would help select suitable officers for the other companies, the initial proposal naming, as well as Gisborne junior, 'Captn. Roberts, one of ye Bagshaws, Mr Rich'd Bateman, Mr Coape, Mr Compton Junr.'.[16] Captain Roberts was presumably a retired officer. The Bagshawes were the family that produced Colonel Samuel of that ilk, whose letters will be familiar to students of the 18th century British Army, but he was already a serving officer at this date: William and Richard Bagshawe were amongst those who subscribed to the association, however.[17]

Plans to provide uniform for the regiment were, based on the initial report of proceedings, fairly rudimentary. Each man enlisting was to receive a new hat and a pair of shoes. Interestingly, the cockade of the former was not to be the usual Hanoverian black, but orange; very clearly, the men were being raised not just to protect the county, nor even the rights of the current monarch, but the rights that had been won when the Glorious Revolution brought William of Orange to the throne. Each private man was to receive a shilling a day for the duration of his service; initially the proposal was that that service was to take him no more than 10 miles outside of the county, but it was later agreed that the only restriction was that the men 'Not to goe out of Gt. Britain'. As a means 'for the better

13   DCA, CS1/316.1, d'Abney to Devonshire, 24 September 1745.
14   DCA, CS1/323.1, Offley to Devonshire, 22 September 1745, postscript.
15   Eardley-Simpson, *Derby and the 'Forty-Five*, p.133 (quoting the *Derby Mercury* of 3 October 1745); Stone, *Highland Army in Derby*, p.83.
16   'Minutes of Meeting as to the Derbyshire Blues', from the cutting book of the late William Bemrose, quoted as an appendix in Eardley-Simpson, *Derby and the 'Forty-Five*, pp.264-266.
17   Derby Museums (DM), DBYMU 1977-748/1, framed subscription list, 28 September 1745.

carrying into execution the design of the Association', a committee, composed of at least five of the major subscribers – defined as those who had pledged at least £25 – was to meet every Friday, alternately at the George and the King's Head.[18] At one of these meetings there seems to have been a backlash in favour of cancelling the subscription scheme and calling out the Militia – Eardley-Simpson attributes this to a pro-Jacobite Tory faction – but this was voted down.[19]

Having thus settled upon their design, the associators now had to convert their subscriptions into arms and uniforms, and to recruit the men to bear them. With Hartington in London and making himself useful by seeing to the supply of arms, Gisborne sought out the other possible figurehead commander for the Blues, Sir Nathaniel Curzon. He was visited at Kedleston on 21 October by Joseph Hayne, Clerk of the Peace at Derby, who provided an account of the meeting, and one William Vernon. A set of proposals was set out for the organisation and recruitment of volunteers, which Hayne was to communicate, via Gisborne, to the Duke. These opened with a calculation of the daily cost of maintaining a company:

That a Captains pay [per] day shall be	0-8-0
A Lieutenants	0-4-0
An Ensign's	0-3-0
That there be 2 Sergts to each Company & that their pay be to each 1-6 p day}	0-3-0
and 2 Corporalls at 1-6 p day	0-2-6
one Drummer at	0-1-3
50 private Men in each Company 1s a piece	2-10-0
Ye Day	3-11-9

Note that the size of the companies had now increased from 50 all ranks to 58. Matters then moved on to the selection of officers, a matter which it was not as easy to resolve as had been assumed at the 28 September meeting. It was now proposed:

That ye Captains shal chuse their Subalterns.
That each private Man shal have 5s advance.
That the Officers which Sr Nathaniel Curzon shall think fit to name shall be appointed & approved at the next meeting.
The soldiers not to be Regimented but be in independent Companies.
That ye Officers pay shal commence from date of their Comissions or from the next meeting; and all their Comissions be of equal date.
That as many of ye Gentlemens Tenants or their Sons above 20 and under 40 as have a mind to list as private Men shal be entertaind.[20]

18   'Minutes of Meeting as to the Derbyshire Blues', in Eardley-Simpson, Derby and the 'Forty-Five, pp.264-266.
19   Eardley-Simpson, Derby and the 'Forty-Five, pp.133-134.
20   DCA, CS1/319.3, Gisbourne to Devonshire, 21 October 1745. Spellings as original.

The resolution to form independent companies rather than a regiment appears to have been settled upon – certainly, there is no talk thereafter of the appointment of any field officers – although the number of companies was at some point increased from 10 to 12. As Curzon had suggested to Hayne and Vernon, a meeting was held the following Friday, 28 October, at the Talbot Inn in Derby with the Duke in attendance. Here the 12 captains were appointed and each issued with £75 of association funds with which to begin the recruitment of their companies.[21] The pay rates agreed with Curzon were adopted, which amounted to a monthly cost of £100 9s 0d per company to which was added a further £20 for bounty money and 'Trophies, by which are meant Halbards, Drums, and other little necessaries', and £50 for clothing. This gave a total cost per company of £195 9s 0d, or £2,345 8s 0d for all 12.[22]

In due course, the complement of 12 captains was filled as follows: 'Wright, Lindley Simpson, Edward Lowe, Rivett, Thornhill, Turner, Bate, Taylor, Hurt, Boothby, Barnes, and Chaworth Hallows'.[23] The Hurts and Boothbys were families of some note in the county; it is not clear which of the many Hurts was made a captain, but it would seem that the Boothby was Brook of that ilk, son of the late Sir William Boothby, Bart, and one of the subscribers to the association. The Rivetts were strong supporters of the local Whig interest with Thomas Rivett being one of the men proposed for a captaincy at the first meeting at the George. Bache Thornhill of Stanton-in-Peak, a lawyer born in 1700, is confirmed by other sources as being the captain named here,[24] and was one of the subscribers to the association. Edward Lowe, of Hazelwood, just south of Belper, whose name, scarcely disguised as 'L-w-', is one of the few to feature in the scurrilous *Chronicle of the Derbyshire Regiment*, was also a subscriber; he was aged around 65 at the time of the Rising, but seems to have thrown himself into the endeavour with the enthusiasm of a younger man and to have taken great pride in his company.[25] Lindley Simpson of Eckington and Chaworth Hallows of Glapwell were both likewise on the list, as was Chambers Bate. Aged only 21 at the time, the last-named was a nephew of the 8th Earl of Exeter, whose Derby townhouse was appropriated as Prince Charles' headquarters when the Jacobites occupied the town, and was newly married to a daughter of the late Thomas Trye of Hardwick.[26] There were two Taylors amongst the subscribers, John and Benjamin, so it is unclear which of them got a company and it has not proved possible to uncover any further information about either. Correspondence confirms that Captain Wright was Thomas Wright of Eyam Hall;[27] he was not amongst the initial subscribers, but this may simply be a result of the distance of his seat from Derby. Of Captains Turner and Barnes, little more can be said and they likewise do not appear amongst the original named subscribers to the association.[28]

---

21   Hutton, *History of Derbyshire*, p.229.
22   'The Establishment of a company of Volunteer Ffoot [sic] in the County of Derby', reproduced in Simpson, *A Collection of Fragments*, Vol.I, p.230.
23   Eardly-Simpson, *Derby in the 'Forty-Five*, p.137, citing an undated memorandum by Joseph Hayne.
24   B. Tacchella (ed.), *The Derby School Register, 1570-1901* (London: Bemrose and Sons, 1902), p.10.
25   A.E.L. Lowe, 'Some account of the family of Lowe of Alderwasley and Denby', *Derbyshire Archaeological Journal*, Vol.3 (1881), p.171.
26   *Gentleman's Magazine*, 1745, p.444; entry for Chambers Bate at *ACAD A Cambridge Alumni Database* <http://venn.lib.cam.ac.uk/>, accessed 9 June 2020.
27   Wright to Hayne, 12 November 1745, in Simpson, *A Collection of Fragments*, Vol.I, p.237.
28   DM, DBYMU 1977-748/1, framed subscription list, 28 September 1745.

However, things did not entirely proceed as planned since Captain Taylor swiftly resigned, which in turn was deemed by Hayne to have invalidated the appointment that he had made for his lieutenant.[29] In a letter of 6 November, Lieutenant George Gretton wrote to enquire of Hayne '…whether the Captain is appointed, because I am in great distress how to act in this Affair in regard to the Men that I have enlisted, it is a great disadvantage to this Affair, because I have refused a great many since you had my Commission…'.[30] From the context, it would seem that Gretton was the lieutenant appointed by Taylor, whose position was in doubt as a result of the captain's resignation. Hayne proposed that a Mr Cotton, of Etwall, be given the vacant company, but Cotton's father refused it on his son's behalf, reiterating a previous refusal by the son in person, Cotton junior then being absent at Thoresby.[31] However, Curzon's later correspondence refers to a 'Captain Buxton', who Eardley-Simpson tentatively identifies as George Buckston who had previously written to Hayne soliciting for a lieutenancy.[32] Aged 24, Buckston had inherited Bradbourne Hall from his father while still a minor; his younger brother Thomas was a regular officer who would later fight at Culloden.[33] It would seem that the good timing of his request meant that he got a vacancy in a higher rank than he had asked for. If George Gretton was indeed the lieutenant who stood to lose out by Taylor's resignation, it seems that he was, after all, retained under the new captain since he is another of the officers identified in the *Chronicle of the Derbyshire Regiment* – not, alas, to his great credit.[34]

To quote Eardley-Simpson, the 12 captains made up a 'far from impressive list'.[35] Few of the big names of the county are seen amongst their ranks, almost to the point that it would seem that such service was shunned. Indeed, Curzon's own proposal that the companies be independent rather than regimented also had the effect of excusing him from accepting the proffered colonelcy by making the issue of appointing field officers null and void. What we see instead is the second tier of county society, with companies going to lesser landed gentry and Derby professional men. None of the men proposed on 28 September as possible officers made it to the final list of captains, and of the four men named at that meeting possibly to command the two Derby companies, only one actually received a company. Young Gisborne is conspicuously absent, and, indeed, his father's role in setting up the companies seems to some extent to have been superseded by Curzon and Hayne once the detailed organisation got underway.

Of the junior officers, very little can be established. George Gretton is one of the few who can be given a name, although it has proved impossible to establish anything more about him. Dropping to the lowest commissioned rank, a Mr Revell was put forward by Curzon to be Buckston's ensign based on the recommendations of 'Mrs Wilmott of Osmaston, and Mrs

---

29   Hayne to Devonshire, 4 November 1745, in Simpson, *A Collection of Fragments*, Vol.I, pp.231-232.
30   Gretton to Hayne, 9 November 1745, in Simpson, *A Collection of Fragments*, Vol.I, p.236.
31   J. Cotton to Hayne, 4 and 5 November 1745, in Simpson, *A Collection of Fragments*, Vol.I, p.235.
32   Buckston to Hayne 3 November 1745 and Curzon to Unknow, 9 November 1745, in Simpson, *A Collection of Fragments*, Vol.I, pp.233, 236; see also Eardley-Simpron, *Derby in the 'Forty-Five*, p.137
33   Stephen Glover and Thomas Noble, *The History of the County of Derby* (Derby: Henry Mozley and Sons, 1828), Vol.II, pp.133-134. In fairness to Curzon in an age of inconsistent spelling, the family had been known as Buxton prior to the archaic 'cks' spelling being deliberately revived by young George.
34   'Ben Shadai', *Chronicle*, pp.7-8.
35   Eardley-Simpson, *Derby in the 'Forty-Five*, p.137.

Mac Cullock'.[36] The Revells of Carnfield were an established landowning family of no great note; however, the young man being recommended, Tristram, was an illegitimate son of Rev. Francis Revell, by a sister of the Derby banker John Heath, who had been permitted to take the family name. Aged about 15, he had become something of a protégé of the Wilmots of Osmaston, with whom the Revells were linked by marriage, so that his connections made up for his having been born on the wrong side of the blanket and gave him a social standing comparable with that of the more senior officers.[37] Conversely, the one ensign identified in the *Chronicle of the Derbyshire Regiment* by something approaching a name was 'Me--lls, of the tribe of St *Giles* ... a man of war from his youth, but a great boaster, moreover he was a publican, and a sinner'.[38] Reading between the satire, the inference would seem to be that previous, and possibly exaggerated, non-commissioned service had here been used to obtain an ensigncy.

Notwithstanding these various difficulties in the appointment of the officers, recruitment of the companies proceeded swiftly, no doubt aided by the seasonal downturn in agricultural work across the county and by the generous bounty. Captain Simpson was able to report his company complete on 7 November, Captain Wright on 12 November; Thornhill's was also complete before 14 November, on which day Hallows 'did not want above four or five' men to complete his.[39] On the 21st of that month Devonshire was able to request that Hayne write to the captains 'to acquaint them that it is my desire that they would hold themselves ready to march w'th their respective Companies immediately upon the receipt of instructions for so doing in writing from me',[40] which would suggest that all 12 companies were by that stage complete. It is not clear to what extent recruitment followed the neat arrangement by hundreds settled upon at the George; more likely the officers recruited men through their own local contacts. The nature of the men raised has been the subject of some speculation, not necessarily to the credit of the volunteers. The scurrilous *Chronicle of the Derbyshire Regiment*, as well as mocking their lack of martial prowess, characterises them as 'striplings, and not able to wield a sword'.[41] Conversely, a contemporary broadside recorded that the men were able to go 'through their exercise to the great satisfaction of all present'.[42]

Mention of the manual exercise brings us to the matter of arms. The search was begun by Gisborne, who had opened negotiations with Birmingham gunsmiths to supplement the 140 muskets – apparently relics from the time of the '15 – that were already to hand.[43] With other local associations also in search of the same essentials, a matter on which Devonshire

---

36   Curzon to Hayne, 9 November 1745, in Simpson, *A Collection of Fragments*, Vol.I, p.236

37   The name is confirmed in Mac Cullock to Hayne, 10 November 1745, in Simpson, *A Collection of Fragments*, Vol.I, p.236, although a typesetter's error has turned 'Triss' into 'Iriss'; see also C.J. Williams, 'The Revell family of Carnfield', *Derbyshire Archaeological Journal*, Vol.91, (1971), p.156.

38   'Ben Shadai', *Chronicle*, p.6; the parish of St Giles is in Normanton, now a suburb of Derby but then a separate village.

39   Simpson to Hayne, 7 November 1745, Wright to Hayne 12 November 1745, Devonshire to Hayne, 14 November 1745, in Simpson, *A Collection of Fragments*, Vol.I, pp.236-238.

40   Devonshire to Hayne, 21 November 1745, in Simpson, *A Collection of Fragments*, Vol.I, pp.245-246.

41   'Ben Shadai', *Chronicle*, p.4.

42   Account of *Derby Mercury*, 12 December 1745, reproduced in Simpson, *A Collection of Fragments*, Vol.I, p.251.

43   DCA, CS1/319.1, Gisborne to Devonshire, 14 September 1745.

corresponded with other magnates as each sought out possible sources of supply, the quest for arms would be a prolonged and difficult one. It became increasingly apparent that local resources would not be sufficient for the various forces being raised – the weapons kept in store at Hull being appropriated for the various units raised in the Ridings of Yorkshire – and that London must be the main source of arms. In arranging this, Devonshire was able to rely on both his son, Lord Hartington, and his son-in-law, William Ponsonby, Viscount Duncannon; the latter, wed to Lady Caroline Cavendish, had served as Chief Secretary for Ireland in conjunction with the Duke's recently-expired tenure as Lord Lieutenant there and was now one of Derby's Members of Parliament. Unravelling this correspondence is not an easy task, for it is complicated by the fact that Hartington and Duncannon were also seeking arms for Devonshire's own regimental project, of which more anon. However, clarity is obtained thanks to a letter of 15 October, in which Duncannon informed the Duke that:

> I have been this morning to wait upon the Duke of Montague about the arms for the two regiments of Derby to know how they are to be supplied, and His Grace has desired me to let you know, that you must write, to the Duke of Newcastle for the Secretary of States order to the master of the ordnance to deliver what arms you have occasion for, signifying the service and <u>particularly</u> the Number of Fire Locks and Bayonets that you want & this His Grace desires you will be exact in for if not, the D of Newcastle will order ten thousand.[44]

Newcastle, it may be inferred, was getting somewhat carried away in his efforts to ensure that sufficient arms were made available to those loyal to the crown.

On 26 October, Hartington was able to inform his father that 'The arms will set out from the Tower on Monday morning, the Steward has been so ill of the Gout that it was impossible for him to take any care about them'.[45] The weapons were to be consigned to Gisborne in Derby. Three days later he could confirm that:

> The arms were loaded in two Waggons at the Tower yesterday, but I believe did not leave London till this morning & will be at Derby on Monday next. There are 28 Chests containing 700 Musquets & Bayonets, 300 & 90 Cartouch Boxes & 900 & 50 Frogs which are things to carry the Bayonets in. The remaining numbers of the two last articles will be sent down as soon as they can be made; for they had no more ready at the Tower; I have directed them to Mr Gisborne & wrote to him to pay for the Carriage which is agreed for at the rate of seven shillings per hundred; I have not seen Sr Robt Wilmot since he was at the Tower for he is gone out of Town, but he sent me an account of the Charge of getting them out of the Ordnance & packing

---

44   DCA, CS1/294.29, Duncannon to the Duke of Devonshire, 15 October 1745; emphasis as original. Note that this letter pre-dates the decision to have 12 independent companies rather than two small regiments.

45   DCA, CS1/260.52, Hartington to Devonshire, 26 October 1745.

up which amounts to £26.8.6 which I will pay him. The Chests are the great expence for they amount to £14.[46]

It would not normally have fallen to the Tower to furnish accoutrements to a regular regiment, since these would have been provided by the regimental colonel out of clothing funds; possibly the opportunity was taken to clear out old items from store.[47]

The arms reached Derby on 30 October, a swifter journey than Hartington's estimate, and were taken into the care of Gisborne.[48] The bulk would seem to have been distributed from there, but eight numbered chests, each containing 25 muskets, plus a 'Little Chest, unnumbered', with a further eight, were sent on to Chatsworth and there distributed to the companies of Captains Simpson, Hallows, Wright, and Thornhill. Packed with these 208 muskets, but rather less evenly distributed, were 128 cartouche boxes and 205 frogs.[49] By 12 November Captain Wright could report from Eyam, well up into the Peak District, that his company had been issued with '52 ffirelocks, 52 ffrogs, and 24 cartouch boxes', corresponding to the contents of chests 10 and 22 as re-packed and sent on from Chatsworth, although he was complaining that he had not yet had a receipt for them.[50] With respect to the shortfall in accoutrements, the Chatsworth accounts confirm that a portion of the men's leatherwork had to be made up locally to compensate for what the Tower could not supply.

With the arms received, along with such accoutrements as were available, and the companies complete, the only remaining point to be addressed was that of clothing. The officers furnished their own uniforms, with one of young Tristram Revell's sponsors seeking to establish whether or not he should present himself to his captain until his clothing was complete.[51] For the non-commissioned officers and drummers, a certain amount of delay had ensued as an allowance for their clothing had been omitted from the original sums issued; or, rather, had been swallowed up as a result of the increase in the number of privates per company.[52] It was subsequently established that clothing two serjeants, two corporals, and one drummer per company would amount to £8 and 15 shillings.[53] This was rather more per head than the allowance for private men, but it is unclear how the dress of the NCOs and drummers differed in terms of quality. The corporals presumably had their shoulder knots and the serjeants their sashes, although, as we have seen, halberds for the latter were accounted for separately.

This aside, however, there is little further that is noted on the matter of the attire of the men, and, for want of evidence to the contrary it would seem to be the case that their

46   DCA, CS1/260.53, Hartington to Devonshire, 29 October 1745. Sir Robert Wilmot, of Osmaston Hall, Derbyshire, had been another of Devonshire's Irish staff and seems to have joined Hartington and Duncannon in acting as a London-based 'fixer' for the Duke.
47   The authors are obliged to Dr Andrew Cormack for this observation.
48   Postscript to Hayne to Devonshire, 4 November 1745, in Simpson, *A Collection of Fragments*, Vol.I, pp.231-232.
49   'Arms &c. Rec'd at Chatsworth Novr. 5 1745', in DCA, C6, Chatsworth Cash Book 1739-1756.
50   Wright to Hayne, 12 November 1745, in Simpson, *A Collection of Fragments*, Vol.I, p.237.
51   Mac Cullock to Hayne, 10 November 1745, in Simpson, *A Collection of Fragments*, Vol.I, p.236
52   Devonshire to Hayne, 14 November 1745, in Simpson, *A Collection of Fragments*, Vol.I, p.238.
53   Circular, Devonshire to Deputy Lieutenants, Justices, and the 12 captains, 23 November 1745, in Simpson, *A Collection of Fragments*, Vol.I, pp.246-247.

clothing progressed without difficulty. As per the initial agreement, the men were issued with a dark blue coat; hats were black, with no mention of lacing but bearing the orange cockade that had also been settled upon at the George. White breeches were apparently issued, and possibly blue woollen stockings also.[54] Insofar as accoutrements are concerned, the Chatsworth account book contains mention of payments for the making of knapsacks, and also specifies cartouche boxes with belts, and, as a separate item, frogs.[55] This combination would suggest a belt carrying a 'belly-box', with a separate frog fitted to hold a bayonet: such an arrangement is seen in the sketches of loyalist volunteers amongst the Penicuik Drawings, and has been postulated as being employed by other locally-raised corps in England and Scotland during the course of the efforts to suppress the Rising.[56] There are passing mentions of swords and sword-belts, but the former were old weapons from the supply that Gisborne had unearthed, and the quantities referred to would not have been sufficient to equip more than a portion of the men raised.[57]

Leaving the Derbyshire Blues proper for a moment, poised and ready to turn out for duty, we now need to consider the men who marched with them from Devonshire's own Chatsworth contingent, and how they came to be raised. The 15 so-called Noblemen's Regiments have been dealt with in detail elsewhere in this work, but, as noted in the Introduction, other magnates expressed an interest in raising such units only for their endeavours to merge into other locally-raised corps. Devonshire, indeed, appears to have been the very first to express an interest in raising a regiment, having done so some time prior to 12 September,[58] only for circumstances to conspire to prevent him from obtaining all the perks of a regular colonelcy.

To begin with, however, all was activity. As early as 24 September, four days prior to the first meeting at the George to form the association that begat the Derbyshire Blues, Devonshire had begun to enlist men at Chatsworth, with 37 on that day alone registering their willingness to serve and receiving a bounty of 10 shillings.[59] However, by early October recruiting had all but ceased, notwithstanding that Devonshire was now offering two Guineas as a bounty (those who had signed up earlier apparently having the difference

---

54   Stone, *Highland Army in Derby*, pp.84-85. Stone's source for the white breeches is not clear; the paragraph dealing with uniforms is cited to Beresford's essay in *Storm and Peace*, but no such detail is therein contained. The suggestion as to blue stockings is supplied by the Charles Edward Stuart Society of Derby, but the original source for this information has been lost. In the absence of any other details, these two points have been followed in reconstructing the uniform for the plate featured in the colour section of this book but should not be considered as definitive.

55   DCA, C/5/A/2, Chatsworth kitchen weekly accounts 1743-1745.

56   Iain Gordon Brown and Hugh Cheape, *Witness to Rebellion. John Maclean's Journal of the 'Forty-Five and the Penicuik Drawings* (East Linton: Tuckwell Press, 1996), pp.64-65; Stuart Reid, *Cumberland's Culloden Army 1745-46* (Oxford: Osprey, 2012), pp.23, 45, and Plate E.

57   DCA, CS1/319.1, Gisborne to Devonshire, 14 September 1745; CS1/319.2, Gisborne to Devonshire, 5 October 1745; C/5/A/2, Chatsworth kitchen weekly accounts 1743-1745.

58   DCA, CS1/320, Herbert to Devonshire, 12 September 1745; he was therefore not, *pace* Christopher Duffy, *Fight for a Throne. The Jacobite '45 Reconsidered* (Solihull: Helion, 2015), p.345 who fails to pick up on the distinction between the two projects with which Devonshire was involved, the originator of the 'Blues' concept.

59   DCA, C6, Chatsworth Cash Book 1739-1756.

made up).[60] Indeed, the Duke's desire to offer a handsome rate of pay may have been one of the difficulties, being one of the points raised by Duncannon in a letter of 10 October, along with the question of appointing officers:

> As to what your Grace desires to be informed in, concerning the recommending of officers for the New regiments. If you will take notice, of the first answer that the King gives to the queries which I sent you, it will set that right and remove all difficulties, for there is not the least regulation or restriction whatsoever, in relation to officers taken out of the army for the King approves of whoever the Colonel recommends. The Duke of Bedford has made Capt: Speed His Lieut: Colonel, Ld Halifax has made Capt: Joseph Dessaux His Lieut: Colonel & the Duke of Kingston has made one His Lieut: Colonel who was never more than a Cornet. This the rest of the army may think hard, but the truth is as I tell your Grace, and I am afraid that it will, some time or other, occasion great discontent amongst the old officers. I could wish your Grace had gone on in the same manner that the others have done, because it would have saved you a great deal of money, and I am very sure that you would have had a much better regiment than any one of them, and I believe some of them have undertaken what they cannot perform, it was always understood by the King, the D of Newcastle and Mr Pelham, that your Grace intended to turn your men into a regular regiment, and that Lord Hartington was to be Colonel, so that should your Grace think of doing it you have nothing to do but to send up a List of your officers to the secretary of state that Commissions may be prepared for the Kings signing, and this is the method that all the others have taken. I think there are 13 or 14 of these New regiments and Mr Pelham thinks it is now full time to put a stop to any more, but as to your Grace you are the very first on the List in the war office, and the 30 out Pensioners are ordered to attend you accordingly, always taking it for Granted, that your Grace intended to raise a regiment as the others have done, but should that be the case, as I observed in the former Letter, your Men must not have any more Pay than the other Foot regiments, as it would occasion mutiny and discontent in the army. As to the answers to the queries which I sent you, Lord Stair forwarded them much with the King, as He thought it was right at this time, to give all the Encouragement that was possible to the Noble men & who offered to raise regiments & it is my opinion that your Grace's example set the whole a going.[61]

The tone of the letter as a whole suggests that the Duke was getting wrapped up over details and thereby risking the progress of the whole project, an impression that is reinforced by a letter from Henry Pelham dated five days earlier outlining the various sorts of troops being raised and inviting Devonshire to 'choose for yourself, whichever is most agreeable to you', and, by implication, to get on with organising it.[62]

---

60   DCA, C/5/A/2, Chatsworth kitchen weekly accounts 1743-1745.
61   DCA, CS1/294.28, Duncannon to Devonshire, 10 October 1745.
62   DCA, CS1/249.26, Pelham to the Duke of Devonshire, 5 October 1745. Pelham's summary from this letter is quoted in the Introduction to this work.

In light of the fact that it was Hartington – altogether more active and politically astute – rather than Devonshire himself who was apparently to have the colonelcy of the putative regiment, much in the way that the Marquis of Granby got that of the regiment raised by his father, it may well be that it was the younger Cavendish who was the real driver behind the project. Certainly, Duncannon's correspondence with the latter would suggest this, as well as indicating that Duncannon had his eye on a commission for himself 'if you think me a proper person to Command any of your men'.[63] Hartington also took a close interest in the Parliamentary debates surrounding the Noblemen's Regiments, and reported back in detail to his father.[64] In a later passage of the letter cited above, Duncannon made clear that it was by Lord Hartington's desire that:

> Drums, Halberts and Pickes [sic] are making, but His Ld ship cannot possibly have them in less than three weeks, there being so great a demand for them. If He wants Colours, Gorgets or accoutrements I should be Glad to know it in time there is no such thing to be had as serjeants[sic] or Corporals, Col de Jean will Lett[sic] me have one serjeant[sic] out of the Horse Grenadiers a very able man and fit to form a regiment, who is to return to His Post when His L'ship has done with Him, I should be Glad to know, if he would have Him sent to Chatsworth.[65]

All, then, seemed to be promising well, with official support and all the trappings of a regular regiment of foot being prepared, with arms to be supplied by the Ordnance, although the impression gained is that the other noble colonels had been swifter off the mark when it came to obtaining experienced aid in training their new commands. Time, however, had run out and Devonshire's efforts were now far behind those of the other magnates, the first of whose regiments were already being taken onto the Establishment. The votes that Hartington so assiduously reported on would seem to have settled the question for good, with only the 15 approved regiments being allowed onto the establishment, and thus the Chatsworth efforts came to naught.

One of the difficulties may simply have been a lack of potential recruits, acknowledged by Duncannon and Hartington to have been a problem almost from the outset, with the former commiserating with the latter 'that men dont [sic] come in to you as fast as might be expected'.[66] Generous bounties notwithstanding, matters were clearly not helped by the fact that Devonshire was looking to recruit in the less populous northern and western parts of the county, whereas the majority of the captains of the 12 Derbyshire Blues companies were based in the south and east. On 13 October, by which time recruiting at Chatsworth

---

63   DCA, CS1/294.26, Duncannon to Hartington, 28 September 1745.
64   DCA, CS1/260.50, Hartington to Devonshire, 22 October 1745; CS1/260.53, Hartington to Devonshire, 29 October 1745; CS1/260.54, Hartington to Devonshire, 31 October 1745; CS1/260.55, Hartington to Devonshire, 2 November 1745; CS1/260.56, Hartington to Devonshire, 5 November 1745.
65   DCA, CS1/294.28, Duncannon to Devonshire, 10 October 1745. Lieutenant Colonel Louis Dejean was then commanding the First Troop of Horse Grenadier Guards.
66   DCA, CS1/294.26, Duncannon to Hartington, 28 September 1745.

had come to an almost complete stop, Joseph Offley wrote from Norton, near Chesterfield, to Hartington:

> As to men we have rais'd here, it is our intention to join his Grace with them, and wish their number larger, as the County raises so few; I can't but think at such a juncture it would be justifiable even to exceed the powers given, and hope, my Lord, orders may immediately be given for raising the men mention'd the last meeting at Derby, as I apprehend in case of a French invasion, it would behove us every one to join the Kings [sic] forces against them – I beg your Lordship will excuse this freedom.[67]

In other words, it would be better in Offley's view for the Cavendishes to throw in their lot with the county association than have two rival enterprises competing for the limited available manpower. This, to the credit of Devonshire and his son, seems to be the course that was taken, with the Duke's position as Lord Lieutenant enabling him to step in and assume control of all the county's forces once it became apparent that the Rising was not going to pass Derbyshire by.

The abortive regimental project was not completely wasted, however. Such men as had been raised at Chatsworth were formed into a single oversized infantry company, with 12 mounted men attached, and local officers were belatedly found to command them, with William Johnson being made captain and Thomas Grammer lieutenant, paid at eight and four shillings per day respectively, both with effect from 29 November. Neither man had any previous military experience; nor did Daniel Grant, who was paid a total of £2 11 shillings for intermittent duty as adjutant 'at several times from ye time he came October 2nd to February 18th'. His duties as adjutant aside, Grant appears to have taken a leading role in recruiting the contingent, receiving a succession of payments which correspond in amount to the bounties being given to recruits – presumably Grant had signed them up and was now claiming the bounty money back, although since the bounties were also credited as paid to each of the soldiers, this would suggest that the sums were inadvertently being charged twice. Grant also had a set of clothes – presumably uniform – paid for out of Chatsworth funds, and received three shillings and five pence expenses for his horse at Retford, which confirms that he accompanied the men when they marched out of Derby.[68] In a post-Rising settling up, calculated separately to the main accounts, he received a further £99 15 shillings, the breakdown of which is not detailed.[69]

On the day after the two officers were appointed, four of the existing volunteers were chosen as serjeants and a further four as corporals, thereby obtaining an increment of sixpence and thruppence respectively over the shilling a day of the privates.[70] In passing, since the only two Chatsworth commissions to be bestowed went to men of obscure background, it may be speculated that the great and good of the county who refused commissions in the Derbyshire Blues did so not through the Jacobite sympathies ascribed to them

---

67   DCA, CS1/323.3, Offley to Hartington, 13 October 1745.
68   DCA, C/5/A/2, Chatsworth kitchen weekly accounts 1743-1745.
69   DCA, C6, Chatsworth Cash Book 1739-1756.
70   DCA, C/5/A/2, Chatsworth kitchen weekly accounts 1743-1745.

by Eardley-Simpson but in the hope that they might instead obtain regular commissions in 'Devonshire's Regiment of Foot': if so, they were sorely disappointed.

The service of the Chatsworth contingent alongside the Derbyshire Blues will be addressed in the final portion of this chapter. However, the accounts and records that were maintained of the men who signed up for the Duke's service enable a much better understanding of the ordinary soldiers than is possible for the Blues, as well as the costs incurred in raising and equipping them. Looking first at the 37 men who came forward on 24 September to declare themselves willing to serve, we have the advantage here that in most cases their ages, places of abode, and occupations were recorded.[71] Of the 34 whose age we know, the youngest was 16 and the oldest 33; the average age was a little over 24 years. There were 12 labourers (32 percent), 11 miners (30 percent), with the remaining trades including butchers, gardeners, weavers, a tailor, a carpenter, and a mason. Two men either had no occupation, or failed to give one. All of the 32 who gave a place of origin were from villages within a radius of six or seven miles extending to the north and west of Chatsworth, or from the market town of Bakewell four miles or so to the southwest. Five came from the estate village of Edensor and were no doubt already in the employ of the Cavendish family; most likely many of the others were too. Comparison with the main pay list indicates that not all of these men did, in fact, fully enter into service, and, of those who did, not all served from 24 September.[72] However, with the caveat that later recruiting was necessarily carried out further afield, they represent the best sample available of the types of men that Devonshire was able to sign up. A little older, perhaps, than the 'striplings' in the Derbyshire Blues, and, judging by the preponderance of miners and labourers, perhaps a hardier set of men into the bargain.

For the bulk of the men, however, we have no such details and the list of payments includes only names, dates of enlistment, wages, and bounties. Twenty-three men were enlisted on 24 September, seven on the 25th, 29 on the 26th, 22 on the 27th, eight on the 28th, one on the 29th, and 28 on the 30th. Three more enlistments on 1 and 2 October completed the results of the initial batch recruiting effort, bringing in a total of 121 men of whom 12 were horsemen. All received the two-Guinea bounty, with two exceptions. James Haymore for some reason only received a Guinea, and the first of the horsemen, John Dale, volunteered to serve without pay. As the only recruit distinguished as 'Mr', Dale was presumably a gentleman and it is to be inferred that he had the charge of the other 11 riders. Subsequent recruiting was rather more ad hoc. One man was signed up on 5 October, receiving only five shillings bounty, but two more who enlisted on the 12th each got £1, three shillings and sixpence. One man joined on 9 November, but received no bounty at all. Thereafter, other than Joseph Ratclife, who signed up as a drummer on 17 October, there was no further recruiting until late November; Ratclife received only five shillings bounty, but was paid the same shilling a day as his fellows. Presumably in response to the reality of the Jacobite threat to the county, enlistment was re-opened in late November, with 10 men signing up on the 26th and five more on the 28th. The bulk of these late-November recruits received only 10 shillings bounty, but one man received £1 and two more got £1 and 2 shillings. Lastly, on 10 December when the Chatsworth men had already completed their brief and inglorious spell

71   DCA, C6, Chatsworth Cash Book 1739-1756.
72   DCA, C/5/A/2, Chatsworth kitchen weekly accounts 1743-1745.

of active service, Jonathan Duckworth was taken on as an extra drummer; he received only five shillings as bounty, but was paid an extra thruppence a day on top of the shilling paid to his fellow drummer, Ratclife.[73]

Bounties and wages aside, the Chatsworth accounts also contain a substantial listing of other costs incurred as a consequence of the family's involvement in the Rising. In total, including the extra payment made later to Daniel Grant, these amount to £2,173, 16 shillings, 4½ pence – equating in modern terms to a little over a quarter of a million pounds.[74] Not all of these were military costs – most conspicuously, £12, one shilling and sixpence 'To Her Grace's Bills whilst at Blyth' – and others, such as charges for messengers, were related more to the Duke's wider role as Lord Lieutenant than to the administration of the men that he had raised. Within the military sphere, the costs break down as follows:[75]

Payments to Daniel Grant: £124, 19 shillings
As noted above, these were mostly not itemised and include unspecified reimbursements to the value of £99, 15 shillings, paid out at a later date.

Payments to Commissioned and Non-Commissioned officers: £135, six shillings
Does not include wage payments to Grant when acting as adjutant, included above. Does include bounty money and wages earned as private men by those who were subsequently made serjeants and corporals. Also includes gratuity of one Guinea to John Dale who otherwise served without pay as a horseman, on the assumption that his 'Mr' status made him, at the least, an NCO-equivalent.

Payments to Rank and File: £1,155, 3 shillings and sixpence
Enlistment bounties and wages of two drummers, 122 infantrymen, and 11 horsemen of the Chatsworth contingent. Includes in addition bounty payments to men who did not, in fact, serve, viz: 'To 75 men that came to offer themselves to enlist, some at 5s apiece and some at 2s/6d', £12, 5 shillings; 'To 10 more men that came to offer themselves' £1, 5 shillings, and payment 'To Mr Thornhill's Gardiner when he came w'th some men by my Lord's order', one Guinea. Also includes extra payments made to all Chatsworth men and to those of the Derbyshire Blues companies upon marching out of Derby, for which see below.

Uniforms, Weapons and Accoutrements: £326, five shillings and eightpence
Examples from this extensive list of charges include: 'To Major Nixon Gunsmith for 50 Bayonets & Scabbards, Making up Eight new Guns Cleaning and Mending those that were Broke &c as by his bill of particulars', £25, five shillings and tuppence; 'To Saml. Ashton for Screws for ye soldiers to Clean their Guns' £1, five shillings; 'To Messers Booth, Bingham, and Bakewell for Hats and Coats for 50 men as by bill', £89, four shillings; 'To Benj. Pidcock covering 100 Single Cartouch Boxes and finding belts at 1s 8d apiece', £8, six shillings and eightpence; 'To Messers Milnes & Co for Gunpowder as by bill', £22, nine shillings, 11½

---

73   DCA, C/5/A/2, Chatsworth kitchen weekly accounts 1743-1745.
74   Calculation by TNA, Currency Converter:1270-2017 at < https://www.nationalarchives.gov.uk/currency-converter/> accessed 28 May 2020.
75   All sums from listing in DCA, C/5/A/2, Chatsworth kitchen weekly accounts 1743-1745.

pence; 'To Benj. Walker Sadler for Furniture making & repairing & other work done for 12 Troop Horses as by bill' £21, 12 shillings, and 10 pence; 'To Thos Fogg making two Great Coats', six shillings; 'To Abram Weldon Shoemaker for 110 Frogs for ye Soldiers at 4d apiece', £1, 16 shillings and eightpence; 'To John Heward for Boots for the Horsemen', £7, 14 shillings and 11 pence.

Training and Equipment: £120, 12 shillings ha'penny
Charges for training relate to three Guineas 'To Lieutenant Longson's Corporal for his trouble helping to instruct the men', and the same for that officer's drummer. There was no Lieutenant Longson in the regular service at that date so most likely this was Lieutenant John Longsdon of Folliott's 61st Foot; that regiment was then in Ireland, where it served for the duration of its short existence, but it is by no means inconceivable that Longsdon was detached on recruiting duty, for which purposes he would, of course, require the services of a corporal and a drummer.[76] Rather more expensive, particularly when calculated on a per-head basis, was 10 Guineas 'To Mr Henry Elliott for instructing 12 horsemen in their exercise'. It is not clear who Mr Elliott was, or where he obtained his expertise. A further £92, five shillings paid for 'nine Horses for ye men', at costs ranging between six and 11 Guineas per animal. Other items classed here under 'equipment' relate to the construction of a cart for ammunition and a second for baggage.

Campaign Expenses: £138, two shillings and fourpence
It is not possible to be completely certain how strictly military some of these payments were – indeed, some, such as 10 shillings and sixpence 'To the poor at Mansfield' were certainly not – but for completeness' sake this list includes all charges incurred by Devonshire, Hartington, and any named officer (including those of the Blues companies) during the 16 days that the contingent was away from Chatsworth, including those for messengers, as well as more overtly military costs such as 'To the Wagoners for the Carriage of the arms &c from Derby to Nottingham their wages only', £5; 'Bill for the Guard room at Retford & for Fire two nights', £1, six shillings; 'To two horses to draw the Baggage Cart to Pentrich', five shillings. Charges relating to removing the Duchess to Blyth in South Yorkshire, along with the plate from Hardwick Hall, are not included.

Grand Total: £2,000, eight shillings 6½ pence
Nearly two-thirds of the total expenditure can therefore be seen to have been made on bounties and wages. Being able to pay the men and so keep them under arms was a challenge for many of the locally-raised corps during the '45, and would later pose problems for the Derbyshire association as we shall see.

Having now considered the raising of the Derbyshire Blues, and of the Chatsworth contingent, and investigated the internal economy of the latter insofar as the surviving accounts permit, it remains to detail the active service – if such is not too strong a term – of the combined Derbyshire forces in December 1745. The main sources for this are the

---

76   Personal communication from Dr J.A Houlding, 30 April 2020.

correspondence at Chatsworth – in particular an account written by Lord Hartington to a Dr R. Newcome on 14 December – and the *Chronicle of the Derbyshire Regiment*. The latter, it is clear, was written by someone well acquainted with the events being described, and, when one gets past the jibes and satire, it chimes with and illuminates Hartington's record. Whilst it cannot be conclusively demonstrated that the *Chronicle* pamphlet is of contemporary composition, the way in which it tallies with contemporary private accounts suggests that it was certainly not put together long after the events described, and the existence of a manuscript copy in the Derby Museums archives implies that it may well have been circulating in that form before it was printed in 1760.[77]

From the outset, it was not intended that the newly-raised provincial forces should directly oppose any Jacobite incursion unless in conjunction with regular forces. As Pelham stated to Devonshire even before the Jacobites had left Edinburgh: 'I doubt your provincial guard, if the Rebels come your way, will not be a sufficient security, I hope you will not think them so, and take care of yourself and family in time'.[78] At that stage, the Prime Minister's hopes were pinned on the forces being assembled at Doncaster and Newcastle under Field Marshal Wade, but as the Jacobites pushed further south a second force was assembled in Staffordshire under HRH the Duke of Cumberland. With his county situated between these two forces, Devonshire was obliged to coordinate his efforts with the commanders of both.

The initial practical contribution that Devonshire was able to make was in breaking up and obstructing the roads through the north-western portion of the Peak District. However, contrary to what has been suggested in some accounts, this work was not assigned to the Derbyshire Blues (who were from the wrong part of the county in any case), nor even to the Chatsworth contingent, but was carried out by civilian workers.[79] As Pelham later wrote to Hartington, 'The Duke [of Cumberland] seems much pleased with your father engaging to break up the roads in Derbyshire, if the times did not require more seriousness, I would crack a joke with you, upon his endeavouring to make Derbyshire roads more uneven than they naturally are'.[80]

Aside from giving the Prime Minister the opportunity to try out his sense of humour, the work, however, was wasted. Contrary to the expectations of the Duke of Cumberland, the Jacobites feinted into Staffordshire before heading towards Derby by way of Leek and Ashbourne. As Cumberland groped to pin down the location of the Jacobite forces, he drew on Devonshire for local knowledge, requesting on 30 November that he procure 'diligent & capable Persons & such as [are] thoroughly acquainted with the roads to observe closely

---

77   DM, DBYMU LDY:44, Book, The Acts of the Blues 1745.

78   DCA, CS1/249.25, Pelham to Devonshire, 28 September 1745.

79   DCA, CS1/327.1, Alexander Barker to Devonshire, [?] November 1745, discusses these plans; none of the named organisers correspond to men from the Chatsworth contingent, whilst reference is made to raising men locally for the purpose at Whalley Bridge and Chapel-en-le-Frith. Duffy, *Fight for a Throne*, p.217, agrees with this line; contrast with Alistair Massie & Jonathan Oates (eds.), *The Duke of Cumberland's Campaigns in Britain and the Low Countries, 1745-1748: A Selection of His Letters* (Stroud: History Press for the Army Records Society, 2018), p.107 which credits the work to the Derbyshire Blues.

80   DCA, CS1/249.31, Pelham to Hartington, 3 December 1745.

the Motions of the Rebels, & to bring or send accounts of them to Him',[81] and later the same day having his secretary, Sir Everard Fawkener, acknowledge 'very thankfully your Graces great vigilance & attention, & as the time is very critical earnestly desires you would use all possible means of getting the earliest notice of the motions of the Rebels, which He would have as soon as speedy communication of as may be'.[82] Three days later, with the Jacobites between Leek and Ashbourne, Cumberland wrote himself from Stone in Staffordshire to update Devonshire on his movements, adding as a postscript 'Should we come your way I hope that we shall find meat & bread for the soldiers'.[83]

All this activity, however, bore primarily on Devonshire in his role as Lord Lieutenant rather than as commander of the county's provincial forces. The Duke, it is true, had waited upon Cumberland at Lichfield on 29 November along with Lord Hartington and had offered the services of his men, but, as Hartington later relayed it, 'His Royal Highness thought himself strong enough, & I believe chose to trust the issue of a Battle entirely to his old Troops, yt were more to be depended upon'.[84] Nevertheless, on the same day Devonshire gave instructions via Hayne for 'all the captains to bring their companies to Derby as soon as possibly they can'. In reporting this to Curzon, Hayne went on to report that 'His Grace is in his military habit in the uniform with his captains, and intends to command the Corps de Garde'.[85] Having returned from their interview with Cumberland, the Duke and his son established their headquarters in Derby at the George and awaited the assembly of their forces, which was completed by the arrival of Edward Lowe's company on the evening of 3 December.[86]

With the men assembled, Devonshire made a payment of sixpence apiece to the private men of the Chatsworth contingent – or at least to most of them; the total accounted for equates to 130 men, which suggests that some may have been absent from the total of 122 foot and 12 horsemen – and paid out a further £1, two shillings and sixpence to each of the 12 captains for the same purpose.[87] No specific reason is given in the accounts for this payment, but it may well have gone to pay for food and drink, for the *Chronicle* notes that 'there was given to each man, a portion of bread and cheese, moreover, they had strong drink in abundance'.[88] Although the companies were reviewed by the Duke on the market-place, it seems that the final assembly of the combined forces took place on the Holmes, an area of open land on the other side of the River Derwent.[89]

At the time that the county forces assembled in Derby, the Jacobite vanguard was in Ashbourne where Lord George Murray had demanded billets for 3,000 men, but the bulk of Prince Charles' forces were still moving up through Leek. There was, therefore, no immediate danger but nor was there any immediate support, since Cumberland was at

81 DCA, CS1/331.1, Fawkener to of Devonshire, 30 November 1745.
82 DCA, CS1/331.2, Fawkener to of Devonshire, 30 November 1745.
83 DCA, CS1/332, Cumberland to Devonshire, 3 December 1745.
84 DCA, CS1/260.58, Hartington to Dr R. Newcome, 14 December 1745.
85 Hayne to Curzon, 29 November 1745, in Simpson, *A Collection of Fragments*, Vol.I, pp.249-250.
86 Account of *Derby Mercury*, 12 December 1745, reproduced in Simpson, *A Collection of Fragments*, Vol.I, p.252.
87 DCA, C/5/A/2, Chatsworth kitchen weekly accounts 1743-1745.
88 'Ben Shadai', *Chronicle*, p.5.
89 'Ben Shadai', *Chronicle*, p.4.

Stone and Wade far away at Boroughbridge in Yorkshire.[90] It is suggested in the *Chronicle* pamphlet that Devonshire sought to meet the Jacobite vanguard 'on the Plains of *Shirley*' – that is to say, near the village of that name, around 10 miles out of Derby in the direction of Ashbourne – but that the men 'hearkened not to the voice of D--h--re' and 'every man took up his weapons and prepared to flee'.[91] Such conduct, if it had been in the Duke's mind, would probably have exposed his men to rout or destruction on 4 December, for the bulk of the Jacobite army was in Derby by the end of that day, having made another of its prodigious marches, and would surely have overwhelmed the 700-odd raw volunteers had it met them along the way. Hartington in his account makes no mention of any such thinking, glossing over the decision by simply noting 'as it was impossible for us to think of resisting their whole force, we retired to Nottingham'.[92] At around 10 o'clock that night, the men marched out by torchlight.[93]

Having been unable to cooperate with Cumberland's army, and with a solo defence of the county town clearly not realistic, the question now remained as to what Devonshire and his men might usefully accomplish. Resurrecting the idea of a rear guard action to delay a Jacobite advance, Hartington recorded that, on the 4th, 'we had some consultations there about maintaining a Pass over a small Brook between the town & Derby, but upon examination it did not prove tenable' – Stone suggests that this brook was probably the River Leen, which flows south through what are now the western suburbs of Nottingham to join the Trent.[94] No thought seems to have been given to securing the strategically more important crossing of the Trent itself at Swarkestone, the bloodless securing of which by the Jacobites marked the 'high-water mark' of Charles' march southwards. A march to Swarkestone, however, would have taken Devonshire and his men towards Cumberland, whereas there seems instead to have been an assumption – perhaps stemming from Cumberland's polite refusal of their help – that the Derbyshire men ought instead to coordinate their efforts with Field Marshal Wade. Seeking as ever to put the worst possible interpretation on events, the *Chronicle* suggests that this stemmed from a reasoning that 'if we join ourselves unto [Cumberland], we shall be in great danger; but if we join ourselves unto W--d--e, then we shall be safe, for behold he is a peaceable man'.[95]

Having considered and then abandoned the idea of making a stand outside Nottingham, the decision was taken to continue the march and move some 15 miles northwards to Mansfield. Before doing so, it was arranged that the arms and gunpowder stored at Nottingham Castle should be taken away for safekeeping since there was otherwise no means of preventing these stores falling into Jacobite hands. This further movement took place on 5 December, presumably in the afternoon as the men had not reached Nottingham until 5 o'clock in the

90 Frank McLynn, *The Jacobite Army in England 1745: The Last Campaign* (Edinburgh, John Donald, 1998), pp.116-117.
91 'Ben Shadai', *Chronicle*, p.4.
92 DCA, CS1/260.58, Hartington to Newcome, 14 December 1745.
93 Account of *Derby Mercury*, 12 December 1745, reproduced in Simpson, *A Collection of Fragments*, Vol.I, p.252.
94 DCA, CS1/260.58, Hartington to Newcome, 14 December 1745; Stone, *Highland Army in Derby*, p.87.
95 'Ben Shadai', *Chronicle*, p.4.

morning of the 5th and were in a state of some fatigue.[96] March discipline does not seem to have been of the best, if the *Chronicle* can be at all trusted on this point. On the night march from Derby to Nottingham, when passing through the village of Borrowash, it is said that 'they made war upon the poultry; moreover they did eat plentifully, and drank much strong drink, and departed, forgetting to pay' – which seems a difficult feat to manage, considering the lateness of the hour, and may well represent an exaggeration.[97] More believable is the story that, on the march to Mansfield, a false report that the Jacobites were almost upon them caused the boastful Ensign 'Me--lls' to reveal his true nature and call out 'halt, ye men in front, for our rear is sorely pressed, and we shall inevitably be cut off', and that, notwithstanding his call being met with derision, something of a panic ensued.[98]

At Mansfield, greater security was provided by the arrival that night of Montagu's Carbineers, summoned up from Loughborough at Devonshire's instigation,[99] and it seemed for a time that this was a position that could be held safely until Wade and his army had come up. However, as Hartington related, 'we had a false alarm that made us move our Quarter again', the circumstances being as follows:

> We had had flying reports most part [sic] of the Day that the Rebels were advancing our way, which we had given no credit to, but on the contrary had sent a Captain with one Company to take Quarters in the Road towards Derby, in order to return there as soon as the Highlanders had left it, imagining that they wou'd have gone, directly for London just as it was growing dark our Captain returned & assur'd us that he had seen the Rebels to the number of three or four Thousand within two miles of the Town, & this being also confirmed by other advices [sic], we thought it was <u>prudent</u> to get out of their way & we went to Retford, which brought us very near the Van Guard of Mr Wade's Army, but upon enquiry the Rebels had never stirrd all that Day from Derby except in small partys[sic], to plunder & seize horses, which made the County people drive off their Cattle in great Bodies which occasiond [sic] that alarm.[100]

Inevitably, given such material, the composer of the *Chronicle* did not have to try hard to make mock of the panicked withdrawal that ensued. The men of Edward Lowe's company, it is claimed, asked 'Captain, what shall we do to be saved, and he answered them run lads run, and he turned his back and fled and they follow'd him. This was done that the words of the Captain might be fulfilled, when he spoke unto *Cope* the Esquire, saying my men will follow me wherever I go'.[101] The narrative does not make it clear whether it was Lowe who was the captain responsible for causing the alarm, or whether he was caught up in the panic at Mansfield. It was no doubt amidst this confusion that Thomas Sharpless, a recent recruit in the Chatsworth contingent, took the opportunity to desert. Sharpless had signed up on

96   Eardley-Simpson, *Derby in the 'Forty-Five*, p.141.
97   'Ben Shadai', *Chronicle*, p.5.
98   'Ben Shadai', *Chronicle*, pp.6-7.
99   Duffy, *Fight for a Throne*, p.229.
100   DCA, CS1/260.58, Hartington to Newcome, 14 December 1745.
101   'Ben Shadai', *Chronicle*, p.7.

28 November, receiving a Guinea as bounty, and had also pocketed a further three shillings in wages since then: altogether, not a bad haul for a week's service.[102]

Hartington makes no mention of the panic, but his account and that of the *Chronicle* do confirm that this removal from Mansfield took place on the afternoon and evening of 5 December, and not the night before, as Christopher Duffy – who also seems to take the *Chronicle* account rather too much at face value – asserts. Nor was it the case that the Blues made their way to Retford by way of Southwell and Newark as Duffy implies.[103] Most likely this route was that taken by Montagu's Carbineers, who were also caught up in the hurried evacuation; payments for guides and carriages confirm that Devonshire's men took a far more direct route by way of Mansfield Woodhouse and Worksop.[104]

Direct or not, the march to Retford was, as narrated in the *Chronicle*'s account, just as disorderly as the departure from Mansfield. After suggesting that the men were rousted out of Mansfield in a state of inebriation, the account continues:

> And one of these men lost in the flight a warlike instrument called a drum, yet he turned not back to look after it.
>
> And Gr--tt--n the Lieutenant, came riding furiously, and he whipped his horse cruelly, saying flee swiftly, for on thy speed dependeth my life.
>
> And he saw not the drum, but rode upon it and burst it, and the noise therefore was like the report of a great gun; and the beast was in a fright and threw his rider on the ground, and he roared terribly, crying oh! I am slain, and the stench of this man was grievous to be born.[105]

Whether or not one takes these added details as fact, gossip, or plain fiction, it is safe to say that, whatever the reality, the lasting popular memory of the Derbyshire Blues was not of their military prowess!

Having made it safely to Retford and belatedly established that the threat to their post at Mansfield had been bovine rather than Jacobite, the remaining sojourn of Devonshire's men was anticlimactic. Devonshire was in contact with Wade,[106] but the latter's troops never came so far south as to link up with the men at Retford. Meanwhile, the Jacobite council of war had made the decision to withdraw northwards rather than continue the march on London, so that, after two nights at Retford, 'As soon as the Scotch were gone we return'd to Derby', as Hartington rather blandly put it.[107] One of the Chatsworth men was left behind sick at Retford, but presumably made his own way back home at a later date since only the deserter Sharpless is recorded as having left the contingent during this time.[108]

102 DCA, C/5/A/2, Chatsworth kitchen weekly accounts 1743-1745.
103 Duffy, *Fight for a Throne*, p.229.
104 DCA, C/5/A/2, Chatsworth kitchen weekly accounts 1743-1745.
105 'Ben Shadai', *Chronicle*, p.8.
106 DCA, CS1/333, Wade to Devonshire, 6 December 1745.
107 DCA, CS1/260.58, Hartington to Newcome, 14 December 1745.
108 DCA, C/5/A/2, Chatsworth kitchen weekly accounts 1743-1745.

Hartington expressed surprise, upon returning to Derby, 'to find they have done so little damage',[109] but one consequence of the Jacobite occupation was that the list of subscribers to the association had been seized, and those who had paid, and could be found, were obliged to make a like contribution to the Jacobite war-chest – 'tho' one half had been paid before', as one such unfortunate associator complained.[110] The result was that there were no funds remaining to keep the 12 Derbyshire Blues companies in pay, and they were accordingly disbanded. The Chatsworth men, however, remained under arms and in pay through until 18 February 1746. Whilst the threat from Scotland had seemingly passed, fears of a French invasion were still seriously entertained,[111] and Devonshire was also concerned that a second Jacobite army had been allowed to form in Scotland while Prince Charles was in England. Writing on 1 January to Hartington, who had returned to London, the Duke remarked that:

> If there be any probability of the rebels returning my opinion is that the well affected in the northern counties should join together wch might raise a consider-able number of men. I think we should soon have the same number as before & I believe more. I think those countries that have been visited by the Rebels do not desire to see them again.[112]

With all this in mind, the men at Chatsworth were retained under arms. However, discipline during this period seems to have fallen off somewhat, in common with the situation in a number of the other units raised for the emergency. In this case, with the men not forming part of the regular British Army, and therefore not subject to the Mutiny Act, maintaining discipline by consent must have represented a particular challenge. George Booth, a 33-year-old labourer, was struck off the list on 1 January, marked as 'Discharged Getting Drunk &c', as was John Plant on the same day 'for behaving ill to ye Capt.'. On 14 January William Bradwell was 'Discharged refusing to Exercise' and on 12 February 25-year-old labourer Jonathan Rippon of Pilsley was 'Dismissed for insulting Capt. Johnson'. The Chatsworth contingent also suffered its only fatality during this period: James Haymore's service came to an end on 29 January, recorded by the pay-list annotation 'This man was lost on ye moor and fell into a Mine (was kill'd)'.[113]

With the disbanding of Devonshire's men at Chatsworth on 18 February, Derbyshire's contribution to the suppression of the Rising came to an end. Little practical benefit had come from the service of the Derbyshire Blues or from Devonshire's abortive regimental project. The Cavendishes, through their lavish expenditure, had affirmed their commit-ment to the status quo, and although the Duke's political career was winding down, that of Hartington – who succeeded his father to become the 4th Duke of Devonshire in December

---

109 DCA, CS1/260.58, Hartington to Newcome, 14 December 1745.
110 DCA, CS1/318.9, A true relation of the behaviour of the rebels in Derby [December 1745] by William Bateman, town clerk, 19 May 1746; see also McLynn, *Invasion of England*, p.123.
111 DCA, CS1/249.33, Pelham to Devonshire, 17 December 1745.
112 DCA, CS1/163.9, Devonshire to Hartington, 1 January 1746.
113 DCA, C/5/A/2, Chatsworth kitchen weekly accounts 1743-1745; additional personal details for Booth and Rippon, who were both amongst the first batch of men to volunteer on 24 September, from DCA, C6, Chatsworth Cash Book 1739-1756.

1755 – continued to flourish with a spell as Lord Lieutenant of Ireland and a brief and unsatisfactory stint as caretaker Prime Minister. Whether those who had served at a lower level obtained any advantage through their service is harder to discover, but one suspects that the benefits were limited considering the lack of respect in which the Derbyshire Blues were held after their disbandment – 'called drivers of cattle unto this very day', according to the *Chronicle*.[114]

Embarrassing though service with the Blues may have been to many, it did not put young Tristram Revell off the idea of a military career. Within months of completing his service as ensign in Captain Buckston's company, his Wilmot patrons had helped him purchase an ensigncy in Reade's 9th Foot on 25 August 1746 and then his step to lieutenant in 1753. The expansion of the Army on the outbreak of the Seven Years War saw him obtain his captaincy, and he served with Lambton's 68th in the descents on the French coast and subsequently with Cornwallis' 24th in Germany. Retiring from the regular service in 1771, he became a major in the Derbyshire Militia two years later, and eventually its lieutenant colonel.[115] Conversely, two of his superior officers forsook the sword for the sake of the Church: Chambers Bate was ordained in 1748, becoming domestic chaplain to his uncle the Earl of Exeter,[116] and Chaworth Hallows in 1757 became Rector of Pleasley.[117] The other officers, insofar as anything more is known of them, settled back into their previous lifestyles.

As for the men who served in the ranks, inevitably even less is known. One closing point may be made however, which relates not to what they did but what they did not do. For all that Eardley-Simpson sought in his history to portray Derbyshire as a hotbed of Jacobitism, the actual support received by Charles and his army was limited. Through the efforts of the association and of Devonshire, not only had such arms as were in store in the county been swept up and carried off, but likewise many of the useful riding horses and, perhaps most importantly, a great many of the county's young men. Whereas over 700 Derbyshire men signed up for the cause of George II, Charles' time in Derby netted him a grand total of three recruits.[118] Simply by denying the Jacobites access to this manpower and material, something at least had been achieved through the mobilisation of the county's resources.

---

114 'Ben Shadai', *Chronicle*, p.8.
115 Williams, 'The Revell family of Carnfield', p.156; obituary notice in *Gentleman's Magazine*, 1797, p.355; personal communication from Dr J.A. Houlding, 8 June 2020.
116 Entries for Chambers Bate at *ACAD A Cambridge Alumni Database* <http://venn.lib.cam.ac.uk/>, and *The Clergy Database* <https://theclergydatabase.org.uk/>, both accessed 9 June 2020.
117 Entry for Chaworth Hallows at *ACAD A Cambridge Alumni Database* <http://venn.lib.cam.ac.uk/>, accessed 9 June 2020.
118 Simpson, *A Collection of Fragments*, Vol.I, p.259.

Appendix I: Organisation and Orders of Battle

Disposition of Forces in British Isles at the Outbreak of the Rising[1]

In Scotland under Lieutenant General Sir John Cope were the following units:
    Gardiner's 13th Dragoons
    Hamilton's 14th Dragoons
    Guise's 6th Foot*
    Lee's 55th Foot (five companies only; remainder at Berwick-upon-Tweed and counted below)
    Murray's 57th Foot
    Lascelles' 58th Foot
    Loudoun's 64th Highlanders (raising)
    Nine additional companies belonging to regiments serving in Flanders: 1st (2), 21st (2), 25th (2), and 43rd (3)

In England were:
    1st and 2nd Troops of Horse Guards
    1st Troop of Horse Grenadier Guards
    1st Foot Guards (18 companies = 2 battalions)
    Coldstream Guards (9 companies = 1 battalion)
    3rd Foot Guards (9 companies = 1 battalion)
    Montagu's 3rd Horse
    Wade's 4th Horse
    St George's 8th Dragoons
    Cobham's 10th Dragoons
    Kerr's 11th Dragoons
    Houghton's 24th Foot*
    Blakeney's 27th Foot*
    Frampton's 30th Foot**
    Richbell's 39th Foot**

---

1   Sourced primarily from C.T. Atkinson, 'Jenkins' Ear, The Austrian Succession War and the 'Forty-Five: Gleanings from the Sources in the Public Record Office', *Journal of the Society for Army Historical Research*, Vol.XXII No 91 (Autumn 1944), pp.280-298, with additional details from Stuart Reid, *Cumberland's Culloden Army 1745-46* (Oxford: Osprey, 2012) and certain of Richard Cannon's regimental histories.

Lee's 55th Foot (five companies)
32 additional companies belonging to regiments serving in Flanders

In Ireland were:
Brown's 5th Horse
Wentworth's 6th Horse
Bowles' 7th Horse
Molesworth's 5th Dragoons
De Grangues' 9th Dragoons
Whitshed's 12th Dragoons
2/1st Royal Regiment of Foot*
Irwin's 5th Foot
Otway's 35th Foot
Bruce's 60th Foot
Folliott's 61st Foot
Battereau's 62nd Foot

* Regiments being brought back up to strength after service in West Indies.
** Regiments having two companies stationed in the Channel Islands and large detachments serving with the fleet in the Channel.

Cope's Army

Of the forces outlined above, the majority of Guise's 6th Foot was garrisoning the Highland forts: Fort William (3 Coys.) Fort Augustus (3 Coys.), Inverness (2 Coys.), Bernera Barracks (1 Coy.), Ruthven Barracks (1 Coy.), Isle of Mull (one officer and 18 men).[2] The weak additional companies of the 1st Royals were sent from Fort Augustus to reinforce the Fort William garrison but were captured by the Jacobites at Highbridge on 16 August. The additional companies of the 21st Royal North British Fusiliers garrisoned Dumbarton Castle and those of Sempill's 25th Foot Stirling Castle.[3]
   Cope took the following forces into the Highlands in August:
Murray's 43rd Highlanders (two additional companies)
Lee's 55th Foot (five companies)
Murray's 57th Foot
Lascelles' 58th Foot (eight companies; two left at Edinburgh Castle)
Artillery train of four 1½-pounder cannon and 4 coehorn mortars

The remaining additional company of Murray's 43rd, that of Captain Duncan Campbell of Inverawe, was sent to Inveraray to support the local magistrates. Gardiner's 13th and

---

2   Arran Johnston, *On Gladsmuir Shall the Battle Be! The Battle of Prestonpans 1745* (Solihull: Helion, 2017), p.74.
3   Reid, *Cumberland's Culloden Army*, p.18.

Hamilton's 14th Dragoons were retained around Edinburgh, initially under Colonel James Gardiner and then under Brigadier Thomas Fowke.[4]

After the failure of his Highland campaign, and the equally dismal performance of the dragoons in the Lowlands, Cope re-concentrated his forces at Dunbar so as to march against the Jacobites who had taken Edinburgh. In shipping his forces back from Inverness, Cope left behind one of the additional companies of Murray's 43rd, that of Captain Aeneas Mackintosh, which had dwindled through desertion to between eight and 15 men.[5] He picked up, however, the two companies of Guise's 6th Foot and three understrength companies of Loudoun's 64th Highlanders.[6] His formal order of battle for the Prestonpans campaign therefore stood as follows (troops given in intended deployment, right to left):[7]

Lieutenant General Sir John Cope, commanding
Brigadier Thomas Fowke, second-in-command
Right Wing, Colonel Peregrine Lascelles
    Gardiner's 13th Dragoons (2 squadrons)
    Lee's 55th Foot (5 companies)
    Lascelles' 58th Foot (8 companies)
    Guise's 6th Foot (2 companies, attached to Lascelles')
Left Wing, Colonel James Gardiner
    Murray's 57th Foot
    Hamilton's 14th Dragoons (2 squadrons)
Corps de Reserve, deployed as a second line
    Gardiner's 13th Dragoons (1 squadron)
    Edinburgh Volunteers
    Highland Battalion (one company 43rd, three companies 64th)
    Hamilton's 14th Dragoons (1squadron)
Artillery Train
    Six 1½-pounder cannon (a pair on each flank of the foot, and a pair between the two wings)
    Four small and two large coehorn mortars (deployed together on the right of the foot)

The rank and file strengths of the regular units stood as follows: the two dragoon regiments together (567); Lee's 55th (291); Murray's 57th (580); Lascelles' 58th and attached companies of Guise's 6th (570); Highland Battalion (183).[8] For details of the Edinburgh Volunteers, see Chapter 4.

---

4   Stuart Reid, *1745: A Military History of the Last Jacobite Rising* (Staplehurst: Spellmount, 1996) p.16.
5   I.A. Davidson, 'Some Notes on the Participation of the Three 'Additional' Companies of Lord John Murray's Highland Regiment During the 1745 Rebellion and its Aftermath', *Journal of the Society for Army Historical Research*, Vol.82, No,331 (Autumn 2004) pp. 255-259 (p.257).
6   Walter Biggar Blakie, *Itinerary of Prince Charles Edward Stuart* (Edinburgh: Scottish Accademic Press, 1975), p.90.
7   Based on a plan in the Royal Collection, RCIN 729153 A Plan of the Battle at Preston-Pans, by William Eyres, at <https://militarymaps.rct.uk/other-18th-19th-century-conflicts/order-of-battle-at-prestonpans-1745-a-plan-of>, viewed 22 June 2020.
8   Blakie, *Itinerary*, p.90.

The actual deployment on the morning of 21 September was not quite as above, due to the sudden nature of the Jacobite assault. All the artillery was on the right, covered by an artillery-guard detached from the foot. The outward picquets of the army were unable to re-join their parent regiments and also fell in on the right. The command distribution with Lascelles and Gardiner in charge of wings does not seem to have been followed. The Highland Battalion was serving as a guard to the army's baggage at Cockenzie House and was captured en-masse after the main action. All of the artillery was lost; the surviving foot and dragoons regrouped at Berwick, where those companies of Lee's 55th with Cope were reunited with the other five.

Reinforcements and Redeployments

Troops were recalled from Flanders in several waves. The first of these, under Lieutenant General Sir John Ligonier, comprised:
  1st Foot Guards (10 companies = one battalion)
  Coldstream Guards (9 companies = one battalion)
  3rd Foot Guards (9 companies = one battalion)
  Sowle's 11th Foot
  Pulteney's 13th Foot
  Howard's 19th Foot
  Bragg's 28th Foot
  Douglas' 32nd Foot
  Johnson's 33rd Foot
  Cholmondeley's 34th Foot

These were battalions whose casualties at Fontenoy had been replaced by drafts, and numbered in total 245 officers and 7,269 other ranks. They disembarked on the Thames from 25 September, with Pulteney's and Cholmondeley's earmarked to join the force being assembled in the north-east of England under Field Marshal George Wade.[9] The Dutch contingent also began to be shipped across at this time, the Regiment de la Rocque narrowly missing arriving in time for Prestonpans and instead joining Cope at Berwick.

Regular forces within the British Isles were also mobilised: Lieutenant General Thomas Wentworth was sent into the north of England with five companies of Blakeney's 27th, two regiments of horse, and the Dutch Regiment Zwitsers van Hirzel, and orders were given for 2/1st Royals and Battereau's 62nd Foot to be brought over from Ireland after being made up to 1,000 men apiece by drafts.[10] Three Provisional Battalions were formed by collecting additional companies per orders of 8 and 9 September, as follows:
  Under Colonel Robert Fraser of 2nd Marines, Coys. of 3rd, 19th, 31st, 33rd, and 37th
  Under Colonel John Duncombe of 8th Marines, Coys. of 4th, 11th, 13th, 28th, 32nd, and 34th

---

9   Atkinson, 'Jenkins' Ear, The Austrian Succession War and the 'Forty-Five', pp.291-292; see also Chapter 2 of this work.
10   Reid, *1745*, p.45.

Under Colonel John Cottrell of 6th Marines, Coys. of 8th, 12th, 20th, 23rd, 36th, and 59th.

Duncombe's Battalion was posted to relieve Houghton's 24th Foot guarding prisoners of war at Plymouth and Cottrell's to relieve Richbell's 39th at Portsmouth (this in lieu of previous orders that would have sent it to garrison Carlisle Castle). Fraser's Battalion was posted to Newcastle-upon-Tyne. The men from Richbell's who were detached with the fleet were ordered to be returned, as were those of Frampton's 30th. The former regiment was to concentrate at Dartford and the latter at Canterbury.[11]

At the end of September, a further reinforcement from Flanders was ordered, comprising:
Provisional Battalion of Foot Guards
Howard's 3rd Foot
Barrell's 4th Foot
Wolfe's 8th Foot
Price's 14th Foot
Fleming's 36th Foot
Munro's 37th Foot
Ligonier's 59th Foot

The Guards went to London to return to their parent regiments, the remaining seven battalions to Newcastle although their passage was hindered by storms. Mounted units were also ordered to return from Flanders, instructions being issued for the recall of:
Ligonier's 8th Horse
1st Royal Dragoons
Bland's 3rd Dragoons
Rich's 4th Dragoons

The last-named was much-reduced, through losses at Melle and in the fall of Ghent. In the event, insufficient horse transports meant that only Ligonier's and Bland's could sail in the first instance. The remaining 11 battalions still on the continent were all also preparing to embark by mid-October, Harrison's 15th and Mordaunt's 18th arriving in the Thames on 7 November.[12]

11   Atkinson, 'Jenkins' Ear, The Austrian Succession War and the 'Forty-Five', pp.291-293; Reid, *1745*, p.58; Reid, *Cumberland's Culloden Army*, p.18; Neil Bannatyne, *History of the Thirtieth Regiment* (Liverpool: Littlebury Bros., 1923) pp.124-125.
12   Atkinson, 'Jenkins' Ear, The Austrian Succession War and the 'Forty-Five', pp.292-293.

Wade's Army

By the first week of November, Wade was able to assemble the bulk of his Anglo-Dutch army around Newcastle, uniting the forces that had sailed to the Tyne with those that had marched up through England. Its organisation stood as follows:[13]

Field Marshal George Wade, commanding
Lieutenant General Lord Tyrawley, second-in-command
Lieutenant Generals Thomas Wentworth and Roger Handasyd; Major Generals Charles Howard, John Huske, and James Oglethorpe

1st Brigade, Brigadier General John Mordaunt
    2/1st Royals
    Wolfe's 8th Foot
    Blakeney's 27th Foot (five companies)
    Munro's 37th Foot
2nd Brigade, Brigadier General James Cholmondeley
    Howard's 3rd Foot
    Pulteney's 13th Foot
    Cholmondeley's 34th Foot
    Ligonier's 59th Foot
    Thornton's Yorkshire Volunteers (attached to Pulteney's 13th Foot; see Chapters 2 and
        6)
3rd Brigade, Brigadier General James Fleming
    Barrell's 4th Foot
    Price's 14th Foot
    Fleming's 36th Foot
    Battereau's 62nd Foot
Mounted Troops
    Montagu's 3rd Horse
    Wade's 4th Horse
    St George's 8th Dragoons
    Georgia Rangers
    Yorkshire Hunters
Artillery Train
    Sixteen 3-pounders
    Eight 1½-pounders

---

13   Jonathan Oates, 'The Responses in North East England to the Jacobite Rebellions of 1715 and 1745' (PhD Thesis, Reading University, 2001), pp.647-648, citing TNA, SP36/70; details of artillery train and identities of Dutch brigadiers from a later order of battle in the Royal Collection, discussed in more detail below: RCIN 730008, Ordre de Bataille de l'Armée commandée par S.E. Le Feldt Marechal Wade 1746, anonymous, at <https://militarymaps.rct.uk/other-18th-19th-century-conflicts/order-of-battle-1746-england-ordre-de-bataille>, viewed 23 June 2020.

Dutch Contingent, General Count Maurice of Nassau, with Lieutenant General
Schwartzenberg and Major General Villattes
1st Brigade, Brigadier Evertsen
    Regiment Zwitsers van Hirzel (3 battalions)
    Regiment Holstein-Gottorp
2nd Brigade, Brigadier Grotenray
    Regiment de la Rocque
    Regiment van Brakel
    Regiment Patot
    Regiment Villattes
Artillery Train
    Ten coehorn mortars

It is not clear what the command arrangements for the mounted troops were. Oglethorpe appears to have had charge of the Georgia Rangers and Yorkshire Hunters, and some accounts credit him with command of all the cavalry but this may be a misunderstanding based on his later command of a mounted flying column, for which see below. Other than the three-battalion Swiss regiment, the Dutch regiments were all of one battalion; it is not clear where the idea that several were of two battalions apiece, repeated by Duffy and Reid, originates.[14] It is noted that one battalion of Dutch was at Berwick; this was presumably the Regiment de la Rocque, which had landed there after failing to reinforce Cope.[15]

One point to notice, which is a recurring organisational feature seen throughout this campaign and also in the continental deployments of the British Army in the 1740s and 1750s, is the very formalised distribution of regiments into brigades by seniority. Thus, in the case above, with three brigades of four battalions each, the senior brigade has the regiments 1st, 4th, 7th, and 10th in seniority, the next the 2nd, 5th, 8th, and 11th, and the junior brigade the 3rd, 6th, 9th, and 12th. This methodology can therefore be applied to suggest the likely brigading of forces where this level of detail is not given in the available sources.

This organisation remained in place for Wade's army until 9 November, when Lieutenant General Handasyd was detached with Prices 14th Foot and Ligonier's 59th Foot in order to reoccupy Edinburgh. Passing Berwick, he added to his infantry the two dragoon regiments that had fled from Prestonpans: Ligonier's (late Gardiner's) 13th and Hamilton's 14th. The Ligonier who had obtained the colonelcy of the 13th Dragoons in the stead of James Gardiner, killed at Prestonpans, was Francis of that ilk, brother of the lieutenant general. Francis Ligonier – unusually – also retained his existing colonelcy of the 59th Foot.[16]

---

14   On this point, and for correct spellings of Dutch unit names, see Marc-Geerdink-Schaftenaar, *For Orange and the States: The Army of the Dutch Republic 1713-1772* (Warwick: Helion, 2018), Part I: Infantry.
15   Christopher Duffy, *Fight for a Throne: The Jacobite '45 Reconsidered* (Solihull: Helion, 2015), p.186.
16   See Reid, *1745*, p.56; N.B. Leslie, *The Succession of Colonels of the British Army From 1660 to the Present Day* (London and Aldershot: Gale and Polden Ltd. for the Society of Army Historical Research, 1974), pp.28, 84.

The main body of Wade's forces therefore underwent a reorganisation, which more closely integrated the Dutch and British troops and is set out in a sketched order of battle in the Royal Collection:[17]

Field Marshal George Wade, commander-in-chief
General Count Maurice of Nassau commanding the Dutch Contingent

First Line, Lieutenant Generals Lord Tyrawley and Schwartzenberg, Major Generals Charles Howard, James Oglethorpe
Right-Wing Cavalry
    St George's 8th Dragoons (1 squadron)
    Montagu's 3rd Horse (1 squadron)
1st Brigade, Brigadier General John Mordaunt
    2/1st Royals
    Cholmondeley's 34th Foot
    Wolfe's 8th Foot
3rd Brigade, unknown commander
    Blakeney's 27th Foot (five companies)
    Munro's 37th Foot
    Barrell's 4th Foot
1st Brigade (Dutch), Brigadier Evertsen
    Regiment Zwitsers van Hirzel (3 battalions)
Left-Wing Cavalry
    Wade's 4th Horse (1 squadron)
    St George's 8th Dragoons (2 squadrons)

Second Line, Lieutenant General Thomas Wentworth, Major Generals John Huske and Villattes
Right-Wing Cavalry
    Montagu's 3rd Horse (2 squadrons)
2nd Brigade, Brigadier General James Cholmondeley
    Howard's 3rd Foot
    Pulteney's 13th Foot
    Fleming's 36th Foot
2nd Brigade (Dutch), Brigadier Grotenray
    Regiment Villattes
    Regiment de la Rocque
    Regiment Holstein-Gottorp
    Regiment van Brakel
Left-Wing Cavalry
    Wade's 4th Horse (2 squadrons)

---

17   RCIN 730008, Ordre de Bataille de l'Armée commandée par S.E. Le Feldt Marechal Wade 1746, anonymous, at <https://militarymaps.rct.uk/other-18th-19th-century-conflicts/order-of-battle-1746-england-ordre-de-bataille>, viewed 23 June 2020. Units given as deployed, right to left.

Corps de Reserve, Colonel Patot (Dutch)
    Battereau's 62nd Foot
    Regiment Patot (Dutch)
Artillery Train
    Sixteen 3-pounders
    Eight 1½-pounders
    Ten coehorn mortars (Dutch)

The Yorkshire Hunters and Georgia Rangers are not included in this listing, but were certainly still present as they were engaged in the action at Clifton on 18 December. The same applies to Thornton's volunteer company, which remained with the army until after Falkirk. The disappearance of Brigadier Fleming from the command structure is also noteworthy. It would seem most likely that he accompanied Handasyd to Scotland: certainly he was there by 12 December, on which date Cumberland noted him as being 'worn out by age and infirmitys'.[18] In the absence of a general officer, it is suggested that the 3rd Brigade would have been under Colonel Sir Robert Munro of the 37th Foot who was the only full colonel present with his regiment in that brigade, Barrell and Blakeney being general officers and serving elsewhere.

Establishing the strength of Wade's forces is somewhat problematic, with newspaper reports at the time crediting him with as many as 14,000 foot and 4,000 cavalry.[19] Individual unit strengths are not available but on 3 December, after the detachment of Handasyd's division, the British foot amounted to 6,701 effectives and 753 sick, for a total of 7,454, while the horse and dragoons amounted to 805 effectives and 111 sick, for a total of 916.[20] It is not clear whether the volunteer horse and foot, or the Georgia Rangers, are included in this total. Insofar as the latter are concerned, there were 128 private rangers at the beginning of the campaign, of whom 88 were still present when the detachment finally sailed for Georgia in May 1746.[21] For an estimate of the strength of the Yorkshire Hunters, see Appendix to Chapter 6; Thornton's Volunteers were still 64-strong at Falkirk (see below) so much have numbered at least that while serving with Wade.

Figures for the Dutch contingent are contradictory. Strengths in October 1745 were given in round numbers as 1,700 for the all three battalions of Hirzel's, and 500 apiece for the five single-battalion regiments, giving a total of 4,200.[22] However, figures for 3 December give 7,159 present, 559 absent, and 909 sick: assuming that the 559 'absent' men refer to Regiment de la Rocque at Berwick, this puts the other battalions well over-strength and so calls the accuracy of these figures into question.[23]

18 Alistair Massie & Jonathan Oates (eds.), *The Duke of Cumberland's Campaigns in Britain and the Low Countries, 1745-1748: A Selection of His Letters* (Stroud: History Press for the Army Records Society, 2018), p.122.
19 Blakie, *Itinerary*, p.95.
20 Figures from Jonathan Oates, 'Field Marshal Wade and the Forty-Five', *Journal of the Society for Army Historical Research*, Vol.84, No.338 (Summer 2006), pp.95-108 (p.103).
21 Duffy, *Fight for a Throne*, p.346.
22 Oates, 'The Responses in North East England to the Jacobite Rebellions of 1715 and 1745', pp.647-648, citing TNA, SP36/70.
23 Figures from Oates, 'Field Marshal Wade and the Forty-Five', p.103.

The Lichfield Army

At the same time as Wade's forces were assembling in the north-east, a second force was being drawn together in the West Midlands under Lieutenant General Ligonier. Nominally subordinate to Wade, this force was in practice independent and command of it was later assumed by Cumberland in person. The composition of this force was somewhat fluid, and a precise order of battle on any given date is difficult to pin down; it would be better to consider this less as a complete army and more as a body of troops that were never fully brought together (although a tentative 'ideal world' brigade structure is suggested below). The following published list, compiled from a variety of primary sources, gives what seems to be the intended composition of this force:[24]

HRH the Duke of Cumberland, commanding
Lieutenant Generals Sir John Ligonier, James St Clair, and the Duke of Richmond
Major Generals Humphrey Bland and Henry Skelton
Brigadier Generals Lord Sempill, William Douglas, and Thomas Bligh

Mounted Troops
    Ligonier's 8th Horse (4 troops)
    Montagu's 9th Carbineers*
    Kingston's 10th Light Horse*
    Bland's 3rd Dragoons
    Cobham's 10th Dragoons
    Kerr's 11th Dragoons
Foot Guards
    1st Foot Guards (1 battalion)
    Coldstream Guards (1 battalion)
    3rd Foot Guards (1 battalion)
Regiments of Foot
    Sowle's 11th Foot
    Skelton's 12th Foot
    Howard's 19th Foot
    Bligh's 20th Foot
    21st Royal North British Fusiliers
    Sempill's 25th Foot
    Beauclerk's 31st Foot
    Douglas' 32nd Foot
    Johnson's 33rd Foot
    Bedford's 68th Foot*
    Montagu's 69th Foot*
    Granby's 71st Foot*
    Cholmondeley's 73rd Foot*

---

24   Massie & Oates (eds.), *Cumberland's Campaigns*, p.108.

Halifax's 74th Foot*
Gower's 77th Foot*
Artillery Train
Two 6-pounders
Fourteen 3-pounders
Two Howitzers

* Newly-raised Noblemen's Regiments.

Cumberland was accompanied throughout this campaign, through to Culloden, by a small escort of hussars in his personal service, numbering at least 16 men.[25]

The 31st is given in this source, as elsewhere, as Handasyd's rather than Beauclerk's; however, Lord Henry Beauclerk had replaced William Handasyd as colonel in April 1745. This situation is further confused by the fact that Roger Handasyd was the longstanding colonel of the 16th Foot, which had also been brought back from Flanders, but this regiment remained around London for the time being. Care therefore needs to be taken when consulting sources that refer simply to 'Handasyd's' at this time, if the regimental number or the colonel's full name is not given. It is not clear whether St Clair or Skelton actually joined the Lichfield Army; St Clair certainly seems to have remained in London. Conversely, although not listed, Lieutenant General Henry Hawley joined the army in the first week of December; his most recent biographer suggests that he could have arrived as early as the 1st or 2nd.[26]

The Foot Guards and the nine 'old' regiments of foot totalled 7,500 men; the new regiments amounted to a further 3,000 men for a total of 10,500 infantry. The mounted forces totalled a further 2,200, of which 800 were accounted for by the two newly-raised regiments.[27] The Foot Guards battalions, which were the three that had come back from Flanders, formed a brigade under Lieutenant Colonel Edward Braddock of the Coldstream Guards, and a return for 1/1st Foot Guards upon returning from that service shows a total of 644 rank and file fit for duty.[28] It is tempting to assume that the nine 'old' regiments of foot were to have formed three brigades under Sempill, Douglas, and Bligh, which would have given these officers the 11th, 20th, and 31st, 12th, 21st, and 32nd, and 19th, 25th, and 33rd respectively. However, if this was indeed the plan then it was overtaken by events, as Douglas was detached with Gower's 77th and 220 men of Bligh's 20th to Chester, to join Cholmondeley's 73rd and the five companies of Blakeney's 27th not with Wade.[29] It is conceivable that these 220 men represented the full effective strength of Bligh's 20th at this time, which had been badly cut up at Melle in July and was one of the regiments originally left behind in Flanders

25   Reid, *Cumberland's Culloden Army*, p.46.
26   Jonathan Oates, *King George's Hangman: Henry Hawley and the Battle of Falkirk 1746* (Warwick: Helion, 2019), p.92.
27   Massie & Oates (eds.), *Cumberland's Campaigns*, p.108.
28   Sir F.W. Hamilton, *The Origin and History of the First or Grenadier Guards* (London: John Murray, 1874), Vol.I, p.132; C.T. Atkinson, 'The Checquers Court MSS', *Journal of the Society for Army Historical Research*, Vol.XXIII, No.95 (Autumn 1945), pp.114-118 (p.116).
29   Massie & Oates (eds.), *Cumberland's Campaigns*, p.108; Reid, *1745*, p.68.

as 'broken'.[30] If, however, this was only a portion of the regiment, then it is not clear where the remainder was.

Cumberland was eventually able to assemble, at or near Stafford, the following units on 1 December, with a view to offering battle at Stonefield to the north of Stone:[31]
> Ligonier's 8th Horse (4 troops, at Stone)
> Kingston's 10th Light Horse (at Cheadle, Uttoxeter, and Congleton)
> Bland's 3rd Dragoons
> Kerr's 11th Dragoons
> Three battalions of Foot Guards
> Sowle's 11th Foot
> Skelton's 12th Foot
> Howard's 19th Foot (reached Stafford 1 December)
> 21st Royal North British Fusiliers
> Sempill's 25th Foot
> Douglas' 32nd Foot
> Johnson's 33rd Foot
> Bedford's 68th Foot
> The Artillery Train

The following general officers were definitely present with this force, being named in a letter of 2 December: Lieutenant Generals John Ligonier, Philip Anstruther, and the Duke of Richmond; Major General Humphrey Bland. Brigadier Generals Bligh and Lord Sempill also appear to have been present but are not specifically named. Of the other regular troops in the vicinity, Cobham's 10th Dragoons had been at Northampton on 30 November, and were moving to join the main body; Beauclerk's 31st Foot was at Coventry – both were under the charge of Brigadier General John Price. Montagu's 9th Carbineers was at Burton-upon-Trent. For the actual dispositions of the remaining Noblemen's Regiments, see Chapter 3.

The Finchley Army

Thanks to Hogarth, and therefore possibly for the wrong reasons, the troops covering London are perhaps the best-known of the forces assembled during the closing weeks of 1745. As with the Lichfield Army, this is perhaps better understood as a potential force that was never quite fully assembled, although, it is possible to piece together its actual composition in a little more detail, and, again, make some informed speculation on its likely organisation had it actually been called upon to defend London. The following order of battle for troops available to defend London in the first week of December 1745 is drawn primarily

30   Atkinson, 'Jenkins' Ear, The Austrian Succession War and the 'Forty-Five', p.292.
31   Frank McLynn, *The Jacobite Army in England 1745: The Final Campaign* (Edinburgh: John Donald, 1998) p.96; Duffy, *Fight for a Throne*, pp.219-220; Cumberland to Newcastle, 2 December 1745, in Massie & Oates (eds.), *Cumberland's Campaigns*, p.111.

from information compiled from a number of published sources, although these contain some discrepancies which are addressed below:[32]

Field Marshal the Earl of Stair, commanding
Lieutenant Generals John Folliott, James St Clair, and the Earl of Albemarle
Major Generals George Reade, Earl of Rothes, Richard Onslow, Henry Pulteney, and George Churchill
Brigadier Generals Sir Charles Paulet, John Jefferys, George Byng, and Daniel Houghton

Household Cavalry, Major General Lord De La Warr
    1st Troops of Horse Guards
    2nd Troops of Horse Guards
    1st Troop of Horse Grenadier Guards
Mounted Troops
    Ligonier's 8th Horse (2 troops)
    1st Royal Dragoons
    Rich's 4th Dragoons (dismounted)
Foot Guards, Lieutenant Colonel Rowland Reynolds
    1st Foot Guards (18 companies = 2 battalions)
    Coldstream Guards (9 companies = 1 battalion)
    3rd Foot Guards (9 companies = 1 battalion)
Regiments of Foot (unit strengths in brackets)
    1/1st Royals (660)
    Mordaunt's 18th Foot (628)
    23rd Royal Welch Fusiliers (611)
    Bragg's 28th Foot (641)
    Richbell's 39th Foot (8 companies; strength unknown)
    Murray's 43rd Highlanders (616)
Artillery Train, Captain John Speedwell
    30-34 pieces of artillery (sources differ on the exact number)

The two troops of Ligonier's 8th Horse amounted to 110 men, the two dragoon regiments between them to 431.[33] The figure of 779 is given for the Household Cavalry; however, this is too large for the three troops in London and so must also include the three expected back from Flanders. The latter had mustered 337 other ranks in July 1745, which suggests that the three home-based troops would have amounted to around 450.[34] Duffy notes that Harrison's 15th Foot was expected at the Tower on 11 December, but this move seems not to have happened: Bragg's 28th were still there on 12 December when orders were sent for

32   List of officers, including brigade commanders for Household Cavalry and Foot Guards given below, from Hamilton, *First or Grenadier Guards*, Vol.I, p.132. Units and strengths from Duffy, *Fight for a Throne*, p.236.
33   Duffy, *Fight for a Throne*, p.236.
34   Atkinson, 'Jenkins' Ear, The Austrian Succession War and the 'Forty-Five', p.294; TNA, SP87/17, 'State of His Majesty's British Forces in the Low Countries July the 16th 1745 N.S'.

them to be relieved by men from the Foot Guards, and by 5 January 1746 Harrison's was in garrison at Dover.[35] Of the six regiments of foot, all bar for the 23rd had been encamped at Dartford in late November, apparently under Houghton since in the above list he is the only brigadier general shown as having a command and a brigade major to assist him. The arrival of a sixth regiment, and the expectation of a seventh, suggests that the foot would have been formed into two brigades if this force actually took to the field.

The strength and deployment of the Foot Guards in the defence of London is problematic. Duffy gives a strength of 1,200 for '17 grenadier companies of the Foot Guards' with the Finchley army, but this is nonsensical as the three regiments only had eight grenadier companies between them (four from the 1st Foot Guards and two apiece from the other regiments). Clearly a portion of the guards were required for duties around the capital; at the Tower as noted above, and at Windsor (until 7 December when two companies of Harcourt's 76th Foot relieved them),[36] so it is unrealistic to assume that all of the London-based companies would have been free to go to Finchley. Some sense is restored by consulting a short analysis published in the *Journal of the Society of Army Historical Research* as long ago as 1949. This notes a newspaper report stating 'On Friday [6 December] on the Rising of the Council at St. James's all the Grenadiers of the three Regiments of Foot Guards, also five Men out of each Company had Orders to march directly to Finchley'. A further extract, this time from a marching order of the same date, subsequently cancelled, specifies '4 of the 5 companies of grenadiers belonging to the 4 batts. of Foot Guards, doing duty under your command in London, to march immediately to St. Albans'.[37] If there were five grenadier companies remaining in London, then it follows that each of the battalions serving with Cumberland contained only one: those in London would therefore amount to three from the 1st Foot Guards and one apiece from the other two regiments, which in turn leaves 15 hat companies from the 1st Foot Guards and eight from each of the other regiments to make up the London contingent. The total strength of all seven battalions of Foot Guards in early December was 4,196,[38] which suggests that the three battalions with Cumberland numbered around 1,836 men and the four in London 2,360. Five grenadier companies, plus five men each from 31 hat companies, amounts to around 485 men so nowhere near Duffy's '1,200', and this drops to around 420 men if one of the grenadier companies was retained in London as is suggested by the marching order. Taking the average company strength, 17 companies of Foot Guards would amount to around 1,120 men, which is closer to Duffy's total, although if that is indeed what was assembled at Finchley then they clearly were not all grenadiers. Bearing in mind that detachments in and around London could only be released for service in the field once they had been relieved by other forces, it is perhaps safest to say that around 2,360 guardsmen were theoretically available to defend the capital, but that half that number was tied down in static garrison duty.

Various local volunteers were, of course, also available to defend the capital, as were London's Trained Bands, but it seems most likely that these would have been employed

---

35   Atkinson, 'Jenkins' Ear, The Austrian Succession War and the 'Forty-Five', pp.294-295.
36   Atkinson, 'Jenkins' Ear, The Austrian Succession War and the 'Forty-Five', p.294.
37   G.R. Mellor, 'Hogarth's "March to Finchley"', *Journal of the Society for Army Historical Research*, Vol.27, No.110 (Summer 1949), pp.48-50 (p.49).
38   Atkinson, 'Jenkins' Ear, The Austrian Succession War and the 'Forty-Five', p.294.

as static garrison troops rather than in the field. A Jacobite army advancing on London would also inevitably have arrived with detachments from the Lichfield army not far behind it. Some indication of the troops that might have been made available can be obtained by looking at those that were instead used to pursue the retreating Jacobites northwards, to which might well be added units like Beauclerk's 31st Foot that were still on the march northwards from London and could have been turned around.[39]

The Pursuit to Carlisle

Once it became apparent that, far from threatening London, the Jacobites were retreating northwards from Derby, troops were sent in pursuit by Cumberland and by Wade, although the former had been wrong-footed and his forces were rather too far to the south and west to have much expectation of catching up with the main body of the Highland Army. Cumberland's 'Corps de Chasse', under his personal command, set off northwards on 7 December composed of the following units:

Ligonier's 8th Horse
Montagu's 9th Carbineers
Kingston's 10th Light Horse
Bland's 3rd Dragoons
Cobham's 10th Dragoons
Kerr's 11th Dragoons
1,000 volunteers from the foot, mounted on locally-obtained horses.

Lieutenant Generals Hawley and the Duke of Richmond accompanied Cumberland, as did Major General Bland; Lieutenant General Ligonier assumed command of the main body of the foot, which remained camped on Meriden Common, between Birmingham and Coventry.[40]

Wade, meanwhile, detached Major General Huske with 4,000 of the fittest foot to march to Penrith via Stainmore, withdrawing the remainder northwards to cover Newcastle-upon-Tyne. The bulk of his mounted troops he detached as a flying column under Major General Oglethorpe to cross the Pennines by way of Blackstone Edge and link up with Cumberland. This force comprised:[41]

Montagu's 3rd Horse
St George's 8th Dragoons
Georgia Rangers
Yorkshire Hunters

39   For further speculation on this point, see Duffy, *Fight for a Throne*, pp.233-234
40   McLynn. *Jacobite Army in England*, p.154; Duffy, *Fight for a Throne*, p.249; Oates, *King George's Hangman*, p.92.
41   Duffy, *Fight for a Throne*, p.150

The combined pursuing forces came up with the Jacobites as the latter were crossing the Shap Fells, engaging the Jacobite rearguard at Clifton on 18 December. The Government forces in that action were deployed as follows:

HRH the Duke of Cumberland, commanding
First Line, Lieutenant General Hawley and Major General Bland
    Bland's 3rd Dragoons
    Cobham's 10th Dragoons
    Kerr's 11th Dragoons
Second Line, Lieutenant General Duke of Richmond
    Ligonier's 8th Horse (detached to left flank)
    Montagu's 9th Carbineers
    Kingston's 10th Light Horse
Right Flank, Major General Oglethorpe
    Montagu's 3rd Horse
    St George's 8th Dragoons
    Georgia Rangers
    Yorkshire Hunters
Reserve (not engaged)
    Mounted volunteers from the regiments of foot.

The 250 dragoons who were dismounted to attack Clifton village were led in that assault by Lieutenant Colonel Philip Honywood of Bland's 3rd Dragoons.[42]
    This force afterwards covered the Siege of Carlisle, which fell on 30 December. Additional forces were brought up for that siege, as follows:[43]

Regiments of Foot, under Brigadier Generals Bligh and Lord Sempill
    Bligh's 20th Foot
    21st Royal North British Fusiliers
    Sempill's 25th Foot
    Bedford's 68th Foot
    Montagu's 69th Foot
    Granby's 71st Foot
    Halifax's 74th Foot
    Liverpool Blues
Artillery
    Ten 18-pounder cannon (ships' guns, brought from Whitehaven)
    Ten coehorn mortars (Dutch, from Wade's army)

---

42   Duffy, *Fight for a Throne*, pp.256-262; Timothy J. McCann, *The Correspondence of The Dukes of Richmond and Newcastle 1724-1750* (Lewes: Sussex Record Society, 1983), p.198; Cumberland to Newcastle 16, 28, and 30 December, Massie & Oates (eds.), *Cumberland's Campaigns*, pp.124, 130-133.
43   Duffy, *Fight for a Throne*, pp.265-268; Atkinson, 'Jenkins' Ear, The Austrian Succession War and the 'Forty-Five', p.295.

War in the Highlands and Far North

Lieutenant General Handasyd had secured Edinburgh and much of Lowland Scotland with his detachment from Wade's army by the time he received orders on 9 December recalling him to Berwick. From this foothold would, in due course, be assembled the army that Hawley would lead to defeat at Falkirk.

Further north, the situation was rather more fluid and dangerous, with a second Jacobite army, including French reinforcements, forming around Aberdeen. At Inverness, Colonel the Earl of Loudoun had the nucleus of a small force built around Mackintosh's additional company of Murray's 43rd Highlanders and two companies of his own 64th Highlanders. To these would be added the 18 Highland Independent Companies as they took to the field. Although often passed over, the action at Inverurie, in which a force of loyal Highlanders was broken up by a Franco-Jacobite column operating out of Aberdeen, was the fifth-largest clash during the course of the '45. The Government forces engaged were as follows:

Independent Companies under Norman MacLeod of MacLeod (clan affinity in brackets)
    John MacLeod's Company (MacLeods of Skye and Harris)
    Norman MacLeod of Waterstein's Company (MacLeods of Skye and Harris)
    Norman MacLeod of Bernera's Company (MacLeods of Skye and Harris)
    Donald MacDonald's Company (MacLeods of Skye and Harris)
    Hugh MacLeod of Geanies' Company (Assynt MacLeods)
    George Munro of Culcairn's Company (Munros)
    Alexander Gunn's Company (Sutherlands)

A further 4-500 men had been raised by the Laird of Grant to accompany this force, but had returned home after Loudoun questioned the legality of them having been called out and stated that he could neither arm nor pay them.[44]

During February and March 1746, as the Jacobites returned to the Highlands in force, a number of the Government garrisons were finally compelled to surrender. After suffering a further embarrassment in the 'Rout of Moy' on 16 February 1746, Loudoun's command was discomfited yet again on 20 March by a Jacobite attack launched across the Dornoch Firth. Gaining some measure of revenge, Captain John MacLeod's company of Loudoun's 64th and Alexander Mackay's Independent Company took part in the action at the Kyle of Tongue on 26 March when a shipment of gold on its way from France to the Jacobites was successfully intercepted, and three locally-raised companies under William Sutherland of Sibberscross successfully ambushed the Earl of Cromartie's Jacobite force at Embo on 15 April.[45]

---

44   I.H. Mackay Scobie, 'The Highland Independent Companies of 1745-47', *Journal of the Society for Army Historical Research*, Vol.20, No.77 (Spring 1941), pp.5-37; Reid, *1745*, pp.85-90.
45   Reid, *1745*, pp.107-118

Hawley's Army

Returning to the main armies, the retreat of the Jacobites from Derby coincided with renewed fears of a French invasion, so that Cumberland was recalled to London and there was a general redeployment southward, with the Channel ports being garrisoned with a mixture of regulars and men of the Noblemen's Regiments. In order to tackle the Jacobites, Lieutenant General Hawley was given the British regiments of foot from what had been Wade's army and placed in command in Scotland. The Dutch contingent was obliged by its parole to return to the continent now that there were French troops in the field with the Jacobites, but plans were afoot to replace them with Hessian troops. The older, less effective, general officers were given postings in England but Huske remained as Hawley's second-in-command. For mounted troops, Hawley had only the two dragoon regiments that had gone to Scotland with Handasyd, with the promise of Cobham's 10th Dragoons to reinforce them. Troops were brought up by stages from Edinburgh to Falkirk, preparatory to a move intended to relieve the Jacobite siege of Stirling Castle. The vanguard of this force marched from Edinburgh on 14 January 1746 under Huske and consisted of:[46]

> Ligonier's 13th Dragoons
> Hamilton's 14th Dragoons
> Price's 14th Foot
> Munro's 37th Foot
> Cholmondeley's 34th Foot
> Ligonier's 59th Foot
> Glasgow Blues

They were followed by three more regiments under Brigadier General Cholmondeley:[47]

> Howard's 3rd Foot
> Barrell's 4th Foot
> Pulteney's 13th Foot

The concentration was only completed on 17 January, with the following forces being available for the resulting Battle of Falkirk fought in the late afternoon of that day (rank and file strengths given in brackets):[48]

---

46 Duffy, *Fight for a Throne*, p.293.
47 Geoff B. Bailey, *Falkirk or Paradise! The Battle of Falkirk Muir 17 January 1746* (Edinburgh: John Donald, 1996), p.79.
48 Order of battle and strengths primarily from Oates, *King George's Hangman*, pp.114-115; details of Artillery Train from Bailey, *Falkirk or Paradise!*, p.79. Duffy, *Fight for a Throne*, p.293, gives 320 as the all-ranks strength for Cobham's 10th Dragoons, from which the figure given is obtained by reversing the usual process of adding 10 percent to turn rank and file strengths into estimated totals; Oates offers 253 rank and file based on a later strength return, but this seem too low.

Lieutenant General Henry Hawley, commanding
1st Brigade, Major General John Huske
    2/1st Royals (532)
    Blakeney's 27th Foot (460)
    Munro's 37th Foot (525)
    Wolfe's 8th Foot (522)
2nd Brigade, Brigadier General John Mordaunt
    Howard's 3rd Foot (554)
    Cholmondeley's 34th Foot (540)
    Ligonier's 59th Foot (318)
    Pulteney's 13th Foot (504)
3rd Brigade, Brigadier General James Cholmondeley
    Barrell's 4th Foot (378)
    Fleming's 36th Foot (426)
    Battereau's 62nd Foot (474)
    Price's 14th Foot (255)
Dragoons, Colonel Francis Ligonier
    Cobham's 10th Dragoons (c.290)
    Ligonier's 13th Dragoons (253)
    Hamilton's 14th Dragoons (266)
Loyal Highlanders, Lieutenant Colonel John Campbell of Mamore
    Regular Highlanders (175)
    Argyll Militia (765)
Volunteers, Colonel Earl of Home
    Glasgow Blues (572)
    Paisley Volunteers (174)
    Edinburgh Volunteer Company (unknown strength)
Artillery Train, Captain Cunningham
    Ten cannon, 6-, 3- and 1½-pounders; 28 gunners and drivers
    Thornton's Yorkshire Volunteers (64)

The regular Highlanders consisted of three companies of Loudoun's 64th Highlanders and one additional company – that of Duncan Campbell of Inverawe – from Murray's 43rd. These, along with the Argyll Militia companies, appear to have acted as a single body under Campbell. The regimental history of the 4th Foot confirms that that regiment, along with the 14th, was brigaded under Cholmondeley, from which appointment the other brigade commanders have been inferred.[49] The employment of Huske as a brigade commander seems unusual for an officer of his senior rank, and was presumably necessitated by the shortage of senior officers.

    The organisation.of the foot as given above reflects the formal brigading by which the regiments were encamped outside Falkirk (with Price's 14th detached in Falkirk town and

---

49   Richard Cannon, *Historical Record of the 4th, or the King's Own, Regiment of Foot from 1680 to 1839* (London: Adjutant General's Office, 1839), pp.45-46.

at Calendar House, along with Cobham's 10th Dragoons),[50] not the ad-hoc manner in which it actually deployed and fought. The actual deployment of the foot was in three lines, the composition of which is here given from right to left:

First Line, Major General John Huske and Brigadier General James Cholmondeley
    Ligonier's 59th Foot
    Price's 14th Foot
    2/1st Royals
    Pulteney's 13th Foot
    Cholmondeley's 34th Foot
    Wolfe's 8th Foot
Second Line, Brigadier General John Mordaunt
    Battereau's 62nd Foot
    Barrell's 4th Foot
    Fleming's 36th Foot
    Munro's 37th Foot
    Blakeney's 27th Foot
Third Line, Lieutenant Colonel George Howard
    Howard's 3rd Foot

A chart in the Royal Collection offers an alternative interpretation of Hawley's order of battle at Falkirk, but a closer inspection reveals the presence of a number of regiments which only joined the defeated army after it retreated to Edinburgh. It is, however, worth reproducing as it reflects the army as it stood immediately prior to Cumberland taking command, and introduces an infantry brigading which remained in force for some time (at least until mid-February; see Chapter 2). This order of battle places the army in four lines, the composition of which is given here from right to left (the brigades are not numbered in the original, but numbers have been added to indicate their relative seniority):[51]

Lieutenant General Henry Hawley, commanding
First Line, Major General John Huske
    [1st] Brigade, Brigadier General James Cholmondeley
        2/1st Royals
        Fleming's 36th Foot
        Pulteney's 13th Foot
    [3rd] Brigade, Brigadier General Lord Sempill
        Blakeney's 27th Foot
        Ligonier's 59th Foot
        Barrell's 4th Foot

50   RCIN 730010, Battle of Falkirk, 1746, James Cunningham [?], 1746 or later, at < https://militarymaps.rct.uk/other-18th-19th-century-conflicts/battle-of-falkirk-1746>, viewed 29 June 2020.
51   RCIN 730009, Order of Battle, 1746, Falkirk [sic], Anonymous, 1746 or later, at < https://militarymaps.rct.uk/other-18th-19th-century-conflicts/order-of-battle-1746-falkirk> viewed 27 June 2020.

Second Line, Brigadier General John Mordaunt
    [2nd] Brigade, Lieutenant Colonel Sir Andrew Agnew of Lochnaw
        Howard's 3rd Foot
        Munro's 37th Foot
        Price's 14th Foot
    [4th] Brigade, Lieutenant Colonel Edward Martin
        Cholmondeley's 34th Foot
        Battereau's 62nd Foot
        Wolfe's 8th Foot
Third Line, Lieutenant Colonel Francis Leighton
    Cobham's 10th Dragoons
    21st Royal North British Fusiliers
    Sempill's 25th Foot
    Kerr's 11th Dragoons
Fourth Line, Lieutenant Colonel John Campbell of Mamore
    Ligonier's 13th Dragoons
    Argyll Militia (and attached regular highlanders, though these are not explicitly mentioned)
    Hamilton's 14th Dragoons

Based on the units included, this arrangement must post-date the arrival of Kerr's 11th Dragoons in Edinburgh on 23 January (Sempill's 25th having arrived there on 17 January and the 21st Royal North British Fusiliers the day after), but pre-date the arrival of Cumberland to take command on the 30th.[52] It should be noted that the chart places the two newly-arrived regiments of foot together in the Third Line, but had Hawley set out from scratch to divide his foot into five brigades this is not where seniority (which is religiously followed in the distribution of the other 12 regiments) would have placed them. This suggests, therefore, that the two new arrivals were 'tacked on' to an existing brigade organisation, which was presumably put into place in the immediate aftermath of the Battle of Falkirk.

The shortage of senior officers to command the brigades is also marked. There were only two full colonels present with their regiments at Falkirk, Sir Robert Munro and Francis Ligonier: the former was killed in the battle and the latter died of an illness, exacerbated by making a campaign in such awful weather, shortly after it. Thus, in the aftermath of these losses, we see significant command appointments given to lieutenant colonels. Of these, Agnew was of the 21st, Martin (given as Martine in the original chart) of the 8th, and Leighton of the 27th. The first and last of these, who would seem to have been the most senior officers of that rank then with the army, were therefore removed from their own regiments to fill command roles. Continuing this trend, they would both later be employed on detached duties away from the main army. The arrival of more senior officers in Scotland for the spring campaign was partially counterbalanced by Brigadier General Cholmondeley

---

52   Dates from Duffy, *Fight for a Throne*, pp.358, 363.

falling ill, leading Cumberland to remark on 5 March of the 'great want of Colonels here', and later to request that Brigadier Generals Bligh and Douglas be sent to join his army.[53]

Cumberland's Army

Upon the Duke of Cumberland replacing Hawley in command, the above order of battle would initially seem to have been maintained. However, as the war moved northwards detachments were made that would have required changes. Lieutenant Colonel Agnew was removed from his brigade to take command at Blair Castle, which he subsequently held against a besieging force of Jacobites under Lord George Murray, and Lieutenant Colonel Leighton was sent to Castle Menzies. Each of these commands amounted to some 300 men, made up of small detachments from various regiments.[54]

As Cumberland and the main army moved by the coastal route to Aberdeen and thence onwards to Banff and Nairn, a second army was assembled to cover the lines of communication and prevent any Jacobite thrust southwards. Originally assembled around Perth and Stirling, this force later moved northwards to Crief and Dunkeld with a view to relieving Agnew's garrison at Blair Castle. It was largely composed of the Hessian contingent, which had completed its disembarkation at Leith on 8 February, with an attached British brigade of dragoons to compensate for the fact that the bulk of the Hessian cavalry had been retained on the continent:[55]

Lieutenant General Prince Frederick of Hesse-Cassel, commanding
Main Body, Lieutenant Generals von Brand and von Mansbach, Major General Wolff von Gaudenberg
    Grenadier-Regiment (830)
    Regiment Mansbach (836)
    Regiment Garde (833)
    Regiment Prinz Friedrich (907)
    Company of Hussars (98)
    Eight 3-pounder cannon
Reserve, Colonel von Rundstedt
    Regiment Prinz Maximillian (829)
    Regiment Donop (833)
    Four 3-pounder cannon
British Dragoons, Major General Earl of Crawford
    St George's 8th Dragoons

---

53   Cumberland to Newcastle, 5 March 1746, Massie & Oates (eds.), *Cumberland's Campaigns*, p.164; Cumberland to Newcastle, 26 March 1746, *ibid.*, p.171.

54   Christopher Duffy, *The Best of Enemies: Germans Against Jacobites, 1746* (London: Bitter Books, 2013), p.64.

55   Duffy, *The Best of Enemies*, p.51-52, 65, 68; Duffy, *Fight for a Throne*, pp.404-406; Jonathan Oates, 'Hessian Forces Employed in Scotland in 1746', *Journal of the Society for Army Historical Research*, Vol.83, No.335 (Autumn 2005), pp.205-214.

Naison's (late Ligonier's) 13th Dragoons
Hamilton's 14th Dragoons

Total strength of the Hessian artillery train was 128 men. Notwithstanding their strength, the Hessian regiments were all organised on a single-battalion basis. Strength figures for the British dragoons are not available, but Naison's 13th and Hamilton's 14th can have mustered no more than 210 and 203 other ranks respectively, deducting their Falkirk casualties from their strengths prior to that battle.[56]

Separately to the above force, Lee's 55th Foot was ordered up from Berwick to Edinburgh in March 1746, and detachments of Johnson's 33rd Foot were transported by sea to reinforce the garrisons in the western Highlands. Regiments of horse were offered to Cumberland, but declined as being unsuited to the terrain.[57]

Meanwhile, the main army under Cumberland received its final reinforcements. Kingston's 10th Light Horse joined at Aberdeen around 6 March,[58] and Bligh's 20th Foot, built up to 573 rank and file, on 25 March. Kingston's 10th Light Horse did not get off to a good start with the army, losing 31 men in the Jacobite attack on Keith on the night of 20 March, along with a further 53 casualties suffered by the Argyll Militia.[59] The arrival of Bligh's 20th completed an organisation of the foot into two lines and a reserve – six, six, and three battalions respectively, just as it would stand at Culloden – with, at this stage, Kingston's 10th Light Horse and Cobham's 10th Dragoons attached to the First Line and Kerr's 11th Dragoons attached to the Second.[60]

The only change to note prior to Culloden is that three colonelcies changed hands. On 6 April Henry Seymour Conway became colonel of the 59th Foot in succession to the dead Francis Ligonier. Three days later Lord George Sackville replaced Thomas Bligh as colonel of the 20th Foot, Bligh moving to the 12th Dragoons, and Louis Dejean became colonel of the 37th Foot in succession to the dead Sir Robert Munro. Dejean had been lieutenant colonel of the 1st Troop of Horse Grenadier Guards; the other two were aides de camp of Cumberland's.[61] With these changes to nomenclature, the organisation of the Government forces at Culloden, as deployed from right to left and with rank-and-file strength shown in brackets, stood as follows:[62]

---

56   Calculation derived from figures in Oates, *King George's Hangman*, pp.114, 140.

57   Cumberland to Newcastle, 9 March 1746, Massie & Oates (eds.), *Cumberland's Campaigns*, pp.165-166.

58   The regiment was 'within a march' on the 5th; Cumberland to Newcastle, 5 March 1746, Massie & Oates (eds.), *Cumberland's Campaigns*, p.162; Cumberland to Major General Campbell, 18 March 1746, *ibid.*, pp.167-168.

59   Reid, *1745*, p.124.

60   Cumberland to Newcastle, 26 March 1746, Massie & Oates (eds.), *Cumberland's Campaigns*, pp.170-171.

61   Leslie, *Succession of Colonels*, pp.62, 76, 84.

62   Compiled from Stuart Reid, 'The British Army at Culloden', in Tony Pollard (ed.), *Culloden: The History and Archaeology of the Last Clan Battle* (Barnsley: Pen & Sword, 2009), pp.62-86; C.T. Atkinson, 'Culloden', *Journal of the Society for Army Historical Research*, Vol.35, No. 141 (March, 1957), pp.18-22; order of battle with strengths in Massie & Oates (eds.), *Cumberland's Campaigns*, p.184.

HRH the Duke of Cumberland, commanding
Lieutenant General Henry Hawley, second-in-command
First Line of Foot, Lieutenant General the Earl of Albemarle
    1st Brigade, Lieutenant Colonel John Ramsey
        2/1st Royals (401)
        Cholmondeley's 34th Foot (399)
        Price's 14th Foot (304)
    3rd Brigade, Brigadier General Lord Sempill
        21st Royal North British Fusiliers (358)
        Dejean's 37th Foot (426)
        Barrell's 4th Foot (325)
Second Line of Foot, Major General John Huske
    2nd Brigade, Lieutenant Colonel George Jackson
        Howard's 3rd Foot (413)
        Fleming's 36th Foot (350)
        Sackville's 20th Foot (412)
    4th Brigade, Colonel Henry Conway ('probably' – see below)
        Sempill's 25th Foot (220)
        Conway's 59th Foot (325)
        Wolfe's 8th Foot (314)
Reserve, or 5th Brigade, Brigadier General John Mordaunt
    Kingston's 10th Light Horse (166)
    Pulteney's 13th Foot (410)
    Battereau's 62nd Foot (364)
    Blakeney's 27th Foot (300)
Dragoons, Major General Humphrey Bland
    Cobham's 10th Dragoons (219)
    Kerr's 11th Dragoons (249)
Loyal Highlanders, Lieutenant Colonel John Campbell of Mamore
    Battalion under John Campbell of Mamore (c.230; detached as baggage guard)
    Battalion under Captain Colin Campbell of Ballimore (c.230)
Artillery Train, Major William Belford
    Company of Captain-Lieutenant John Goodwin (77) with:
    Ten 3-pounder cannon
    Six Coehorn mortars

The artillery was deployed with the 3-pounders in pairs in the gaps between the battalions of the First Line, and the Coehorns in the interval between the First Line and Second. The total rank and file strength of the eight Highland companies present was 460, but company strengths are not available: see Chapter 5 for the composition of Ballimore's battalion.

The 1st and 2nd Brigades seem to have been notionally commanded by Albemarle and Huske respectively; bearing in mind their higher positions commanding the whole line, the name of the senior battalion commander has been given in each case. Stuart Reid places the 4th Brigade as 'probably' under the newly-promoted Colonel Conway. If this is incorrect – and it is by no means certain whether the news of Conway's colonelcy had reached the army in Scotland when the battle was fought; that of Sackville's and Dejean's certainly had not, as Cumberland used the old colonel's names in his victory dispatch – then the brigade's senior battalion commander would have been Lieutenant Colonel George Stanhope of the 59th Foot.[63]

The bulk of the dragoons, and Ballimore's four Highland companies, took part in the move to outflank the Jacobite right; one squadron of Cobham's 10th was detached to the opposite flank, where it was joined by Kingston's 10th Light Horse (which had initially been deployed with one squadron on either flank of Mordaunt's three regiments of foot). Pulteney's 13th Foot was taken from the 5th Brigade to extend the right flank of the First Line, and Battereau's 62nd to extend the right flank of the Second.

Too late to take part in the battle, a reinforcement of four battalions under Major General Henry Skelton was shipped to Aberdeen by way of Leith. It comprised:

Skelton's 12th Foot
Handasyd's 16th Foot
Mordaunt's 18th Foot
Houghton's 24th Foot

The last-named regiment had been in garrison at Bristol; the other three were in London as of 5 January 1746. Orders for the dispatch of these troop to Scotland were sent on 22 March, and they were 'hourly expect[ed]' at Inverness on 23 April.[64] Even as this reinforcement was awaited, however, the army was already being broken up to begin the pacification of the Highlands, which brings this outline of its formal order of battle to its conclusion.

---

63   Seniority calculated from dates of commissions from TNA, WO64/9, 'Army List 1736' (in fact, lists officers during 1742-1743, with additions to 1751).
64   Cumberland to Newcastle, undated and 23 April 1746, Massie & Oates (eds.), *Cumberland's Campaigns*, pp.175, 192; Atkinson, 'Jenkins' Ear, The Austrian Succession War and the 'Forty-Five', p.295.

Appendix II: Regimental Colonelcies

In the index which follows, regiments other than Household troops are listed under the names of their colonels. For the aid of readers more familiar with numerical designations, this pair of tables lists the regiments of cavalry and infantry by seniority and gives the names of their colonels (including any changes during the Rising).[1] In addition, the station of each regiment at the time of the outbreak of the Rising is given. For the colonels of the Noblemen's Regiments, see pp.86-92 of this work.

Cavalry Colonelcies

Unit	Colonel	Station
1st Troop of Horse Guards	Earl De La Warr	England
2nd Troop of Horse Guards	Lord Cadogan	England
3rd Troop of Horse Guards	Lord Tyrawley	Flanders
4th Troop of Horse Guards	Earl of Crawford	Flanders
1st Troop of Horse Grenadier Guards	Richard Onslow	England
2nd Troop of Horse Grenadier Guards	Earl of Harrington	Flanders
Royal Horse Guards	Duke of Somerset	Flanders
2nd Horse	Philip Honywood	Flanders
3rd Horse	Duke of Montagu	England
4th Horse	George Wade	England
5th Horse	John Brown	Ireland
6th Horse	Thomas Wentworth	Ireland
7th Horse	Phineas Bowles	Ireland
8th Horse	John Ligonier	Flanders
1st Dragoons (Royals)	Henry Hawley	Flanders

---

1   Sourced from Leslie, *Succession of Colonels*, pp.1-84; TNA WO64/9, 'Army List 1736'. The list of colonels in Reid, *Cumberland's Culloden Army*, pp.35-38 contains a number of errors, particularly with respect to the Marine Regiments.

Unit	Colonel	Station
2nd Dragoons	Earl of Stair	Flanders
3rd Dragoons	Humphrey Bland	Flanders
4th Dragoons	Robert Rich	Flanders
5th Dragoons	Viscount Molesworth	Ireland
6th Dragoons	Earl of Rothes	Flanders
7th Dragoons	John Cope	Flanders
8th Dragoons	Richard St George	England
9th Dragoons	Henry de Grangues	Ireland
10th Dragoons	Viscount Cobham	England
11th Dragoons	Lord Mark Kerr	England
12th Dragoons	Samuel Whitshed; Thomas Bligh from 6 April 1746	Ireland
13th Dragoons	James Gardiner; Francis Ligonier from 1 October 1745; Peter Naison from 3 March 1746	Scotland
14th Dragoons	Archibald Hamilton	Scotland

Infantry Colonelcies

Regiment	Colonel	Station
1st Foot Guards	HRH Duke of Cumberland	Flanders (1 Bn); England (2 Bns)
Coldstream Guards	Earl of Albemarle	Flanders (1 Bn); England (1 Bn)
3rd Foot Guards	Earl of Dunmore	Flanders (1 Bn); England (1 Bn)
1st Foot (Royals)	James St Clair	Flanders (1 Bn); Ireland (1 Bn)
2nd Foot	Thomas Fowke	Gibraltar
3rd Foot	George Howard	Flanders
4th Foot	William Barrell	Flanders
5th Foot	Alexander Irwin	Ireland
6th Foot	John Guise	Scotland
7th Royal Fusiliers	William Hargrave	Gibraltar
8th Foot	Edward Wolfe	Flanders
9th Foot	George Reade	Minorca
10th Foot	Francis Columbine	Gibraltar
11th Foot	Robinson Sowle; William Graham from 7 February 1746	Flanders

Regiment	Colonel	Station
12th Foot	Henry Skelton	Flanders
13th Foot	Henry Pulteney	Flanders
14th Foot	John Price	Flanders
15th Foot	Henry Harrison	England
16th Foot	Roger Handasyd	Flanders
17th Foot	John Wynyard	Minorca
18th Foot	John Mordaunt	Flanders
19th Foot	Charles Howard	Flanders
20th Foot	Thomas Bligh; Lord George Sackville from 9 April 1746	Flanders
21st Royal North British Fusiliers	Duke of Argyll	Flanders
22nd Foot	Richard O'Farrell	Minorca
23rd Royal Welch Fusiliers	John Huske	Flanders
24th Foot	Daniel Houghton	England
25th Foot	Lord Sempill	Flanders
26th Foot	Philip Anstruther	Minorca
27th Foot	William Blakeney	England
28th Foot	Philip Bragg	Flanders
29th Foot	Francis Fuller	Gibraltar
30th Foot	Charles Frampton	England
31st Foot	Lord Henry Beauclerk	Flanders
32nd Foot	William Douglas	Flanders
33rd Foot	John Johnson	Flanders
34th Foot	James Cholmondeley	Flanders
35th Foot	Charles Otway	Ireland
36th Foot	James Fleming	Flanders
37th Foot	Robert Munro; Louis Dejean from 9 April 1746	Flanders
38th Foot	Robert Dalzell	West Indies
39th Foot	Edward Richbell	England
40th Foot	Richard Philipps	Nova Scotia
42nd Foot	James Oglethorpe	Georgia
41st Foot (Royal Invalids)	Tomkyn Wardour	Dispersed
43rd Foot (Highlanders)	Lord John Murray	Flanders
44th Foot (1st Marines)	George Churchill	Sea Service
45th Foot (2nd Marines)	Robert Fraser	Sea Service

Regiment	Colonel	Station
46th Foot (3rd Marines)	Anthony Lowther; Robinson Sowle from 7 February 1746	Sea Service
47th Foot (4th Marines)	George Byng	Sea Service
48th Foot (5th Marines)	James Cochrane	Sea Service
49th Foot (6th Marines)	John Cottrell	Sea Service
50th Foot (7th Marines)	Henry Cornwall	Sea Service
51st Foot (8th Marines)	John Duncombe	Sea Service
52nd Foot (9th Marines)	Charles Paulet	Sea Service
53rd Foot (10th Marines)	John Jefferys	Sea Service
54th Foot	William Graham; James Kennedy from 7 February 1746	Minorca
55th Foot	John Lee	Scotland/ England
56th Foot	Hugh Warburton	Gibraltar
57th Foot	Thomas Murray	Scotland
58th Foot	Peregrine Lascelles	Scotland
59th Foot	Francis Ligonier; Henry Seymour Conway from 6 April 1746	Flanders
60th Foot	John Bruce	Ireland
61st Foot	John Folliot	Ireland
62nd Foot	John Battereau	Ireland
63rd Foot	Edward Trelawney	Jamaica
64th Foot (Highlanders)	Earl of Loudoun	Scotland, Raising
65th Foot	William Shirley	Cape Breton
66th Foot	William Pepperell	Cape Breton

Select Bibliography and Further Reading

Specific sources have been given in each of the chapters: the following is a list of titles of particular merit or which cover a wide range of the topics dealt with in this book. Many of the 18th-century titles listed are now available digitally.

Books

Anon., *The Report of the Proceedings and Opinions of the Board of General officers in the examination into the Conduct, behaviour and Proceedings of Lieutenant General Sir John Cope* (Dublin: George Faulkner, 1749).

Bailey, Geoff B., *Falkirk or Paradise! The Battle of Falkirk Muir 17 January 1746* (Edinburgh: John Donald, 1996).

Black, R., *The Campbells of the Ark: The Men of Argyll in 1745: The Outer Circle* (Edinburgh, John Donald, 2017).

Blackmore, David, *British Cavalry in the Mid-18th Century* (Nottingham: Partizan Press, 2008).

Blackmore, David, *Destructive & Formidable: British Infantry Firepower 1642-1765* (London: Frontline Books, 2014).

Brown, Iain, and Cheape, Hugh, *Witness to Rebellion: John Mclean's Journal of the Forty Five and the Penicuik Drawings* (East Linton: Tuckwell Press, 1996).

Cormack, Andrew, 'These Meritorious Objects of the Royal Bounty': The Chelsea Out-pensioners in the Early Eighteenth Century* (London: Privately Published, 2017).

Douglas, F., *History of the Rebellion in 1745 and 1746* (Aberdeen: F. Douglas and W. Murray, 1755).

Duffy, Christopher, *Fight for a Throne: The Jacobite '45 Reconsidered* (Solihull: Helion, 2015).

Duffy, Christopher, *The Best of Enemies: Germans Against Jacobites, 1746* (London: Bitter Books, 2013).

Geerdink-Schaftenaar, Marc, *For Orange and the States: The Army of the Dutch Republic 1713-1772* (Warwick: Helion, 2018), Part I: Infantry.

Guy, A.J., *Oeconomy and Discipline – Officership and Administration in the British Army, 1714-1763* (Manchester: Manchester University Press, 1985).

Henderson, Andrew, *History of the Rebellion* (London: R. Griffiths, 1748).

Houlding, J.A., *Fit for Service: The Training of the British Army, 1715-1795* (Oxford: Clarendon, 1981).

Johnston, Arran, *On Gladsmuir Shall the Battle Be! The Battle of Prestonpans 1745* (Solihull: Helion, 2017).

Lawson, Cecil C.P., *A History of the Uniforms of the British Army* (London: Norman Military Publications, 1963), Vol.II.

McLynn, Frank, *The Jacobite Army in England 1745: The Final Campaign* (Edinburgh: John Donald, 1998).

Marchant, John, *History of the Present Rebellion* (London: R. Walker, 1746).

Massie, Alastair, & Oates, Jonathan, (eds.), *The Duke of Cumberland's Campaigns in Britain & the Low Countries 1745-1748: A Selection of His Letters* (Stroud: The History Press for The Army Records Society, 2018),

Oates, Jonathan, *King George's Hangman: Henry Hawley and the Battle of Falkirk 1746* (Warwick: Helion, 2019).

Oates, Jonathan, *The Jacobite Campaigns: The British State at War* (Abingdon: Routledge, 2016).

Pollard, Tony (ed.), *Culloden: The History and Archaeology of the Last Clan Battle* (Barnsley: Pen & Sword, 2009).

Ray, James, *A Journey through part of England and Scotland along with the Army 2nd Edn* (London: Printed for T. Osborne, 1747).

Ray, James, *History of the Rebellion* (Edinburgh, Unknown Publisher, 1754).

Reid, Stuart, *1745: A Military History of the Last Jacobite Rising* (Spellmount: Staplehurst, 1996).

Reid, Stuart, *Cumberland's Army, the British Army at Culloden* (Leigh-on-Sea: Partizan Press, 2006).

Reid, Stuart, *Cumberland's Culloden Army 1745-46* (Oxford: Osprey, 2012).

Tomasson, K. & Buist, F., *Battles of the '45* (London: Batsford, 1978).

Journal Articles

Atkinson, C.T., 'Culloden', *Journal of the Society for Army Historical Research*, Vol.35, No. 141 (March 1957), pp.18-22.

Atkinson, C.T., 'Jenkins' Ear, The Austrian Succession War and the 'Forty-Five: Gleanings from the Sources in the Public Record Office', *Journal of the Society for Army Historical Research*, Vol.XXII No 91 (Autumn 1944), pp.280-298.

Luff, P.A., 'The Noblemen's Regiments: Politics and the 'Forty-Five', *Bulletin of the Institute of Historical Research*, Vol. LXV (1992), pp.54-73.

Oates, Jonathan, 'Hessian Forces Employed in Scotland in 1746', *Journal of the Society for Army Historical Research*, Vol.83, No.335 (Autumn 2005), pp.205-214.

Scobie, I.H. Mackay, 'The Argyll or Campbell Militia, 1745-6', *Journal of the Society for Army Historical Research*, Vol.24, No.97 (Spring 1946), pp.12-29.

Scobie, I.H. Mackay, 'The Highland Independent Companies of 1745-47', *Journal of the Society for Army Historical Research*, Vol.20, No.77 (Spring 1941), pp.5-37.

Online Resources

Royal Collections Trust, Map Collection of George III, Jacobite Wars, < https://militarymaps.rct.uk/other-18th19th-century-conflicts/jacobite-wars>

Stennis Historical Society 'Cantonment Register of the British Army in Scotland, 1746-52', Version 1.2, 13/01/19, <bit.ly/StennisHS>

Index of Regiments and Corps

General Index

From Reason to Revolution – Warfare 1721-1815

http://www.helion.co.uk/published-by-helion/reason-to-revolution-1721-1815.html

The 'From Reason to Revolution' series covers the period of military history 1721–1815, an era in which fortress-based strategy and linear battles gave way to the nation-in-arms and the beginnings of total war.

This era saw the evolution and growth of light troops of all arms, and of increasingly flexible command systems to cope with the growing armies fielded by nations able to mobilise far greater proportions of their manpower than ever before. Many of these developments were fired by the great political upheavals of the era, with revolutions in America and France bringing about social change which in turn fed back into the military sphere as whole nations readied themselves for war. Only in the closing years of the period, as the reactionary powers began to regain the upper hand, did a military synthesis of the best of the old and the new become possible.

The series will examine the military and naval history of the period in a greater degree of detail than has hitherto been attempted, and has a very wide brief, with the intention of covering all aspects from the battles, campaigns, logistics, and tactics, to the personalities, armies, uniforms, and equipment.

Submissions

The publishers would be pleased to receive submissions for this series. Please contact series editor Andrew Bamford via email (andrewbamford18@gmail.com), or in writing to Helion & Company Limited, Unit 8 Amherst Business Centre, Budbrooke Road, Warwick, CV34 5WE

Titles

No 1   *Lobositz to Leuthen. Horace St Paul and the Campaigns of the Austrian Army in the Seven Years War 1756-57* Translated with additional materials by Neil Cogswell (ISBN 978-1-911096-67-2)

No 2   *Glories to Useless Heroism. The Seven Years War in North America from the French journals of Comte Maurés de Malartic, 1755-1760* William Raffle (ISBN 978-1-1911512-19-6) (paperback)

No 3   *Reminiscences 1808-1815 Under Wellington. The Peninsular and Waterloo Memoirs of William Hay* William Hay, with notes and commentary by Andrew Bamford (ISBN 978-1-1911512-32-5)

No 4   *Far Distant Ships. The Royal Navy and the Blockade of Brest 1793-1815* Quintin Barry (ISBN 978-1-1911512-14-1)

No 5   *Godoy's Army. Spanish Regiments and Uniforms from the Estado Militar of 1800* Charles Esdaile and Alan Perry (ISBN 978-1-911512-65-3) (paperback)

No 6   *On Gladsmuir Shall the Battle Be! The Battle of Prestonpans 1745* Arran Johnston (ISBN 978-1-911512-83-7)

No 7   *The French Army of the Orient 1798-1801. Napoleon's Beloved 'Egyptians'* Yves Martin (ISBN 978-1-911512-71-4)*

No 8   *The Autobiography, or Narrative of a Soldier. The Peninsular War Memoirs of William Brown of the 45th Foot* William Brown, with notes and commentary by Steve Brown (ISBN 978-1-911512-94-3) (paperback)

No 9   *Recollections from the Ranks. Three Russian Soldiers' Autobiographies from the Napoleonic Wars* Translated and annotated by Darrin Boland (ISBN 978-1-912174-18-8) (paperback)

No 10   *By Fire and Bayonet. Grey's West Indies Campaign of 1794* Steve Brown (ISBN 978-1-911512-60-8)

No 11   *Olmütz to Torgau. Horace St Paul and the Campaigns of the Austrian Army in the Seven Years War 1758-60* Translated with additional materials by Neil Cogswell (ISBN 978-1-911512-72-1)

* indicates 'Falconet' format paperbacks, page size 248mm x 180 mm, with high visual content including colour plates; other titles are hardback monographs unless otherwise noted.